Absolutely Every

Bed & Breakfast
*Almost

OREGON

EDITED BY CARL HANSON

SASQUATCH BOOKS
SEATTLE

Copyright ©1999 by Sasquatch Books
All rights reserved. No portion of this book may be reproduced or utilized in any form, or by any electronic, mechanical, or other means without the prior written permission of the publisher.

Printed in the United States of America.
Distributed in Canada by Raincoast Books Ltd.
03 02 01 00 99   5 4 3 2 1

Cover design: Jane Jeszeck
Cover illustration: Michael Skott/The Image Bank
Interior design: Alan Bernhard
Composition: Alan Bernhard
Editor: Carl Hanson
Copy editor: Christine Clifton-Thornton

ISSN 1522-3906
ISBN 1-57061-189-0

Sasquatch Books
615 Second Avenue
Seattle, Washington 98104
(206) 467-4300
books@SasquatchBooks.com
http://www.SasquatchBooks.com

CONTENTS

ABSOLUTELY EVERY BED & BREAKFAST SERIES xiii
HOW TO USE THIS BOOK xiv

ADAMS	Bar M Dude Ranch	1
ALBANY	Brier Rose Inn Bed & Breakfast	1
APPLEGATE	Applegate River Lodge	1
ASHLAND	A-Dome Studio Bed & Breakfast.	2
	Adams Cottage Bed & Breakfast	3
	Albion Inn	3
	Anne Hathaway's Cottage	3
	Antique Rose Inn.	4
	Arden Forest Inn	5
	Ashberry Inn	5
	Ashland Patterson House.	5
	Ashland's English Country Cottage	6
	Ashland's Main Street Inn	7
	Bayberry Inn	7
	Cadbury Cottage	7
	Chanticleer Inn	8
	Clarity Cottage and Suite.	8
	Colonel Silsby's Bed & Breakfast Inn	8
	Coolidge House Bed & Breakfast	9
	Country Willows B&B Inn.	10
	Cowslip's Belle Bed & Breakfast	11
	Daniel's Roost Bed & Breakfast.	12
	Fadden's Inn	12
	Grapevine Inn	13
	Green Springs Inn	13
	Hersey House and Bungalow.	14
	Iris Inn, The.	15
	Jessell House	16
	Laurel Street Inn	16
	Lithia Rose Bed & Breakfast	16
	Lithia Springs Inn	17
	McCall House Bed & Breakfast.	17
	Morical House Garden Inn	18
	Mousetrap Inn	18
	Mount Ashland Inn	18

	Neil Creek House Bed & Breakfast 20
	Nightin' Gail's Inn 20
	Oak Hill Country Bed & Breakfast 21
	Oak Street Cottages 21
	Oak Street Station Bed & Breakfast 21
	Parkside Cottage 21
	Pedigrift House Bed & Breakfast 21
	Peerless Hotel 23
	Pinehurst Inn at Jenny Creek 23
	Queen Anne Bed & Breakfast 24
	Redwing Bed & Breakfast, The 24
	Rock Garden Inn 25
	Romeo Inn 25
	Royal Carter House Bed & Breakfast 26
	Shrew's House 26
	Summer Place Inn 26
	Waterside Inn 27
	Weisinger's Vineyard Cottage 27
	Wimer Street Inn 28
	Winchester Country Inn 28
	Wolfe Manor Inn 28
	Woods House Bed & Breakfast Inn, The 29
ASTORIA	Astoria Inn Bed & Breakfast 31
	Benjamin Young Inn 32
	Clementine's Bed & Breakfast 33
	Columbia River Inn B&B 33
	Franklin Street Station Bed & Breakfast 33
	Grandview Bed & Breakfast 34
	Rosebriar Hotel 35
AURORA	Inn at Aurora 36
AZALEA	Havenshire Bed & Breakfast 37
BAKER CITY	A Demain "Until Tomorrow" Bed & Breakfast 38
	Baer House B&B 39
	Grant House 39
	Powder River Bed & Breakfast 40
BANDON	Bailey's Cedar House Bed & Breakfast 41
	Bandon Beach House 41
	Beach Street Bed & Breakfast 41
	Historic River House, The 42
	Lighthouse Bed & Breakfast 42
	Pacific House 42

BEAVERTON	Aloha Junction Inn & Gardens Bed & Breakfast	43
	Brautigam House at Kensington Park, The	44
	Yankee Tinker Bed & Breakfast, The	44
BEND	Country Inn The City	45
	Cricketwood Country B&B	45
	Gazebo	46
	Juniper Acres Bed & Breakfast	46
	Lara House Bed & Breakfast	47
	Mill Inn Bed & Breakfast	48
	Sather House Bed & Breakfast, The	49
	Swallow Ridge	49
	Villa Genovese	49
BLUE RIVER	Drift Inn Bed & Breakfast	49
	Osprey Inn	50
	River's Edge Inn	50
BRIDAL VEIL	Bridal Veil Lodge Bed & Breakfast	51
BRIDGEPORT	Bruno Ranch Bed & Breakfast	51
BRIGHTWOOD	Brightwood Guesthouse Bed & Breakfast	51
	Maple River	53
BROOKINGS	Brookings South Coast Inn	53
	Chart House Lodge, Outfitter and B&B	54
	Chetco River Inn	54
	Holmes Sea Cove Bed & Breakfast	55
	Lowden's Beachfront B&B	55
	Pacific View Bed & Breakfast	55
	Sea Dreamer Inn	56
BROWNSVILLE	Atavista Farm Bed & Breakfast	57
BURNS	Blue Bucket Inn at 3E Ranch Bed & Breakfast	58
	Sage Country Inn Bed & Breakfast	59
CANNON BEACH	Cannon Beach Hotel	60
	St. Bernards, a Bed & Breakfast	61
	Stephanie Inn	62
CAVE JUNCTION	Erin Lodge	62
CLOVERDALE	Hudson House Bed & Breakfast	62
	Sandlake Country Inn	63
COOS BAY	Blackberry Inn Bed & Breakfast	63
	Coos Bay Manor Bed & Breakfast	63
	Old Tower House B&B, The	64
	This Olde House	64
COQUILLE	The Barton House	65

CORBETT	Chamberlain House Bed & Breakfast 65
CORVALLIS	Ashwood, The 65
	Bed & Breakfast on the Green, A 66
	Chapman House Bed & Breakfast................ 67
	Courtyard Inn 67
	Hanson Country Inn, The 67
	Harrison House Bed and Breakfast............... 67
	MacPherson Inn Bed & Breakfast................ 69
COTTAGE GROVE	Apple Inn Bed & Breakfast 69
	Carousel House Bed & Breakfast 69
	Lily of the Field Bed & Breakfast 69
DALLAS	Historic Henkle House Bed & Breakfast........... 70
	Woodridge Haven Bed & Breakfast............... 70
DAYTON	Wine Country Farm........................... 70
DAYVILLE	Fish House Inn 71
DEPOE BAY	Channel House Bed & Breakfast................. 72
	Gracie's Landing Bed & Breakfast................ 72
DETROIT	Repose & Repast 72
DUFUR	Balch Hotel 73
ECHO	Tolemac Inn.................................. 73
ELGIN	Pinewood.................................... 74
ELKTON	Elkqua Lodge 74
ELMIRA	McGillivray's Log Home Bed & Breakfast........... 75
ENTERPRISE	George Hyatt House Bed & Breakfast Inn, The 76
	Lozier's Country Loft Bed & Breakfast 76
	Tickled Trout 76
EUGENE	A-1 Krumdieck Kottage........................ 77
	Atherton Place............................... 77
	Camille's Bed & Breakfast 77
	Campbell House, a City Inn 77
	Excelsior Inn 78
	Fort Smith Bed & Breakfast 78
	Getty's Emerald Garden Bed & Breakfast.......... 79
	Kjaer's House in the Woods..................... 79
	Maryellen's Guest House Bed & Breakfast 80
	McGarry House Bed & Breakfast 80
	McKenzie View, a Riverside Bed & Breakfast 80
	Moloney's Inn Bed & Breakfast................... 81
	Oval Door Bed & Breakfast Inn, The 81
	Pookie's Bed 'n Breakfast on College Hill 82

	Secret Garden 84
	Tuscany Inn 84
FLORENCE	Blue Heron Inn 85
	Edwin K Bed & Breakfast 86
	Johnson House Bed & Breakfast 87
	Oak Street Victorian B&B 87
FOREST GROVE	Gaslight Inn, The 88
	Main Street Bed & Breakfast 89
FORT KLAMATH	Horseshoe Ranch 90
	Sun Pass Ranch 90
FOSSIL	Bridge Creek Flora Bed & Breakfast Inn 91
	O'Brien House 91
	Wild River Ranch Bed & Breakfast 91
FRENCHGLEN	Frenchglen Hotel 92
GARDINER	Gardiner Guest House 93
GLENDALE	Mount Reuben Inn 93
GLIDE	Steelhead Run B&B/Fine Art Gallery 93
GOLD BEACH	Endicott Gardens Bed & Breakfast 94
	Inn at Nesika Beach 94
	Tu Tu Tun Lodge 95
GOLD HILL	Rogue River Guest House 96
	Willowbrook Inn 96
GOVERNMENT CAMP	Falcon's Crest Inn 97
	Mount Hood Manor 98
GRAND RONDE	Granny Franny's Farm 98
GRANTS PASS	Flery Manor 99
	Home Farm 101
	Ivy House, The 101
	Lawnridge House 102
	Pine Meadow Inn Bed & Breakfast 102
	Weasku Inn 104
HALFWAY	Clear Creek Bed & Breakfast 105
HAMMOND	Officers Inn Bed & Breakfast 105
HOOD RIVER	Avalon Bed and Breakfast 105
	Beryl House Bed & Breakfast 106
	Brown's Bed & Breakfast 106
	Cottonwood Bed & Breakfast 107
	Gorge View Bed & Breakfast 107
	Hackett House 108
	Hood River Hotel and Pasquale's Ristorante 108

	Inn at the Gorge—Bed & Breakfast 110
	Lakecliff Estate Bed & Breakfast................. 110
	Panorama Lodge B&B........................ 111
	State Street Inn 111
Ione	Woolery House Bed & Breakfast................ 112
Jacksonville	Historic Orth House B&B "The Teddy Bear Inn".... 112
	Jacksonville Inn 114
	McCully House Inn, The...................... 115
	Touvelle House, The 115
	Wells Ranch House Bed & Breakfast, The 115
John Day	Sonshine B&B 116
Joseph	Chandlers' Bed, Bread & Trail Inn 117
	Tamarack Pines Inn 118
Junction City	Black Bart Bed & Breakfast..................... 118
Kerby	Kerbyville Inn 118
Kimberly	Land's Inn Bed & Breakfast..................... 119
Klamath Falls	Boarding House Inn........................... 119
	Iron Gate Estate Bed & Breakfast................ 119
	Thompsons' Bed & Breakfast.................... 120
La Grande	Countryside Inn Bed & Breakfast 121
	Stang Manor Inn 121
La Pine	Diamond Stone Guest Lodge & Gallery 122
Lafayette	Kelty Estate Bed & Breakfast 123
Lakeview	Heryford House Bed & Breakfast 123
Langlois	Floras Lake House by the Sea.................... 123
Leaburg	Marjon Bed & Breakfast Inn 124
Lincoln	Spyglass Inn................................. 125
Lincoln City	Brey House "Ocean View" Bed & Breakfast Inn 125
	Enchanted Cottage 126
	Ocean Memories—A Touch of Elegance on the Oregon Coast 126
	Pacific Rest Bed & Breakfast.................... 127
	Young's B&B—Tastes of Yesterday................ 127
Manzanita	Arbors Bed & Breakfast, The.................... 128
Maupin	C&J Lodge Bed & Breakfast 129
McMinnville	Baker Street Bed & Breakfast 129
	Gahr Farm B&B Cottage....................... 130
	Mattey House Bed & Breakfast.................. 131
	Orchard View Inn Bed & Breakfast............... 131
	Steiger Haus Bed and Breakfast 132

	Williams House Bed & Breakfast. 133
	Youngberg Hill Vineyard & Inn 133
MEDFORD	Carpenter Hill Inn. 135
	Under the Greenwood Tree Bed & Breakfast 135
	Whispering Pines. 135
MILL CITY	Ivy Creek Bed & Breakfast 136
	Morrison Cottage. 136
MILWAUKIE	Historic Broetje House 136
MITCHELL	Historic Oregon Hotel Bed & Breakfast 137
MONMOUTH	Howell's Bed & Breakfast 138
MOSIER	Cherry Hill Farm. 139
	Mosier House Bed & Breakfast, The. 139
MOUNT HOOD	Mount Hood Bed & Breakfast. 140
	Mount Hood Hamlet. 141
	Old Parkdale Inn Bed & Breakfast, The 141
NEHALEM	Nehalem River Inn 142
	Redwood Inn. 142
NEW PINE CREEK	Honker Inn Bed & Breakfast. 142
NEWBERG	Entheos Estate. 142
	Partridge Farm. 143
	Smith House Bed & Breakfast. 143
	Springbrook Hazelnut Farm Bed & Breakfast. 144
NEWPORT	Green Gables Bed & Breakfast 145
	Newport Belle Bed & Breakfast. 146
	Oar House Bed & Breakfast 146
	Ocean House. 147
	Sea Cliff Bed & Breakfast 148
	Solace by the Sea Bed & Breakfast 148
	Sylvia Beach Hotel. 149
	Tyee Lodge Oceanfront Bed & Breakfast 150
NORTH BEND	2310 Lombard Bed & Breakfast 151
	Itty Bitty Inn Motel Bed & Breakfast 151
OAKLAND	Beckley House Bed & Breakfast 152
OCEANSIDE	Sea Rose Bed & Breakfast 152
OREGON CITY	Ainsworth House Bed & Breakfast 153
	Tolle House 153
OTIS	Lake House Bed & Breakfast, The 154
	Salmon River Bed & Breakfast 155
OXBOW	Hell's Canyon Bed & Breakfast 155
PACIFIC CITY	Eagle's View Bed & Breakfast 155

PENDLETON	Dorie's Inn 157
	Parker House Bed & Breakfast, The 157
	Place Apart Bed & Breakfast Inn, A 158
PORT ORFORD	Home by the Sea Bed & Breakfast 160
	Steelblue Chameleon Lodge 160
PORTLAND	Abernathy's Bed & Breakfast 161
	Century Garden Bed & Breakfast 161
	Clinkerbrick House 162
	Gedney Gardens 162
	General Hooker's Bed & Breakfast 162
	Georgian House Bed & Breakfast 163
	Heron Haus 164
	Holladay House Bed & Breakfast 165
	Hostess House Bed & Breakfast 166
	Irvington Inn 167
	Kennedy School 167
	Knott Street Inn Bed & Breakfast 167
	Lion & Rose Victorian B&B, The 167
	Macmaster House Circa 1895 168
	Pittock Acres Bed & Breakfast................... 168
	Portland Guest House 168
	Portland's White House Bed & Breakfast 169
	Sauvie Island Bed & Breakfast................... 169
	Sullivan's Gulch B&B.......................... 170
	Terwilliger Vista Bed & Breakfast 171
	Three B's at Market 172
	Tudor House Bed & Breakfast................... 172
	Villa Bed & Breakfast, A 172
	Westlund's River's Edge Bed & Breakfast 172
	Woven Glass Inn, The 172
PRAIRIE CITY	Strawberry Mountain Inn 173
PRINEVILLE	Elliott House, The............................ 174
PROSPECT	Prospect Historical Hotel/Motel and Dinnerhouse ... 176
RAINIER	1888 House 177
REDMOND	Llast Camp Llamas Bed & Breakfast.............. 177
ROSEBURG	Hokanson's Guest House 177
	House of Hunter 178
	Umpqua House, The 178
SALEM	Bethel Heights Farm Bed & Breakfast 179
	Bookmark Bed & Breakfast 179

	Cotton Wood Cottage Bed & Breakfast 179
	Eagle Crest Bed & Breakfast 180
	Marquee House 180
	Meadow View Inn Bed & Breakfast 182
	State House Bed & Breakfast 182
	Stone Lion Inn 182
	Vista Park Bed & Breakfast 183
SANDY	Brookside Bed & Breakfast 184
	Fernwood at Alder Creek 184
SCAPPOOSE	Barnstormer Bed & Breakfast 184
	Malarkey Ranch Inn B&B 185
SEASIDE	10th Avenue Inn 185
	Anderson's Boarding House Bed & Breakfast 186
	Country River Inn 187
	Custer House Bed & Breakfast 188
	Gilbert Inn Bed & Breakfast 189
	Guest House Bed & Breakfast, The 190
	Riverside Inn B&B 190
	Sand Dollar B&B 190
	Sea Side Inn 191
	Summer House Bed & Breakfast 192
SHERIDAN	Brightridge Farm Bed & Breakfast 192
	Middle Creek Run Bed & Breakfast 194
	Sheridan Country Inn 195
SILVERTON	Abiqua Creek Farms Bed & Breakfast 195
	Egg Cup Inn Bed & Breakfast, The 196
	Marvin Gardens Guest House 196
SISTERS	Conklin's Guest House, a Bed & Breakfast 197
	Hospitality House 198
	Rags to Walkers Guest Ranch 199
	Squaw Creek 200
SIXES	Sixes River Hotel 200
STAYTON	Bird & Hat Inn—B&B 201
	Our Place in the Country Bed & Breakfast 202
SUBLIMITY	Silver Mountain Bed & Breakfast 202
SUMMER LAKE	Summer Lake Inn 202
SUMPTER	Sumpter Bed & Breakfast 203
THE DALLES	Boarding House 203
	Captain Gray's Guest House 203
	Columbia House, The 203
	Windrider Inn 204

TILLAMOOK	Blue Haven Inn	204
	Whiskey Creek Bed & Breakfast	205
VALE	1911 Sears & Roebuck Home	206
VERNONIA	Vernonia Inn	207
VIDA	McKenzie River Inn	207
WALDPORT	Cliff House—Yaquina John Point	207
WELCHES	Doublegate Inn B&B	208
	Old Welches Inn Bed & Breakfast	209
	Suite River Bed & Breakfast	210
WEST LINN	Riverbend House	210
	Swift Shore Chalet Bed & Breakfast	211
WESTFIR	Westfir Lodge, a Bed & Breakfast Inn	211
WESTON	Tamarack Inn Bed & Breakfast	212
YACHATS	Burd's Nest Inn B&B	213
	Kittiwake Bed & Breakfast	213
	Morning Star	214
	New England House Bed & Breakfast	215
	Oregon House, The	215
	Sanderling Bed & Breakfast, The	215
	Sea Quest Bed & Breakfast	215
	Serenity Bed & Breakfast	216
	Ziggurat Bed & Breakfast	216
YONCALLA	Tuckaway Farm Inn	217

INDEX *219*

ABSOLUTELY EVERY BED & BREAKFAST SERIES

Welcome to *Absolutely Every° Bed & Breakfast: Oregon*, a comprehensive guide to virtually every bed and breakfast establishment in Oregon. We've done the work for you: Everything you need to know in choosing a bed and breakfast is included on these pages, from architectural style to atmosphere, from price range to breakfast variety. Listings are in alphabetical order by town, so locating the perfect stay at your destination is a snap, and the simple format makes comparing accommodations as easy as turning the page. So whether you're looking for an elegant Victorian experience, a seaside bungalow adventure, or a rustic farmhouse getaway, *Absolutely Every° Bed & Breakfast: Oregon* (*°Almost*) will help you find it.

In addition to Oregon, the *Absolutely Every* series covers Arizona, Colorado, New Mexico, Southern California, Northern California, Texas, and Washington; look for the latest edition of each in your local bookstore. Each guide in the series lists small- and medium-sized inns, hotels, and host homes that include breakfast in the price of the room. The lists of B&B establishments are compiled from a variety of sources, including directories, chambers of commerce, tourism bureaus, and the World Wide Web. After gathering a complete list, the editors send each innkeeper a survey, asking for basic lodging information as well as those special details that set them apart. The completed surveys are then examined and fact-checked for accuracy before inclusion in the book. The *°Almost* in the series title reflects the fact that a small number of innkeepers may choose not to be listed, may neglect to respond to the survey and follow-up phone calls, or are not listed because of negative reports received by the editors.

The editors rely on the honesty of the innkeepers in completing the surveys and on feedback from readers to keep the *Absolutely Every Bed & Breakfast* series accurate and up-to-date. (*Note:* While innkeepers are responsible for providing survey information, none are financially connected to the series, nor do they pay any fees to be included in the book.) Please write to us about your experience at any of the bed and breakfasts listed in the series; we'd love to hear from you.

Enjoy your bed and breakfast experience!

—The editors, *Absolutely Every Bed & Breakfast*

How to Use This Book

Absolutely Every Bed & Breakfast: Oregon is organized alphabetically by town and by establishment name, and includes a comprehensive index. The concise, at-a-glance format of the complete bed and breakfast listings covers fifteen categories of information to help you select just the right bed and breakfast accommodation for your needs. This edition offers you a choice of establishments in cities, towns, and outlying areas.

THE BED & BREAKFAST LISTINGS

Note that although specifics of each establishment have been confirmed by the editors, details such as amenities, decor, and breakfast menus have been provided by the innkeepers. Listings in this guide are subject to change; call to confirm all aspects of your stay, including price, availability, and restrictions, before you go. Some bed and breakfast listings offer only selected information due to lack of response or by request of the innkeeper; complete listings include the following information.

Establishment name
Address: Note that street addresses often vary from actual mailing addresses; confirm the mailing address before sending a reservation payment.
Telephone numbers: Includes any toll-free or fax numbers.
Innkeeper's Languages: Languages spoken other than English.
Location: Directions from the nearest town, highway, or landmark.
Open: Notice of any seasonal or other closures.
Description: Overview of architecture, furnishings, landscaping, etc.
Rooms: Number of rooms with private bathrooms vs. shared baths; availability of suites and/or additional guesthouses; and the innkeeper's favorite room.
Rates: Range of room prices, which vary based on private or shared bathroom, season, and individual room amenities. Also noted here are any minimum stay requirements and cancellation policies (usually two weeks' notice is required for a full refund).

Breakfast: Description of breakfast served (full, continental, continental plus, or stocked kitchen).
Credit cards: Indicates which, if any, credit cards are accepted. Note that credit cards may be listed for reservation confirmation purposes only; be prepared to pay by check or cash.
Amenities: Details any special amenities that are included.
Restrictions: Lists any restrictions regarding smoking, children, and pets. Also listed here are any resident pets or livestock.
Awards: Any significant hospitality or historic preservation awards received.
Reviewed: Publications in which the B&B has been reviewed.
Rated: Indicates whether the B&B has been rated by institutions such as the American Automobile Association (AAA), American Bed & Breakfast Association (ABBA), or the Mobil Travel Association.
Member: Indicates membership in any professional hospitality associations or organizations.
Kudos/Comments: Comments from guests who have stayed in the establishment.

ADAMS

BAR M DUDE RANCH

48840 Bar M Lane, Adams, OR 97810   541-566-3381
The Baker Family, Innkeepers

ALBANY

Time and I-5 have both bypassed Albany, which is probably a blessing. Once you get off the freeway (ignore the smell of the nearby pulp mill), you'll discover a fine representative of the small-town Oregon of an earlier era, with broad, quiet streets, neat houses, and a slow pace. Once an important transportation hub in the Willamette Valley, the town has an unequaled selection of historic homes and buildings in a wide variety of styles, many of them lovingly restored. The covered bridges that were so characteristic of this area are disappearing. From 450, their number has dwindled to fewer than 50, but that's still more than in any other state west of the Mississippi.

BRIER ROSE INN BED & BREAKFAST

206 Seventh Avenue SW, Albany, OR 97321   541-926-0345
WEBSITE www.skipnet.com/~brierrose

APPLEGATE

Situated along the Applegate River, about 20 miles southwest of Medford on Highway 238, Applegate is well positioned for exploring Oregon Caves National Monument and the Rogue River and Siskiyou National Forests.

APPLEGATE RIVER LODGE

15100 Highway 238, Applegate, OR 97530   541-846-6690
Richard & Joanna Davis, Innkeepers
WEBSITE www.moriah.com/inns

LOCATION   Halfway between Medford and Grants Pass on scenic Highway 238.

OPEN	All year
DESCRIPTION	A 1997 two-story log and timber lodge overlooking the historic Pioneer Bridge and Applegate River, with decor based on themes of those who influenced settlement of the Applegate Valley, such as the logging, cattle, and gold mining industries, as well as American Indian and others.
NO. OF ROOMS	Seven rooms with private bathrooms. Try the Cattle Man Room.
RATES	June through October, rates are $125-145 for a single or double, $145 for a suite, and $1,000 for the entire lodge. November through May, rates are $95-115 for a single or double, $115 for a suite, and $800 for the entire lodge. There is no minimum stay and cancellation requires 48 hours' notice for a full refund.
CREDIT CARDS	MasterCard, Visa
BREAKFAST	Continental breakfast is served in the lobby and includes bagels and cream cheese, Danish, homemade cinnamon rolls, fruit, juice, coffee, tea, and hot chocolate. Dinner is also available.
AMENITIES	All rooms with two-person Jacuzzi tubs, decks overlooking the river, all rooms air-conditioned, handicapped access, raft trips and free pickups downriver, fishing poles, gold pans, CD players in rooms, large lobby area with balcony and sitting room, game tables and books.
RESTRICTIONS	Smoking on decks only, no pets. Smoky is the resident six-toed cat.

ASHLAND

The remarkable success of the Oregon Shakespeare Festival, now well over 50 years old, has transformed this sleepy town into one with, per capita, the best tourist amenities in the region. Visit the Exhibit Center, where you can clown around in costumes from plays past. There are also lectures and concerts at noon, excellent backstage tours each morning, Renaissance music and dances nightly in the courtyard—plus all the nearby daytime attractions of river rafting, picnicking, and historical touring.

A-DOME STUDIO BED & BREAKFAST

8550 Dead Indian Memorial Road, Ashland, OR 97520   541-482-1755
German spoken
WEBSITE www.mind.net/adome

LOCATION	Fifteen minutes outside of Ashland.
DESCRIPTION	A handcrafted dome with knotty pine interior, rock fireplace, and antiques.

NO. OF ROOMS	Two suites with private bathrooms.
RATES	Year-round rates are $100-110 for a double. There is a two-night minimum stay on weekends and cancellation requires 14 days' notice.
CREDIT CARDS	No
RESTRICTIONS	No smoking, no pets, children are welcome.
MEMBER	Oregon Bed & Breakfast Guild

ADAMS COTTAGE BED & BREAKFAST

737 Siskiyou Boulevard, Ashland, OR 97520   541-488-5405

ALBION INN

34 Union Street, Ashland, OR 97520   541-488-3905

ANNE HATHAWAY'S COTTAGE

586 E Main Street, Ashland, OR 97520   541-488-1050
Kate Jackson & Chuck Keil, Resident Owners   800-643-4434
French spoken   FAX 541-482-1969
EMAIL AnnesBed@opendoor.com   WEBSITE www.opendoor.com/AnnesBed

LOCATION	Half a block southeast of downtown.
OPEN	All year
DESCRIPTION	A restored 1908 two-story boarding house on the County Historic Register.
NO. OF ROOMS	Five rooms with private bathrooms. Try the JT Currie Suite.
RATES	June through September, rates are $90-115 for a single or double, and suites are $160-210. March through October, rates are $75-95 for a single or double, and suites are $130-180. Call for rates from November through February. There is no minimum stay and cancellation requires 15 days' notice.
CREDIT CARDS	MasterCard, Visa
BREAKFAST	Full breakfast is served in the dining room and includes coffee, scones, and entreés.

AMENITIES	Central air-conditioning; robes; flowers.
RESTRICTIONS	No smoking, no pets; children are welcome in the JT Currie Suite.
MEMBER	Oregon Bed & Breakfast Guild

ANTIQUE ROSE INN

91 Gresham Street, Ashland, OR 97520   541-482-6285
Kathleen Buffington, Innkeeper   888-282-6285
EMAIL antiquebnb@aol.com   WEBSITE www.wvi.com/~dhull/antiquebnb

LOCATION	From I-5, take either of the Ashland exits; the inn is three blocks south of the Oregon Shakespeare Theatre on Main Street. Turn right on Gresham Street and go one block.
OPEN	Main house is open March through October. The cottage is open year-round.
DESCRIPTION	An 1888 three-story Victorian inn with antique Victorian lace, four-poster beds, and intricate woodwork, listed on the National and State Historic Registers.
NO. OF ROOMS	Four rooms with private bathrooms. Try the Rose Room.
RATES	June through October, rates are $117-137 for a single or double and $159 for the cottage. November through May, rates are $87-107 for a single or double and $119 for the cottage. There is a two-night minimum stay during summer weekends and holidays. A one-night deposit is due within seven days of booking and cancellation requires three weeks' notice.

Antique Rose Inn, Ashland

CREDIT CARDS	American Express, MasterCard, Visa
BREAKFAST	Full multicourse breakfast is served in the dining room and includes fresh juice, fruit, home-baked muffins and cinnamon rolls, and an entrée such as crab soufflé or fresh peach crepes.
AMENITIES	Flowers, robes, sherry, candy, wine, lotions and perfumes, scripts of plays, soft drinks, early coffee and tea, air conditioning, sauna and Jacuzzi, fireplace in cottage and the Rose Room, clawfoot tubs, antiques, down comforters, beautiful gardens, gazebo.
RESTRICTIONS	No smoking, no pets. Children over 10 are welcome. Mickey, Alex, Fred, and Kitten are the four resident cats.
REVIEWED	*The Best Places to Kiss in the Northwest, Fodor's, Best Places to Stay in the Pacific Northwest*
MEMBER	Oregon Bed & Breakfast Guild, Professional Association of Innkeepers International
AWARDS	Ashland Distinguished Preservation Award 1996, by the City of Ashland Historic Commission

ARDEN FOREST INN

261 W Hersey Street, Ashland, OR 97520   541-488-1496
WEBSITE www.afinn.com

KUDOS/COMMENTS   "Tasteful, charming, comfortable—they've created a gem of an inn."

ASHBERRY INN

527 Chestnut Street, Ashland, OR 97520   541-488-8000
WEBSITE www.abbnet.com/ or www.innsite.com/obbg

ASHLAND PATTERSON HOUSE

639 N Main Street, Ashland, OR 97520   541-482-9171
Nancy Tuggle, Innkeeper   888-482-9171
EMAIL tuggle@mind.net   FAX 541-488-8597
WEBSITE www.mind.net/patterson

LOCATION   Seven-tenths of a mile north of the plaza in downtown Ashland.

Ashland Patterson House, Ashland

OPEN	All year
DESCRIPTION	A 1910 two-story Craftsman inn with casual country decor.
NO. OF ROOMS	Four rooms with private bathrooms. Try the Cottage.
RATES	June 15 through October 15, rates are $80-110 for a single or double. October 16 through June 14, rates are $60-90 for a single or double. There is a minimum stay during weekends. Inquire about a cancellation policy.
CREDIT CARDS	American Express, Discover, MasterCard, Visa
BREAKFAST	Full healthy vegetarian breakfast is served.
AMENITIES	Robes, air conditioning, sherry.
RESTRICTIONS	Pets (mature dogs) accepted. Children over 10 are welcome.
MEMBER	Ashland Bed & Breakfast Network, Professional Association of Innkeepers International

ASHLAND'S ENGLISH COUNTRY COTTAGE

271 Beach Street, Ashland, OR 97520
Brian & Shorley Wallace, Innkeepers
EMAIL bwallace@cdsnet.net
WEBSITE www.ashlandbb.com

541-488-4428
800-760-4428
FAX 541-482-4780

LOCATION   South of the theaters 0.7 mile.

OPEN	All year
DESCRIPTION	A 1940 two-story Tudor lodge set back from the main street, decorated in English country style, with lots of flowers, a private garden, and decks.
NO. OF ROOMS	Five rooms with private bathrooms. Try the Daisy Room.
RATES	High-season rates are $99-109 for a single or double and $495 for the entire cottage. Regular-season rates are $89-99 for a single or double and $445 for the entire cottage. There is a minimum stay during weekends and holidays and cancellation requires 14 days' notice.
CREDIT CARDS	Discover, MasterCard, Visa
BREAKFAST	Full breakfast is served in the dining room or on the deck and includes a fruit dish, a main egg course, homemade rolls, muffins or scones, homemade jams, and more.
AMENITIES	Air conditioned, one room is handicapped accessible, guest TV and video tapes, library, afternoon tea.
RESTRICTIONS	No smoking, no pets, children over 12 are welcome. Tuppy is the resident poodle.
MEMBER	Ashland Bed & Breakfast Network, Oregon Bed & Breakfast Guild

ASHLAND'S MAIN STREET INN

142 N Main Street, Ashland, OR 97520   541-488-0969

BAYBERRY INN

438 N Main Street, Ashland, OR 97520   541-488-1252
Harriet Maher, Innkeeper   800-795-1252

CADBURY COTTAGE

353 Hargadine Street, Ashland, OR 97520   541-488-5970

CHANTICLEER INN

120 Gresham, Ashland, OR 97520
Pebby Kuan, Innkeeper
EMAIL rooster@mind.net

541-482-1919
800-898-1950
WEBSITE www.ashlandbnb.com

CLARITY COTTAGE AND SUITE

868 A Street, Ashland, OR 97520
Emeral Clarity & Betty Camner, Innkeepers
EMAIL clarity@mind.net

541-488-2457
888-488-2457
WEBSITE www.mind.net/claritycottage

COLONEL SILSBY'S BED & BREAKFAST INN

111 N Third Street, Ashland, OR 97520
Rosemary A. Silva, Innkeeper
EMAIL silsbys@mind.net
WEBSITE www.mind.net/colsilsbys

541-488-3070
800-927-3070
FAX 541-482-5791

LOCATION	From north I-5, take exit 19 and follow signs into Ashland. Turn left on Second Street, and take a right on Third Street to the corner of "C" Street and Third Street. From south I-5, take exit 14 to Ashland. Take a right on Siskiyou, turn right on Third Street, and drive one block.
OPEN	All year
DESCRIPTION	A 1896 two-story Queen Anne Victorian inn with antique and lace decor.
NO. OF ROOMS	Four rooms with private bathrooms. Rosemary recommends the Princess Suite.
RATES	May through October, rates are $81-125 for a single or double, $112.50-185 for a suite, and the entire B&B rents for $545 per night for up to 12 people. November through April, rates are $67.50-110 for a single or double, $99-170 for a suite, and the entire B&B rents for $400 per night for up to 12 people. There is no minimum stay and cancellation requires 15 days' notice.
CREDIT CARDS	American Express, MasterCard, Visa
BREAKFAST	Full breakfast is served in the dining room and includes freshly squeezed orange juice, fresh fruit, award-winning scones and

Colonel Silsby's Bed & Breakfast Inn, Ashland

	muffins, and a gourmet entrée. Vegetarian and other special diets can be accommodated.
AMENITIES	Air conditioning, in-room telephone, port in the evenings, cookies, fresh flowers.
RESTRICTIONS	No smoking, no pets, children over 9 are welcome.
REVIEWED	*The Official Guide to American Historic Inns*
MEMBER	Oregon Bed & Breakfast Guild, Oregon Bed & Breakfast Association
AWARDS	Jackson Country Fair, scones & muffins, 1998

COOLIDGE HOUSE BED & BREAKFAST

137 N Main Street, Ashland, OR 97520
The Parkers, Innkeepers
WEBSITE *www.coolidgehouse.com*

541-482-4721
800-655-5522

COUNTRY WILLOWS B&B INN

1313 Clay Street, Ashland, OR 97520
Dan Durant, Innkeeper
EMAIL *willows@willowsinn.com*
WEBSITE *www.willowsinn.com*

541-488-1590
800-WILLOWS
FAX 541-488-1611

LOCATION	Take exit 14 off I-5. Turn west onto Highway 66. Take a left at the first traffic signal onto Tolman Creek Road. Take a right at the blinking red light onto Siskiyou. Take the second left onto Clay Street and follow to the end of the road.
OPEN	All year
DESCRIPTION	An 1896 two-story farmhouse on 5 acres, a separate cottage, and a barn built in 1899, decorated with comfortable rural elegance.
NO. OF ROOMS	Nine rooms with private bathrooms. Try the Pine Ridge Suite.
RATES	High-season rates are $95-195 for a single or double, $135-195 for a suite, and $150 for the guesthouse. Regular-season rates are $76-156 for a single or double, $108-156 for a suite, and $120 for the guesthouse. There is no minimum stay and cancellation requires 15 days' notice with a $20 charge. For groups renting three or more rooms, 30 days' notice is required.
CREDIT CARDS	American Express, Discover, MasterCard, Visa
BREAKFAST	Full breakfast is served at private tables in stages and includes fresh-squeezed juices or smoothies, great coffee, fruit, baked goods, homemade granola, and a variety of sweet and savory dishes such as stuffed French toast or eggs Benedict.
AMENITIES	Each room with Turkish cotton robes, hair dryers, iron/ironing board, telephones with data ports, guest directories, French-milled and glycerine soaps, shampoo, bubble bath, shower caps, fresh flowers, "welcome" fruit baskets.
RESTRICTIONS	No smoking, no pets, children over 12 are welcome. Aristotle and Bear are the resident Morgan horses, Portia and Cleopatra are the Nubian goats, Beatrice and Florence are the bunnies. "We also have a pond with ducks and geese. Guests love the animals. They bring back the flavor of the original farmhouse."
REVIEWED	*The Best Places to Kiss in the Pacific Northwest, Northwest Best Places, Recommended Country Inns, Best Places to Stay in the Pacific Northwest*
MEMBER	Oregon Bed & Breakfast Guild, Ashland Area Association of the Oregon Bed & Breakfast Guild, Professional Association of Innkeepers International
RATED	AAA 3 Diamonds, Mobil 3 Stars, Best Places to Kiss in the Pacific Northwest 4 Lips, Northwest Best Places 3 Stars

KUDOS/COMMENTS "They do it all right! The new suite is incredible!" "Perfect—setting, decor, ambience, food, and delightful innkeepers." "1896 farmhouse on 5 white-fenced acres, romantic and scenic."

COWSLIP'S BELLE BED & BREAKFAST

159 N Main Street, Ashland, OR 97520
Jon & Carmen Reinhardt, Innkeepers
EMAIL stay@cowslip.com
WEBSITE www.cowslip.com/cowslip

541-488-2901
800-888-6819
FAX 541-482-6138

LOCATION	From I-5, take exit 19 to Ashland and drive south into town on Main Street. The B&B is on the right between Laurel and Bush Streets. To park, turn right onto Bush Street, drive half a block, and turn right down the alley to the rear of the B&B.
OPEN	All year
DESCRIPTION	A 1913 two-story Craftsman bungalow and carriage house decorated with a comfortable and eclectic mix of antiques and oriental rugs.
NO. OF ROOMS	Four rooms with private bathrooms. Try the Rosebud Suite.
RATES	June through October, rates are $115-140 for a single or double and $140 for a suite. November through May, rates are $105 for a single or double and $105 for a suite. There is no minimum stay and cancellation requires 30 days' notice.
CREDIT CARDS	No
BREAKFAST	Full breakfast is served in the dining room and includes fresh juice, coffee, tea, homemade baked goodies, a main entrée (such as walnut wheat-germ pancakes with fresh blackberries and homemade blackberry sauce, Dutch apple French toast, shrimp turnovers with sherry sauce, Dutch babies with brandied peach sauce, or green chile egg puff), a fresh fruit dish, and a choice of breakfast meats.
AMENITIES	Turndown service with chocolates on pillows, private entrances, pond with waterfall, off-street parking, coffee, tea, sherry, biscotti, great cookies from the Reinhardt's cookie business, free use of the Ashland Racquet and Fitness Club (with indoor pool, tennis courts, weight room, saunas, and Jacuzzis), rooms with decks, air conditioning.
RESTRICTIONS	No smoking, no pets, children over 9 are welcome.
REVIEWED	Northwest Best Places; The Best Places to Kiss in the Northwest; Weekends for Two in the Pacific Northwest; 50 Romantic Getaways; America's Favorite Inns, B&Bs, & Small Hotels

DANIEL'S ROOST BED & BREAKFAST

1920 E Main Street, Ashland, OR 97520　　541-482-0121
Michele Martin & Daniel Fischer, Innkeepers　　800-215-9031
EMAIL michmar101@aol.com　　FAX 541-482-7493

LOCATION	From I-5, take exit 14 and turn right (north) onto Highway 66. Take a right at the first traffic signal onto Tolman Creek Road, which dead-ends on East Main Street. Turn left. The B&B is between Clay and Walker Streets, the second house on the left after the red barn.
OPEN	May through October
DESCRIPTION	A mid-1980s one-story ranch house decorated with Chippendale antiques, nestled on 2 acres with a creek and pond and views of pasture and mountains.
NO. OF ROOMS	Two rooms and suite shares 1½ bathrooms.
RATES	Rates are $100-110 for a single or double and $130-150 for a suite with two beds. Additional guests are $25 per person. Add $10 for Friday- and Saturday-night stays and reduce 10 percent for stays longer than four days. There is a three-day minimum stay and cancellation requires 14 days' notice.
CREDIT CARDS	MasterCard, Visa
BREAKFAST	Full breakfast is served in the dining room and includes juice, fruit, bread, a main dish, coffee, and tea.
AMENITIES	Flowers, comforters, robes, small refrigerators, air conditioning, large outdoor areas for eating and relaxing, creeks and pond.
RESTRICTIONS	No smoking, no pets, children over 10 are welcome. Roxie is the friendly Lab/Rott mix. Roxie will bark a greeting when guests arrive—a leisurely hello makes her an instant friend.
REVIEWED	*America's Favorite Inns, B&Bs, & Small Hotels; America's Historic Inns*
MEMBER	Oregon Bed & Breakfast Guild

FADDEN'S INN

326 N Main Street, Ashland, OR 97520　　541-488-0025
WEBSITE www.abbnet.com/fadden/index.html

GRAPEVINE INN

486 Siskiyou Boulevard, Ashland, OR 97520
Shirley Grega, Innkeeper
WEBSITE www.mind.net/grapevineinn

541-482-7944

GREEN SPRINGS INN

11470 Highway 66, Ashland, OR 97520
Pam Marsh & Diarmuid McGuire, Innkeepers
EMAIL gsprings@cdsnet.net

541-482-0614
800-572-9172
FAX 541-488-3942

LOCATION	Take exit 14 from I-5 at Ashland and travel east on Highway 66 toward Klamath Falls. Green Springs Inn is 17.5 miles east of and about 2,500 feet above Ashland.
OPEN	All year
DESCRIPTION	A 1981 two-story rustic, cedar-sided guest house, plus a separate eight-room lodge and small restaurant, all situated in an evergreen forest near the Pacific Crest Trail.
NO. OF ROOMS	Eight rooms with private bathrooms.
RATES	May through October, rates are $69-79 for a single or double and $89-109 for a suite (with a Jacuzzi). November through April, rates are $59-69 for a single or double and $79-99 for a suite (with a Jacuzzi). There is no minimum stay and cancellation requires three days' notice for a full refund.
CREDIT CARDS	American Express, Discover, MasterCard, Visa
BREAKFAST	Full breakfast is served in the dining room and includes eggs any style, omelets, sourdough or whole-wheat pancakes, breakfast burritos, and more. Lunch and dinner are also available.
AMENITIES	The Forest Room, a spacious, round room with picture windows opening into the surrounding woods, available for retreats, weddings, and other group functions; all guest rooms air conditioned; room 1 is fully handicapped accessible; all buildings wheelchair accessible.
RESTRICTIONS	No smoking, pets and children are welcome. Tara is the resident black Lab. Tara escorts guests on hikes.
REVIEWED	*Northwest Best Places, Northwest Budget Traveler*

HERSEY HOUSE AND BUNGALOW

451 N Main Street, Ashland, OR 97520
Paul & Terri Mensch, Innkeepers
EMAIL innkeeper@herseyhouse.com
WEBSITE www.herseyhouse.com

541-482-4563
888-3HERSEY
FAX 541-488-9317

LOCATION	Exit I-5 at Valley View Road (exit 19), and travel west on Valley View Road to the traffic light at the bottom of the hill. Turn left onto Highway 99 (North Main Street), and go two blocks past the traffic light at Maple Street. Hersey House is located on the right at the corner of North Main and Nursery Streets.
OPEN	All year
DESCRIPTION	A 1904 two-story Craftsman inn with a spacious front porch, an English country garden, hardwood floors, period furnishings, and antiques. The Bungalow is a private, contemporary guest cottage built in the 1940s and renovated in 1992.
NO. OF ROOMS	Five rooms with private bathrooms. Try the Eastlake.
RATES	June through early October, rates are $115 for a single or double and $140 for the bungalow. November through April, rates are $75

Hersey House and Bungalow, Ashland

	for a single or double and $99 for the bungalow. There is a two-night minimum stay in the bungalow and cancellation requires 21 days' notice.
CREDIT CARDS	American Express, Discover, MasterCard, Visa
BREAKFAST	Full breakfast is served in the house. Early morning coffee or tea service (ready by 7:30 a.m.) precedes a bountiful breakfast. In the Bungalow, a continental breakfast is served that includes fresh-baked muffins or coffeecake, coffee and tea, and oranges for fresh-squeezed juice.
AMENITIES	In-room private baths, bedside reading lamps, telephones with data ports, individually controlled heat and air conditioning, down comforters, fresh flowers in season from the garden, home-baked cookies and iced tea in the afternoon.
RESTRICTIONS	No smoking, no pets, children over 12 are welcome. Ophir and Kira are the resident golden retrievers. "They function as the official greeters, and are more than happy to take guests on a walk before breakfast!"
REVIEWED	*America's Favorite Inns, B&Bs and Small Hotels; Recommended Country Inns*
MEMBER	Oregon Bed & Breakfast Guild, Ashland Area Association of the Oregon Bed & Breakfast Guild
RATED	AAA 2 Diamonds

THE IRIS INN

59 *Manzanita Street, Ashland, OR 97520* 541-488-2286
Vicki & Greg Capp, Innkeepers 800-460-7650
Some Spanish spoken FAX 541-488-3709
EMAIL *IrisInnBB@aol.com* WEBSITE *www.datacor.com/irisinn.ccxn*

LOCATION	From I-5 north or south, take exit 19. Proceed 0.25 mile to the stoplight and Highway 99. Turn left, go 1.6 miles, and turn right onto Manzanita Street. The inn is the first house facing Manzanita.
OPEN	All year
DESCRIPTION	A 1905 two-story Victorian inn decorated with antiques and warm colors.
NO. OF ROOMS	Five rooms with private bathrooms.
RATES	High-season rates are $91-110 for a single or double. Regular-season rates are $60-90 for a single or double. There is no minimum stay and cancellation requires 20 days' notice.
CREDIT CARDS	MasterCard, Visa

BREAKFAST	Full, elegant breakfast is served in the dining room. Some of the favorites include eggs Benedict with smoked salmon, cheese blintz, rhubarb muffins, Belgium waffles loaded with fresh berries, crepes, and buttermilk scones, plus fresh-ground coffee and teas served with fruit juices and smoothies. "Great conversations!"
AMENITIES	Custom robes for each room, fresh flowers in the rooms/common areas, wine and sherry in the evening, central air conditioning, custom soaps for each room, help with tickets to the various events in the area and with dinner reservations.
RESTRICTIONS	No smoking, no pets. Rosie, Pinto, Buckwheat, Sophie, Stripe, Fric, and Frac are the resident cats.
REVIEWED	*Best Places to Stay in the Pacific Northwest, Official Guide to American Historic Inns, National Trust Guide to Historic Bed & Breakfasts, Inn and Travel: Guide for Business and Leisure Travelers*
MEMBER	Professional Association of Innkeepers International, Oregon Bed & Breakfast Guild

JESSELL HOUSE

541 Holly Street, Ashland, OR 97520   541-488-0588

LAUREL STREET INN

174 N Main Street, Ashland, OR 97520   541-488-2222

LITHIA ROSE BED & BREAKFAST

163 Granite Street, Ashland, OR 97520   541-482-1882
WEBSITE www.mind.net/lithiarose   800-354-9914

LITHIA SPRINGS INN

2165 W Jackson Road, Ashland, OR 97520
EMAIL lithia@mind.net
WEBSITE www.ashlandinn.com

541-482-7128
800-482-7128

LOCATION	Two miles from the theaters of the Oregon Shakespeare Festival.
DESCRIPTION	A country inn on 8 acres with flower and organic vegetable gardens.
NO. OF ROOMS	All rooms and cottages with private bathrooms.
RATES	Year-round rates are $95-125 for a double, $195 for the Parisian Suite, and the cottages rent for $145-175. Ask about specials.
BREAKFAST	Full country breakfast includes fresh-baked breads and scones, buttermilk biscuits, muffins, an egg dish, sausage or bacon, bananas Foster or strawberry shortcake, orange juice, and Starbucks coffee.
AMENITIES	Hot springs–fed whirlpools in every room.
RATED	AAA 3 Diamonds

MCCALL HOUSE BED & BREAKFAST

153 Oak Street, Ashland, OR 97520
Bobbie & Ed Bludau, Innkeepers
EMAIL mccall@jeffnet.org

541-482-9296
800-808-9749 (reservations)
WEBSITE www.mccallhouse.com

LOCATION	Near Lithia Park, one block from the Oregon Shakespeare Festival.
DESCRIPTION	A restored 1883 Italianate manor and carriage house, listed on the National Historic Register.
NO. OF ROOMS	Eight rooms with private bathrooms.
RATES	Please call for current rates. There is a two-night minimum stay on weekends from June through September. Cancellation requires 30 days' notice less a $15 fee per room.
BREAKFAST	Full country breakfast is served in the dining room.
RESTRICTIONS	No smoking, no pets, children over 11 are welcome.

Morical House Garden Inn

668 N Main Street, Ashland, OR 97520　　　　　541-482-2254
Gary & Sandye Moore, Innkeepers　　　　　　800-208-0960
WEBSITE www.garden-inn.com

LOCATION	Close to the theaters of the Oregon Shakespeare Festival.
DESCRIPTION	A restored 1882 Eastlake Victorian farmhouse decorated with period antiques, stained-glass windows, and woodwork, and situated on 2 landscaped acres.
NO. OF ROOMS	Seven rooms with private bathrooms.
RATES	Call for current rates and cancellation information.
CREDIT CARDS	American Express, Discover, MasterCard, Visa
BREAKFAST	Full breakfast is served in the dining room or on the sun porch and includes fresh ingredients from the Northwest.
AMENITIES	Baby grand piano, fireplace, central air conditioning and heating, gardens with ponds, waterfalls, and a bird sanctuary.
RESTRICTIONS	No smoking, no pets (boarding is available at a nearby kennel), children over 12 are welcome.
KUDOS/COMMENTS	"Beautiful setting, great breakfast—and Gary folds the napkins in the darnedest shapes!" "The two garden rooms are beautiful. Sandy and Gary are wonderful hosts." "Warm and witty innkeepers who provide attention to details in food preparation, service, and the inn's decor. Wonderful garden!" "Beautiful gardens! Great host."

Mousetrap Inn

312 Helman Street, Ashland, OR 97520　　　　541-482-9228
EMAIL mousetrapinn@stealthcom.com　　　　　800-460-5453
WEBSITE www.stealthcom.com/mousetrapinn

Mount Ashland Inn

550 Mount Ashland Road, Ashland, OR 97520　　541-482-8707
Chuck & Laurel Biegert, Resident Owners　　　　800-830-8707
EMAIL mtashinn@teleport.com　　　　　　　　FAX 541-482-1775
WEBSITE www.mtashlandinn.com

Mount Ashland Inn, Ashland

LOCATION	South of Ashland on I-5, take exit 6 and follow signs to Mount Ashland Ski Area. The inn is 5.5 miles from I-5 on the way to the ski area.
OPEN	All year
DESCRIPTION	A 1987 four-story handcrafted log lodge with early American antiques and spectacular mountain views.
NO. OF ROOMS	Five rooms with private bathrooms. Try the Sky Lake Suite.
RATES	June 1 through October 31 and December 17 through January 2, rates are $94-110 for a single or double and $115-190 for a suite. The entire B&B rents for $809. November through April (on non-holidays and weekdays), rates are $74-90 for a single or double and $95-165 for a suite. The entire B&B rents for $679. There is a minimum stay on weekends and holidays, and cancellation requires 15 days' notice.
CREDIT CARDS	Discover, MasterCard, Visa
BREAKFAST	Full breakfast features a two- or three-course gourmet meal, individually presented and served.
AMENITIES	Rooms with robes, hairdryers, wineglasses, slippers; hot tub and sauna outdoors; common area with hot and cold beverages and snacks; complimentary snowshoes, cross-country skis, sled, and mountain bikes; discounted downhill ski lift passes; shuttle for hiking, skiing, and biking.
RESTRICTIONS	No smoking, no pets, children over 10 are welcome. The resident golden retrievers Whistler and Aspen often accompany guests on

	hikes on the Pacific Crest Trail right outside the front door, while Steamboat the cat prefers to rest up at the inn.
REVIEWED	*Weekends for Two in the Pacific Northwest*, Fodor's *West Coast*, *The Best Places to Kiss in the Northwest*, *Northwest Best Places*
MEMBER	Oregon Bed & Breakfast Guild, Professional Association of Innkeepers International, Oregon Lodging Association
RATED	AAA 3 Diamonds, Mobil 3 Stars, *Best Places to Kiss* 3 Lips

NEIL CREEK HOUSE BED & BREAKFAST

341 Mowetza Drive, Ashland, OR 97520   541-482-6443
Paul & Gayle Negro, Innkeepers   800-460-7860
EMAIL *neilcrk@mind.net*   WEBSITE *www.mind.net/neilcrk*

DESCRIPTION	A contemporary inn nestled into the foothills of the Cascade and Siskiyou Mountains on 5 acres with a creek and pond.
NO. OF ROOMS	Two rooms with private bathrooms and a family suite with private bathrooms.
RATES	November through May, rates are $85 for a double and $150 for the family suite. June through October, rates are $100 for a double and $175 for the family suite. Cancellation requires 14 days' notice for a full refund.
BREAKFAST	Full breakfast is served in the dining room or on the deck.
AMENITIES	Down comforters, fruit basket, fresh flowers, pool, gazebo, pond, lawn bowling, badminton, croquet, volleyball, space for seminars and retreats.
RESTRICTIONS	No smoking, no pets, children over 12 are welcome. Jezabelle is the resident pooch.
MEMBER	Oregon Bed & Breakfast Guild, Professional Association of Innkeepers International, Ashland Bed & Breakfast Network, Oregon Lodging Association
KUDOS/COMMENTS	"Delightful retreat a few miles outside of town. (It's where I'd go to escape.)"

NIGHTIN' GAIL'S INN

117 N Main Street, Ashland, OR 97520   541-482-7373

Oak Hill Country Bed & Breakfast

2190 Siskiyou Boulevard, Ashland, OR 97520
Linda Johnson, Innkeeper
EMAIL *oakhill@mind.net*

541-482-1554
800-888-7434
FAX 541-482-1378

Oak Street Cottages

236 Oak Street, Ashland, OR 97520

541-488-3778

Oak Street Station Bed & Breakfast

239 Oak Street, Ashland, OR 97520

541-482-1726

KUDOS/COMMENTS "Beautifully appointed with very high-quality linens, wonderful food, and charmingly gracious and unpretentious hosts."

Parkside Cottage

171 Granite Street, Ashland, OR 97520

541-482-2320

Pedigrift House Bed & Breakfast

407 Scenic Drive, Ashland, OR 97520
Dorothy & Richard Davis, Innkeepers
EMAIL *pedigrift@opendoor.com*
WEBSITE *www.opendoor.com/pedigrift*

541-482-1888
800-262-4073
FAX 541-482-8867

LOCATION   Six blocks north of downtown Ashland on the corner of Wimer Street and Scenic Drive, two blocks up from North Main Street.

OPEN   All year

DESCRIPTION   An 1888 two-story Queen Anne Victorian inn, completely restored in 1994 and tastefully decorated with traditional and antique furnishings. Listed on the National Historic Register.

Pedigrift House Bed & Breakfast, Ashland

NO. OF ROOMS	Four rooms with private bathrooms.
RATES	May through October, rates are $125 for a single or double. November through April, rates are $85 for a single or double. There is a two-night minimum stay from June through September and cancellation requires 15 days' notice.
CREDIT CARDS	MasterCard, Visa
BREAKFAST	Full breakfast is served in the dining room and typically includes juice, fresh fruit plate, an entrée such as French toast or an egg dish, fresh-baked pastry, and a side of breakfast meat. Fresh cobbler is served daily.
AMENITIES	Complimentary soft drinks and wine available in guest refrigerator, fresh flowers in all rooms, fireplace in living room with matching leather love seats, many magazines and books, central air conditioning.
RESTRICTIONS	No smoking, no pets, children over 12 are welcome.
REVIEWED	*America's Favorite Inns and B&Bs of the West Coast, The Best Places to Kiss in the Northwest*
MEMBER	Oregon Bed & Breakfast Guild, Ashland's Bed & Breakfast Network, Professional Association of Innkeepers International
RATED	Mobil 2 Stars

PEERLESS HOTEL

243 Fourth Street, Ashland, OR 97520 541-488-1082
EMAIL *peerless@mind.net* 800-460-8758
WEBSITE *www.mind.net/peerless*

LOCATION	In Ashland's historic railroad district, three blocks from downtown.
DESCRIPTION	A restored European-style red-brick inn and restaurant decorated with antiques and Oriental rugs.
RATES	Please call for current rates and cancellation information. Gift certificates are available.
CREDIT CARDS	American Express, MasterCard, Visa
BREAKFAST	Full breakfast is served every day from June 15 through October 15 and on weekends only during the rest of the year, at which time continental breakfast is served on weekdays.
AMENITIES	Turndown service, honor bars, porch, garden, air conditioning, rooms with Jacuzzis or clawfoot tubs, rooms with 30-channel cable music system, on-site restaurant with room service.
RESTRICTIONS	No smoking inside, no pets, children over 14 are welcome.
KUDOS/COMMENTS	"Small, eight-room inn, nicely furnished and very elegant. Adjacent restaurant serves fine dinners."

PINEHURST INN AT JENNY CREEK

17250 Highway 66, Ashland, OR 97520 541-488-1002
Mike & Mary Jo Moloney, Innkeepers FAX 541-488-1002
EMAIL *mikemoloney@grrtech*

LOCATION	Twenty-three miles east of Ashland on Highway 66.
OPEN	February 14 through January 1
DESCRIPTION	A 1923 two-story log country inn with rustic interior and antiques. The first-floor restaurant has an old wood-burning stove, and there is a large stone fireplace in the front room.
NO. OF ROOMS	Six rooms with private bathrooms. The Moloneys recommend room 6.
RATES	Year-round rates are $75-95 for a single or double and $105 for a suite. There is no minimum stay and cancellation requires seven days' notice.
CREDIT CARDS	Discover, MasterCard, Visa

Pinehurst Inn at Jenny Creek, Ashland

BREAKFAST	Full breakfast is served in the dining room and includes anything from the restaurant's menu. Lunch and dinner are also available.
RESTRICTIONS	No smoking, no pets, children over 10 are welcome. Tags and Bucket are the resident cats.
REVIEWED	*The Best Places to Kiss in the Northwest, The Official Guide to American Historic Inns, Northwest Best Places, Flyer's Recreation Guide*

QUEEN ANNE BED & BREAKFAST

125 N Main Street, Ashland, OR 97520　　　541-482-0220
Elaine Martens, Innkeeper　　　800-460-6818

THE REDWING BED & BREAKFAST

115 N Main Street, Ashland, OR 97520　　　541-482-1807
Jerry Madsen & Jorge Perez, Innkeepers
EMAIL ORRedwing@aol.com

LOCATION	One block north of Ashland's plaza, two blocks from the Oregon Shakespeare Festival's theaters.
OPEN	All year

DESCRIPTION	A 1911 two-story Craftsman inn with original woodwork and lighting fixtures.
NO. OF ROOMS	Three rooms with private bathrooms. The best room is Titania's Glade.
RATES	June through October rates are $110-125 for a single or double. November and March rates are $75 for a single or double. April and May, rates are $90. There is a two-night minimum stay on weekends and cancellation requires 10 days' notice.
CREDIT CARDS	MasterCard, Visa
BREAKFAST	Full breakfast is served in the dining room and includes fresh fruit, breads and muffins, hot entreés, and juice, coffee, or tea.
AMENITIES	Robes for guests, new central air-conditioning system, and catering available for special events.
RESTRICTIONS	No smoking, no pets. Medea is the resident Oriental shorthair cat.
MEMBER	Ashland Bed & Breakfast Network, Oregon Bed & Breakfast Guild, Professional Association of Innkeepers International

ROCK GARDEN INN

561 Rock Street, Ashland, OR 97520   541-488-3965

ROMEO INN

295 Idaho Street, Ashland, OR 97520   541-488-0884
Don & Deana Politis, Innkeepers   800-915-8899
EMAIL *romeoinn@msn.com*   FAX 541-488-0817
WEBSITE *www.romeoinn.com*

LOCATION	From the plaza, proceed south on Main Street, turn right on Gresham Street, left on Iowa Street, and right on Idaho Street. The inn is on the corner of Idaho and Holly Streets.
OPEN	All year
DESCRIPTION	An elegant 1932 two-story Cape Cod inn set among pines and beautiful gardens in a quiet residential neighborhood near downtown.
NO. OF ROOMS	Six rooms with private bathrooms. Try the Stratford Suite.
RATES	May through October, rates are $130-180 for a single or double and $165-180 for a suite. November through April, rates are $95-150

	for a single or double and $150 for a suite. There is no minimum stay and cancellation requires 30 days' notice.
CREDIT CARDS	MasterCard, Visa
BREAKFAST	Full three-course breakfast is served in the dining room and may include fresh-squeezed orange juice, cranberry pecan scones, and ham soufflés with chili potatoes. The menu changes daily.
AMENITIES	Afternoon snack, king-size beds, robes, telephones, bedtime chocolates, air conditioning, outdoor swimming pool and Jacuzzi, gardens, refreshments available 24 hours, meeting facilities.
RESTRICTIONS	No smoking, no pets, children over 12 are welcome. Cleo is the resident cat.
REVIEWED	*Northwest Best Places, Best Places to Stay in the Pacific Northwest, The Great Towns of America, The Best Places to Kiss in the Northwest*
MEMBER	Oregon Bed & Breakfast Guild, Professional Association of Innkeepers International, Oregon Lodging Association
RATED	AAA 3 Diamonds, Mobil 3 Stars

ROYAL CARTER HOUSE BED & BREAKFAST

514 Siskiyou Boulevard, Ashland, OR 97520   541-482-5623

SHREW'S HOUSE

570 Siskiyou Boulevard, Ashland, OR 97520   541-482-9214
Laurence & Laura Shrewsbury, Innkeepers
WEBSITE *www.shrews.com*

SUMMER PLACE INN

534 Siskiyou Boulevard, Ashland, OR 97520   541-488-5650

WATERSIDE INN

70 Water Street, Ashland, OR 97520   541-482-3315

WEISINGER'S VINEYARD COTTAGE

3150 Siskiyou Boulevard, Ashland, Oregon 97520   541-488-5989
German and Spanish spoken   800-551-9463
EMAIL *john@weisingers.com*   FAX 541-488-5989
WEBSITE *www.weisingers.com*

LOCATION	From I-5, take exit 14 onto Highway 66 and go west about 0.5 mile. Take a left at Tolman Creek Road. Where the road ends, take a left onto Siskiyou Boulevard. Watch for the Weisinger's Winery sign on the right side of the road.
OPEN	All year
DESCRIPTION	A 1948 one-story country cottage—a restored apple storage building—nestled in the middle of a lovely vineyard, which is part of the Weisinger's of Ashland Winery. From the cottage, you have a bird's-eye view of the grapes and winery operations.
NO. OF ROOMS	A one-bedroom cottage.
RATES	High-season rate is $150; low-season rates are $110-125. There is a minimum stay from June through October. Cancellation requires 14 days' notice.
CREDIT CARDS	MasterCard, Visa
BREAKFAST	A food and wine basket with pastries and coffee is included the first night.
AMENITIES	Guests receive a gift basket containing a bottle of wine, cheese, crackers, coffee, pastries, wine soap, wine jelly, corkscrew; hot tub on deck; gas free-standing stove in the living room; air conditioning.
RESTRICTIONS	No smoking, no pets, no children. Chardonnay and Kitty are the resident Lab and Manx cat. They are extremely friendly and calm and have their own web pages (www.weisingers.com/pets.htm).
REVIEWED	*The Best Places to Kiss in the Northwest*
RATED	*Best Places to Kiss* 3.5 Lips

WIMER STREET INN

75 Wimer Street, Ashland, OR 97520 541-488-2319
WEBSITE www.abbnet.com

WINCHESTER COUNTRY INN

35 S Second Street, Ashland, OR 97520 541-488-1115
WEBSITE www.winchesterinn.com

KUDOS/COMMENTS "Victorian country inn. Wonderful restaurant. Downtown Ashland."

WOLFE MANOR INN

586 B Street, Ashland, OR 97520 541-488-3676
Sybil & Ron Maddox, Innkeepers 800-801-3676
WEBSITE www.wolfemanor.com FAX 541-488-4567

LOCATION   Turn north at the Safeway on Siskiyou Boulevard and go one block. Jog left on East Main, then right on Fifth Street. Go two blocks to B Street. Look for the inn on the corner of Fifth and B Streets.

OPEN   January 12 through November 15

DESCRIPTION   A 1910 two-story Craftsman inn located in a quiet neighborhood convenient to downtown Ashland, restored with traditional decor.

Wolfe Manor Inn, Ashland

NO. OF ROOMS	Five rooms with private bathrooms. Try Alyce's Alcove.
RATES	May 26 through October 15, rates are $99-129 for a single or double. October 16 through February 27, rates are $79. There is a minimum stay during weekends and holidays during May through October. Cancellation requires 30 days' notice less a $15 fee.
CREDIT CARDS	American Express, Diners Club, Discover, MasterCard, Visa
BREAKFAST	Full breakfast is served in the dining room and includes fresh-squeezed orange juice, choice of hot beverage, seasonal fresh fruit, hot and cold cereals, fresh-baked muffins and scones, and a breakfast entrée.
AMENITIES	A 24-hour snack and beverage center, bathrobes, air conditioning, port, truffles.
RESTRICTIONS	No smoking, no pets, children over 12 are welcome. There are several "timid but very affectionate" tabby cats roaming the premises.
REVIEWED	*The Best Places to Kiss in the Northwest*
MEMBER	Oregon Bed & Breakfast Association, Oregon Bed & Breakfast Guild, Ashland's Bed & Breakfast Network, Professional Association of Innkeepers International, American Bed & Breakfast Association, Oregon Lodging Association, National Bed & Breakfast Association
RATED	ABBA 3 Crowns

THE WOODS HOUSE BED & BREAKFAST INN

333 N Main Street, Ashland, OR 97520
Francoise & Lester Roddy, Innkeepers
EMAIL woodshse@mind.net
WEBSITE www.mind.net/woodshouse/

541-488-1598
800-435-8260
FAX 541-482-8027

LOCATION	Take exit 19 off I-5 and turn right onto Valley View Road. Take a left onto Highway 99 heading toward Ashland center. Go 2 miles; the inn is on the right between Wimer and Manzanita Streets.
OPEN	All year
DESCRIPTION	A 1908 two-story Craftsman inn and adjacent carriage house on 0.5 acre of gardens, decorated with English antiques and Victorian and romantic touches.
NO. OF ROOMS	Six rooms with private bathrooms. The Roddys recommend the Bouquet Room.
RATES	June through October, rates are $100-120 for a single or double. November through May, rates are $75-105 for a single or double.

The Woods House Bed & Breakfast Inn, Ashland

	There is a two-night minimum stay and cancellation requires 21 days' notice for a full refund.
CREDIT CARDS	Discover, MasterCard, Visa
BREAKFAST	Full breakfast is served on china with silver, crystal goblets, and fine linens in the dining room, guestrooms, or the garden during summer. Breakfast includes fresh fruit plates, fresh-baked hot breads (scones, muffins, cinnamon rolls), and a hot entrée (alternates between sweet and savory), plus juice and hot beverages.
AMENITIES	Roses from the garden, fresh cookies all day, lots of good books and places to curl up and read, book of local restaurants' menus (hosts will make reservations for you); TV, fax, data ports, guest refrigerator, laundry facilities.
RESTRICTIONS	No smoking, no pets, children over 12 are welcome. Jasmine is the resident Newfoundland. Katie and Funny Face are the resident cats, a Flamepoint and calico, respectively.
REVIEWED	*Northwest Best Places; America's Favorite Inns, B&Bs & Small Hotels; Best Places to Stay in the Pacific Northwest; Fodor's B&Bs, Country Inns, & Other Weekend Pleasures*
MEMBER	Ashland's Bed & Breakfast Network, Professional Association of Innkeepers International

ASTORIA

Founded in 1811 by John Jacob Astor's fur traders, Astoria lays claim to being the oldest permanent American settlement west of the Rockies. Today this town at the mouth of the Columbia River is like a museum without walls. Well-maintained Victorian homes line the hillside along Franklin, Grand, and Irving. The bustling waterfront—once the locale of canneries and river steamers—is now an active port for oceangoing vessels and fishing boats. The Columbia River Maritime Museum is the finest of its kind in the Northwest. Restored small craft are displayed in the Great Hall, and seven thematic galleries depict different aspects of the region's maritime history. Six miles southwest of Astoria, Lewis and Clark's 1805–6 winter encampment is re-created at the Fort Clatsop National Memorial.

ASTORIA INN BED & BREAKFAST

3391 Irving Avenue, Astoria, OR 97103　　　503-325-8153
Mickey Cox, Innkeeper　　　　　　　　　　800-718-8153
WEBSITE www.moriah.com/astorinn/

LOCATION	Astoria is approximately 2 hours from Portland and about 3½ hours from Seattle. Once in Astoria, the B&B is 1.5 miles from downtown.
OPEN	All year
DESCRIPTION	An 1890 three-story Victorian farmhouse inn that sits in a quiet residential area on a hill overlooking the Columbia River.
NO. OF ROOMS	Four rooms with private bathrooms.
RATES	May through September, rates are $70-85 for a single or double. October through April, rates are $60-75 for a single or double. There is no minimum stay and cancellation requires 48 hours' notice.
CREDIT CARDS	Discover, MasterCard, Visa
BREAKFAST	Full breakfast is served and includes an egg dish, meat, fruit or vegetables, juice, coffee, and tea.
AMENITIES	Snapple and water in rooms; cookies, candy, coffee, and tea always available.
RESTRICTIONS	No smoking, no pets, no children. Wrinkles is the resident English bulldog. She is blind and a bit deaf and thinks everyone is there just to see her.
REVIEWED	Fodor's, The Rough Guide
MEMBER	Oregon Bed & Breakfast Guild, Oregon Lodging Association

BENJAMIN YOUNG INN

3652 Duane Street, Astoria, OR 97103　　　　503-325-6172
Carolyn Hammer, Innkeeper　　　　　　　　800-201-1286
French and limited Spanish spoken
EMAIL benyoung@willapabay.org
WEBSITE www.ohwy.com/or/b/benyoung.htm

LOCATION	East of Astoria near Highway 30 and 37th Street. Turn south on 37th, go one block, and turn right on Duane Street.
OPEN	All year
DESCRIPTION	An 1888 three-story Victorian Queen Anne inn on a 0.75-acre estate with a domed cupola, sunny front porch, original carriage house, and stained-glass windows. Listed on the National and State Historic Registers.
NO. OF ROOMS	Five rooms with private bathrooms. Carolyn recommends the Fireplace Room with the double Jacuzzi.
RATES	Year-round rates are $65-80 for a single or double and $100-135 for a suite. Stay three nights and the fourth night is free. The entire inn rents for $450-500, depending on the season. There is a two-night minimum stay during holiday and festival weekends and cancellation requires seven days' notice.

Benjamin Young Inn, Astoria

CREDIT CARDS	American Express, Diners Club, Discover, MasterCard, Visa
BREAKFAST	Full breakfast served in the dining room, which overlooks the Columbia River, features fresh local berries and other fruits, fresh-baked breads, hot egg and griddle dishes, coffee, and tea. Lunch, dinner, and special meals are also available, as is catering for groups of eight to 100.
AMENITIES	Robes in the Dorothy Room, flowers and candy, piano, fireplace, stereo in large living room, afternoon coffee or tea, fruit and homemade cookies, off-street parking, storage for bikes, near pier and sea lions, catering for weddings available.
RESTRICTIONS	No smoking, no pets
REVIEWED	Fodor's The Pacific Northwest's Best Bed & Breakfasts
MEMBER	Astoria–Warrenton Bed & Breakfast Association

CLEMENTINE'S BED & BREAKFAST

847 Exchange Street, Astoria, OR 97103
Judith Taylor, Innkeeper & Chef
EMAIL jtaylor@clementinesbb.com
WEBSITE www.clementines-bb.com

800-521-6801

COLUMBIA RIVER INN B&B

1681 Franklin Avenue, Astoria, OR 97103
Karen Nelson, Innkeeper

503-325-5044
800-953-5044

FRANKLIN STREET STATION BED & BREAKFAST

1140 Franklin Avenue, Astoria, OR 97103

503-325-4314
800-448-1098

Grandview Bed & Breakfast, Astoria

GRANDVIEW BED & BREAKFAST

1574 Grand Avenue, Astoria, OR 97103   503-325-5555
Charleen Maxwell, Innkeeper   800-488-3250
WEBSITE *www.moriah.com/grandview*

LOCATION	Astoria is about two hours from Portland.
OPEN	All year
DESCRIPTION	A 1896 four-story Victorian bed & breakfast.
NO. OF ROOMS	Seven rooms with private bathrooms; two rooms with two shared bathrooms. Charleen recommends the Gazebo Room.
RATES	March 17 through October 31, rates are $69-96 for a single or double with a private bathroom, $45-65 for a single or double with a shared bathroom, and $93-159 for a suite. Ask about low-season rates. There is no minimum stay and a 24-hour cancellation policy.
CREDIT CARDS	Discover, MasterCard, Visa
BREAKFAST	Breakfast includes a hot beverage, orange juice, fruit bowl, muffins, and smoked salmon with cream cheese and bagels.
AMENITIES	Snacks, hot cocoa, teas.

RESTRICTIONS	No smoking, no pets, children over 8 are welcome in two rooms and children over 10 in all rooms. No liquor, beer, or wine on premises. Kearsarge is the resident German shepherd.
REVIEWED	*Fodor's, Quick Escapes in the Pacific Northwest, Lonely Planet*
MEMBER	Oregon Lodging Association

ROSEBRIAR HOTEL

636 14th Street, Astoria, OR 97103
Anthony & Teresa Tavoloni, Innkeepers
EMAIL rosebriar@oregoncoastlodgings.com
WEBSITE www.oregoncoastlodgings.com/rosebriar

503-325-7427
800-487-0224
FAX 503-325-6937

LOCATION	Corner of 14th and Franklin, one block up the hill from the southwest corner of downtown Astoria.
OPEN	All year
DESCRIPTION	An elegant 1902 three-story neoclassic Georgian hotel, a local historic landmark and former convent, restored to period and traditionally furnished.
NO. OF ROOMS	Eleven rooms with private bathrooms. Try the Carriage House.
RATES	June through September, rates are $65-135 for a single or double, $95 for a suite, $135 for the carriage house, and $991-1049 for the entire inn. October through May, rates are $39-109 for a single or double, $59-89 for a suite, $79-109 for the carriage house, and $619-847 for the entire inn. There is a two-night minimum stay on weekends and during high season and cancellation requires seven days' notice.
CREDIT CARDS	American Express, Diners Club, Discover, MasterCard, Visa
BREAKFAST	Full gourmet breakfast is served restaurant-style in the dining room. The menu changes daily. Catering is also available.
AMENITIES	The former chapel seats 50 and is perfect for weddings, conferences, and retreats; on-site catering is available; the Carriage House is handicapped accessible; fireplaces; spas.
RESTRICTIONS	No smoking, no pets
REVIEWED	*Fodor's*
MEMBER	Oregon Bed & Breakfast Guild, Oregon Lodging Association

AURORA

In 1856, Dr. William Keil brought a group of Pennsylvania Germans to establish a communal settlement. Called the Harmonites, the commune faded away after the death of its founder; today most people come to the town, on the National Register of Historic Places, to comb through the myriad antique stores that occupy the many clapboard and Victorian houses along the highway. The Old Aurora Colony Museum offers tours that recount the communal history of the town. History-minded visitors will also enjoy Champoeg State Park, site of one of the first settlements in the Willamette Valley and now a fine place to picnic, hike, or bike along the river. And rose lovers will want to wander a few miles farther up the river (west on Champoeg Road and across Highway 219) to Heirloom Old Garden Roses, one of the country's premier commercial growers of old garden roses.

INN AT AURORA

15109 Second Street NE, Aurora, OR 97002　　　503-678-1932
Fay & Dave Weaver, Innkeepers　　　888-799-1374
EMAIL fdweaver@teleport.com　　WEBSITE www.innataurora.aurora.or.us

LOCATION	Aurora is halfway between Portland and Salem, just east of I-5. Take exit 278 and travel east along Ehlen Road until it turns into Main Street in Aurora. Turn left onto Second Street near the center of town. Cross Highway 99E and go past the Aurora Colony Museum to the end of Second Street.
OPEN	All year
DESCRIPTION	A 1995 two-story colonial inn located in the National Historic District and designed to reflect the old Aurora Colony, with traditional decor flavored with antiques and quilts.
NO. OF ROOMS	Four rooms with private bathrooms.
RATES	Year-round rates are $89-119 for a single or double and $119 for a suite. There is no minimum stay and cancellation requires 14 days' notice.
CREDIT CARDS	American Express, MasterCard, Visa
BREAKFAST	Full breakfast is served in the dining room and includes fresh fruit, juice, quiche, coffeecake or muffins, coffee and tea, Dutch baby pancakes, sausage, and fruit. Early morning coffee, tea, and lattes are available.
AMENITIES	Air conditioning, robes and jetted tub in suite, cable TV, data ports for computers, phones, complimentary beverages in rooms, early morning coffee and tea before breakfast, cookies and tea in living room.
RESTRICTIONS	No smoking, no pets, no children.

Inn at Aurora, Aurora

REVIEWED *The Romantic Pacific Northwest*

MEMBER Associated Bed & Breakfasts of Mount Hood and Northern Willamette Valley, Oregon Bed & Breakfast Guild, Mid-Willamette Valley Bed & Breakfast Association

AZALEA

Azalea is perched on I-5 just north of the Cow River and below Canyon Creek Pass, about 30 miles north of Grants Pass.

HAVENSHIRE BED & BREAKFAST

1098 Hogum Creek Road, Azalea, OR 97410   541-837-3511
Evelyn Jones, Innkeeper

LOCATION Take I-5 south to exit 88, go right 0.9 mile to Starveout Circle Road, turn right and go 2 miles. Take a left on Hogum Circle Road and go 1 mile, keeping to the right. Look for signs along the way.

OPEN All year

DESCRIPTION A 1981 one-and-a-half-story English Tudor decorated to the seasons, with country furnishings and handmade toys, dolls, needlework, and other crafts. "The upstairs brings back one's childhood," says Evelyn.

NO. OF ROOMS One room with a private bathroom and one room shares two bathrooms.

RATES	Year-round rates are $65 for a double with a private bathroom and $60 for a double with a shared bathroom (a price that has remained the same for 12 years!). Cancellations result in the $20 deposit being held as credit for a return visit within the year.
CREDIT CARDS	No
BREAKFAST	Full breakfast is served in the dining room and may include fruit, juice, bacon, and French toast. The menu changes with each visit.
AMENITIES	Air conditioning; nature walks; wildflowers in spring; cookies, tea or coffee; two creeks; lots of gold mining history on the property from the 1865 Hogum Creek Mine.
RESTRICTIONS	No smoking, ask about pets and children. There is one outside cat roaming the property. He hides when strangers are around.
REVIEWED	*Country Innformation*

BAKER CITY

Baker's restful city park, old-time main street, and mature shade trees may give it a Midwest flavor, but the backdrop is decidedly Northwest. Located in the valley between the Wallowas and the Elkhorns, Baker makes a good base camp for forays into the nearby mountain Gold Rush towns. The Oregon Trail Interpretive Center, 4 miles east of I-84 on Highway 86, is worth the detour. The multimedia walk-through brings the Oregon Trail experience to life. Open every day except Christmas and New Year's Day. The Elkhorn Mountains, west of Baker, contain most of the old mining towns, which you can tour on a 100-mile loop from Baker (some on unpaved roads). The deserted towns of Granite, Bourne, Bonanza, and Whitney are well worth visiting. There's a restored narrow-gauge steam train in the now revitalized ghost town of Sumpter that operates between Memorial Day and Labor Day.

A DEMAIN "UNTIL TOMORROW" BED & BREAKFAST

1790 Fourth Street, Baker City, OR 97814   541-523-2509
Pat & Kristi Flanagan, Innkeepers
WEBSITE *www.activeaccess.com/ademain*

LOCATION	Five-and-a-half hours from Portland off I-84.
DESCRIPTION	A restored two-story Victorian inn decorated with period antiques.
RATES	Please call for current rates. Cancellation requires seven days' notice.

BREAKFAST	Full breakfast is served by candlelight in the dining room or on the balcony.
AMENITIES	Fresh flowers, turndown service, feather beds, goose-down comforters and pillows.
RESTRICTIONS	No smoking, no pets, well-behaved children are welcome.

BAER HOUSE B&B

2333 Main Street, Baker City, OR 97814 541-524-1812
Judy & Nick Greear, Innkeepers
EMAIL *baerhouse@triax.com*
WEBSITE *www.triax.com/baerhouse*

LOCATION	From I-84, take exit 304 west for 0.5 mile, then south (left) on Main Street for one block.
OPEN	All year
DESCRIPTION	An 1882 two-story Victorian Italianate host home with Victorian and country decor, near the path of the Oregon Trail.
NO. OF ROOMS	One room with private bathroom, and two rooms share one bathroom. Try the Anthony Room.
RATES	Year-round rates are $65-80 for a single or double with a private bathroom, $55-65 for a single or double with a shared bathroom, $50-60 for a suite, and the entire B&B rents for $220-260. There is no minimum stay and cancellation requires 48 hours' notice or a $35 fee.
CREDIT CARDS	American Express, Discover, MasterCard, Visa
BREAKFAST	Full breakfast is served in the dining room and includes juice, fresh fruit, meat, and specialties such as Italian apple bake or decadent French toast.
AMENITIES	Upstairs kitchenette and laundry facilities, robes, meeting facility, historic-district walking tour.
RESTRICTIONS	No smoking, no pets, children over 12 are welcome.

GRANT HOUSE

2525 Third Street, Baker City, OR 97814 541-523-6685
EMAIL *granthbb@triax.com* 800-606-7468

POWDER RIVER BED & BREAKFAST

HCR 87, Box 500, Baker City, OR 97814   541-523-7143
Phil & Danae Simonski, Innkeepers   800-600-7143
Some Spanish and some German spoken
EMAIL *powdergs@eoni.com*

LOCATION	From exit 304 in Baker City, go west on Campbell Street to the first traffic light and turn left onto Main Street. Go through three more traffic lights and under the overpass. From the overpass, the B&B is exactly 1 mile on the right.
OPEN	All year
DESCRIPTION	A 1962 two-story modern guesthouse furnished with antiques and set in a large yard with formal gardens and fruit trees.
NO. OF ROOMS	Two rooms with private bathrooms.
RATES	Year-round rates are $50-60 for a single or double. There is no minimum stay and cancellation requires one week's notice.
CREDIT CARDS	MasterCard, Visa
BREAKFAST	Full breakfast is served in the dining room. Entrées include sourdough waffles with barbecued sausage. All dietary needs are accommodated.
AMENITIES	Guided fishing trips, full-line tackle shop, meeting facilities for up to 18, handicapped access.
RESTRICTIONS	No smoking, pets and children are welcome. Winer and Squatter are the resident outdoor cats.
REVIEWED	*Where to Stay in Oregon*
MEMBER	Oregon Lodging Association, Baker County Bed & Breakfast Association

BANDON

The town of Bandon looks and feels newly painted, freshly scrubbed, and friendly. Some locals believe Bandon sits on a "ley line," an underground crystalline structure that is reputed to be the focus of powerful cosmic energies. Certainly there's magic here. Begin exploring in Old Town, where there are a number of galleries. The best beach access is from the south jetty or Face Rock Viewpoint on Beach Loop Road. This route parallels the ocean in view of weather-sculpted rock formations and is a good alternative to Highway 101 (especially if you're on a bike). Just north of Bandon, Bullards Beach State Park occupies an expansive area crisscrossed with hiking and biking trails that lead to uncrowded, driftwood and kelp-cluttered beaches. Good windsurfing beaches abound on the river and ocean side of the park. Bandon's cranberry bogs make it one of the nation's largest producers.

BAILEY'S CEDAR HOUSE BED & BREAKFAST

2226 Seven Devils Road, Bandon, OR 97411 541-347-3356
Glen & Joanne Bailey, Innkeepers

BANDON BEACH HOUSE

2866 Beach Loop, Bandon, OR 97411 541-347-1196
Steve & Adrienne Casey, Innkeepers FAX 541-347-1204
EMAIL beachhouse@harborside.com WEBSITE www.bandonbeach.com

LOCATION	On the ocean, 90 miles from the Oregon-California border.
DESCRIPTION	An oceanfront inn decorated with contemporary and antique furnishings.
NO. OF ROOMS	All rooms with private bathrooms.
RATES	Winter rates are $140 for a double; summer rates are $160 for a double. Cancellation requires 14 days' notice for a full refund.
CREDIT CARDS	No
BREAKFAST	Continental breakfast is served in the Great Room and includes fruit, homemade breads, cereals, egg dishes, coffee, and tea.
AMENITIES	Rooms with river-rock fireplaces; lounge chairs perfect for contemplating the unusual rock formations offshore.
RESTRICTIONS	No smoking, no pets, no children
MEMBER	Professional Association of Innkeepers International
KUDOS/COMMENTS	"Awesome! Even chocolate chip cookies and a freshly laid fire in your room each evening."

BEACH STREET BED & BREAKFAST

200 Beach Street, Bandon, OR 97411 541-347-5124
Ray & Sharon, Innkeepers
WEBSITE www.beach-street.com

THE HISTORIC RIVER HOUSE

Route 1, Box 890-10, Bandon, OR 97411
EMAIL garrison@mail.coos.or.us

541-347-1414
888-221-6936

LIGHTHOUSE BED & BREAKFAST

650 Jetty Road, Bandon, OR 97411
Shirley Chalupa, Innkeeper
EMAIL lthousbb@harborside.com   WEBSITE www.morian.com/lighthouse

541-347-9316

LOCATION	At the mouth of the Coquille River, four blocks from Old Town.
OPEN	All year
DESCRIPTION	A 1980 two-story contemporary inn with some antiques and some modern decor.
NO. OF ROOMS	Five rooms with private bathrooms.
RATES	Year-round rates are $95-155 for a single or double and $155 for a suite. November 1 through May 1 features a 15 percent discount for multiple-night stays. There is no minimum stay and cancellation requires one week's notice.
CREDIT CARDS	MasterCard, Visa
BREAKFAST	Full breakfast is served in the dining room and includes fresh fruit, juice, egg dishes, potatoes, bacon or ham, muffins or other breads, cereal, coffee, milk, and tea.
AMENITIES	Wine in the evening.
RESTRICTIONS	No smoking, no pets, children over 12 are welcome by prior arrangement.
REVIEWED	*Northwest Best Places, The Best Places to Kiss in the Northwest, National Geographic Traveler, Laniers Bed & Breakfast Inns and Guesthouses, Fodor's*
KUDOS/COMMENTS	"Gorgeous. And Shirley can cook!"

PACIFIC HOUSE

2165 Beach Loop Drive, Bandon, OR 97411
K Thompson, Innkeeper
EMAIL pacific@harborside.com
WEBSITE www.moriah.com/pacific

541-347-9526

BEAVERTON

Settled in 1868 as a railroad town and named in honor of the bountiful beavers that once populated the area, Beaverton today is a center of agriculture and light industry. A few of the local celebrations include the Tigard Festival of Balloons, A Taste of Beaverton, and the Verboort Sausage Festival. Other food fetes include Blueberry, Strawberry, and Onion Festivals; the Tualatin Crawfish Festival; and the Founders Day Corn Roast. Portland is just minutes to the northeast.

ALOHA JUNCTION INN & GARDENS BED & BREAKFAST

5085 SW 170th Avenue, Beaverton, OR 97007
Sandra Eimers, Innkeeper
EMAIL alohajunction@juno.com
WEBSITE www.moiriah.com/inns

503-642-7236
888-832-5251
FAX 503-642-7236

LOCATION	On the west side of Beaverton approximately 14 miles west of Portland and 8 miles east of Hillsboro. Take Highway 26 to Murray Boulevard (exit 67), south to Farmington Road, west to SW 170th Avenue, and go north.
OPEN	All year
DESCRIPTION	A 1920s-era two-story farmhouse renovated with country cottage decor on 2 tranquil acres of green fields, flowers, and herb gardens.
NO. OF ROOMS	One room with a private bathroom, and three rooms share two bathrooms. Sandra recommends Belle's Boudoir.
RATES	Year-round rates are $75 for a single or double with a private bathroom, $59-65 for a single or double with a shared bathroom, $110 for a suite, and $230 for the entire B&B. There is no minimum stay and cancellations require a courtesy call with no penalty assessed.
CREDIT CARDS	Discover, MasterCard, Visa
BREAKFAST	Full, energizing breakfast is served in the dining room or on the veranda. Breakfast begins with a "fast-start jolt" of famous Northwest coffee and servings of regional specialties. Many of the ingredients are grown on-site in the organic garden. Special diets (vegetarian, diabetic, etc.) are accommodated by request. Brown-bag picnic lunches are also available
AMENITIES	Bouquet in room, robes, airport pickup and delivery, fax, photocopying, email, word processing, laundry service, complimentary refreshment upon arrival, therapeutic queen mattresses, TV/VCR, phone, handicapped access, ample parking for large vehicles (RVs), gazebo, hot tub, fragrant garden, self-serve area with refrigerator and microwave.

RESTRICTIONS	No smoking inside (there is a designated area outside). Winnie is the resident pooch, a Rhodesian Ridgeback. Also a rabbit named Rosie and several goats roaming the property.
MEMBER	Inns of Washington County

THE BRAUTIGAM HOUSE AT KENSINGTON PARK

19655 SW Jaylee Street, Beaverton, OR 97007   503-649-8033
Hans & Lore Brautigam, Innkeepers

THE YANKEE TINKER BED & BREAKFAST

5480 SW 183rd Avenue, Beaverton, OR 97007   503-649-0932
Jan & Ralph Wadleigh, Innkeepers   800-846-5372
EMAIL yankeetb7b@aol.com   503-649-0932
WEBSITE www.yankeetinker.com

LOCATION	One mile south of the 185th Avenue and Route 8 intersection.
OPEN	All year
DESCRIPTION	A 1970 one-story ranch-style B&B with colonial decor.
NO. OF ROOMS	One room with a private bathroom, and two rooms with two shared bathrooms.
RATES	Year-round rates are $75 for a single or double with a private bathroom and $50-65 for a single or double with a shared bathroom. There is no minimum stay and cancellation requires 72 hours' notice.
CREDIT CARDS	American Express, Diners Club, Discover, MasterCard, Visa
BREAKFAST	Full breakfast is served in the dining room and includes fresh-ground coffee, fresh-squeezed orange juice, and seasonal fruit with gingered yogurt. Entreés include peaches and cream and French toast.
AMENITIES	Cut flowers; robes; chocolates; guest refrigerators stocked with complimentary soft drinks, beer, and wine; air conditioning, handicapped-friendly.
RESTRICTIONS	No smoking, no pets
REVIEWED	Hidden Oregon
MEMBER	Oregon Bed & Breakfast Guild, Oregon Lodging Association, Professional Association of Innkeepers International
KUDOS/COMMENTS	"Great hosts, well-kept house and garden. They serve wine in the evening."

BEND

Bend was a quiet, undiscovered high-desert paradise until a push in the 1960s to develop recreation and tourism tamed Bachelor Butte (later renamed Mount Bachelor) into an alpine playground. Then came the golf courses, the airstrip, the bike trails, the river-rafting companies, the hikers, the tennis players, the rock hounds, and the skiers. Bend's popularity and its population (more than 50,000) have been on a steady increase ever since, propelling it into serious-destination status. Part of the charm of the town comes from the blinding blue sky and the pine-scented air. The other part of its appeal is its proximity to Mount Bachelor Ski Area (22 miles southwest of Bend). The High Desert Museum is an outstanding nonprofit center for natural and cultural history, located 4 miles south of Bend, that includes live-animal educational presentations.

COUNTRY INN THE CITY

1776 NE Eighth Street, Bend, OR 97701   541-385-7639

KUDOS/COMMENTS   "Lovely home, friendly, warm, fun! Good food!"

CRICKETWOOD COUNTRY B&B

63520 Cricketwood Road, Bend, OR 97701-9748   541-330-0747
Cristi Edmonston, Innkeeper   877-330-0747
                                           FAX 541-330-0747

LOCATION	Northeast 8 miles from historic downtown Bend.
OPEN	All year
DESCRIPTION	A 1989 two-story ranch-style home with country pine furnishings. Located on 10 acres with a small farm; eight minutes from historic downtown.
NO. OF ROOMS	One room with a private bathroom, and two rooms share 1½ bathrooms.
RATES	Year-round rates are $90 for a single or double with a private bathroom and $65-70 for a single or double with a shared bathroom. The entire B&B rents for $250 and up. There is a two-night minimum stay on the second weekend in July and holidays, and cancellation requires 14 days' notice.
CREDIT CARDS	Discover, MasterCard, Visa
BREAKFAST	Full breakfast is served in the dining room. Catering is available for additional meals.

AMENITIES	Flowers, robes, snack basket, Jacuzzi-style tub in private room, soda and juices, air-conditioning, hot homemade soup available on winter afternoons, pet boarding in barn available at additional cost.
RESTRICTIONS	No smoking, and no pets indoors. Bear is the long-haired cat and Pismo, the resident Border collie.

GAZEBO

21679 Obsidian Avenue, Bend, OR 97702   541-389-7202
Gale & Helen Estergreen, Innkeepers

JUNIPER ACRES BED & BREAKFAST

65220 Smokey Ridge Road, Bend, OR 97701   541-389-2193
Vern & Della Bjerk, Innkeepers
EMAIL *verndella@prodigy.net*

LOCATION	From Bend, drive northwest on Highway 20 for 6 miles and turn right on Smokey Ridge Road.
OPEN	All year
DESCRIPTION	A 1991 two-story lodge-style log home with country decor on 9.5 acres of wooded property with mountain views.
NO. OF ROOMS	Two rooms with private bathrooms.
RATES	Year-round rates are $70 for a double. There is a two-night minimum stay during weekends and cancellation requires seven days' notice.

Juniper Acres Bed & Breakfast, Bend

Lara House Bed & Breakfast, Bend

CREDIT CARDS	No
BREAKFAST	Full gourmet breakfast is served in the dining room and includes fresh coffee, tea, exotic juice drinks, fresh muffins or rolls, fruit or cereal, plus a main course such as an egg dish, waffles, or stuffed French toast.
AMENITIES	Rooms are air conditioned, refreshments in the afternoon or evening, walks along a country lane, large visiting and reading area, TV in rooms.
RESTRICTIONS	No smoking, no pets
REVIEWED	America's Wonderful Little Hotels & Inns

LARA HOUSE BED & BREAKFAST

640 NW Congress, Bend, OR 97701
Doug & Bobbye Boger, Innkeepers

541-388-4064
800-766-4064
FAX 541-388-4064

LOCATION	Take Highway 97 into Bend, turn west onto Franklin Avenue, go 0.9 mile, and turn left onto Louisiana. The B&B is on the corner of Louisiana and Congress.
OPEN	All year
DESCRIPTION	A 1910 three-story Craftsman inn with oak floors, a large brick fireplace, and casual, cozy decor.

NO. OF ROOMS	Six rooms with private bathrooms. Try the Drake Room.
RATES	Year-round rates are $55-75 for a single, $75-110 for a double, and $600 for the entire B&B. There is a minimum stay during holidays and cancellation requires 14 days' notice.
CREDIT CARDS	Discover, MasterCard, Visa
BREAKFAST	Full breakfast is served in the dining room or sun room overlooking the gardens and includes juice, coffee, tea, and an entrée such as sun-dried tomato quiche with fruit bread and fruit cup or stuffed French toast with fruit sauce. Early coffee is available.
AMENITIES	Afternoon snack, hot tub on raised deck, large spa towels, winter ski guide, ceiling fans in guestrooms.
RESTRICTIONS	No smoking inside, well-behaved children are welcome.
REVIEWED	*Best Places to Stay in the Pacific Northwest*, *The Best Places to Kiss in the Northwest*, *Fodor's*

MILL INN BED & BREAKFAST

642 NW Colorado Avenue, Bend, OR 97701   541-389-9198
Ev & Carol Stiles, Innkeepers   FAX 541-330-0966
EMAIL stiles@coinet.com

LOCATION	Coming from the north, take the Mount Bachelor Freeway entrance. Go to the first stoplight and turn right onto Colorado. Go six blocks to the corner of Bond and Colorado.
OPEN	All year
DESCRIPTION	A 1990 two-story rectangular inn with modern decor.
NO. OF ROOMS	Five rooms with private bathrooms, and five rooms share two bathrooms.
RATES	Year-round rates are $50-65 for a single or double with a private bathroom and $40-50 for a single or double with a shared bathroom. There is no minimum stay and cancellation requires 48 hours' notice.
CREDIT CARDS	MasterCard, Visa
BREAKFAST	Full breakfast is served in the dining room and includes juices, fresh fruit, cereals, and an entrée of the day, plus coffee, tea, hot chocolate, hot cider, or milk.
AMENITIES	Hot tub on back deck, fireplace in living room, air conditioning.
RESTRICTIONS	No smoking, no pets

THE SATHER HOUSE BED & BREAKFAST

7 NW Tumalo Avenue, Bend, OR 97701
Robbie Giamboi, Innkeeper
WEBSITE www.moriah.com/sather

541-388-1065
FAX 541-330-0591

SWALLOW RIDGE

65711 Twin Bridges Road, Bend, OR 97701
EMAIL bluesky@teleport.com

541-389-1913

VILLA GENOVESE

222 Urania Lane, Bend, OR 97702
Dominic & Patricia Genovese, Innkeepers
EMAIL villagenov@aol.com

541-318-3557
FAX 541-388-4439

BLUE RIVER

Not surprisingly, the Blue River flows past here on its way to hooking up with the McKenzie River. Nearby in the Willamette National Forest, the 1,200-acre Blue River Lake, a pricey project of the U.S. Corps of Engineers, is a hot spot for outdoor recreation.

DRIFT INN BED & BREAKFAST

51592 McKenzie Highway, Blue River, OR 97413
Mel Crabb & Carolyn Gabriel, Innkeepers
EMAIL driftnfish@aol.com

541-822-3822

LOCATION   East of Eugene. Head east on Highway 126 (McKenzie Highway) toward Blue River. Watch for milepost 40. Go 0.5 mile farther to driveway on right. Yellow mailbox with "Drift Inn B&B" across from driveway.

OPEN   All year

DESCRIPTION	A 1950 two-story cottage with mountain cabin decor.
NO. OF ROOMS	One room with a private bathroom and one room with a shared bathroom. The innkeepers recommend the downstairs room with the private bathroom.
RATES	Year-round rates are $50 per person for a double room. There is no minimum stay. Reservations require 50 percent nonrefundable deposit.
CREDIT CARDS	No
BREAKFAST	Full breakfast is served in the dining room. Special meals include a fish fry if a fishing trip is booked.
AMENITIES	Arrangements for professionally guided drift boat, fishing, and sight-seeing trips; whitewater rafting; fly-tying lessons; golf; hiking and cross-country skiing excursions. Massage therapy also an option.
RESTRICTIONS	No smoking, pets are negotiable. Shadow and Sandy are the resident dogs; also two cats.

Osprey Inn

McKenzie Bridge, Blue River, OR 97413   541-822-8186
WEBSITE www.osprey-inn.com

DESCRIPTION	A two-story inn along the McKenzie River.
NO. OF ROOMS	Three rooms with private bathrooms.
RATES	Please call for current rates and cancellation information.
BREAKFAST	Full breakfast is served in the dining room, in the guestrooms, or on the gazebos.
AMENITIES	Great Room with stone fireplace and wet bar, deck, picnic tables, lounge chairs.
AWARDS	1997 Best Bed & Breakfast, McKenzie River Chamber of Commerce

River's Edge Inn

91241 Blue River Drive, Blue River, OR 97413   541-822-3258
WEBSITE www.pond.net~bnbassoc/

BRIDAL VEIL

BRIDAL VEIL LODGE BED & BREAKFAST

46650 E Historic Columbia River Highway, 503-695-2333
Bridal Veil, OR 97010
EMAIL Lbslater@aol.com

BRIDGEPORT

BRUNO RANCH BED & BREAKFAST

US Highway 245, Bridgeport, OR 97819 541-446-3468

BRIGHTWOOD

Just west of Portland, Brightwood lies along scenic Highway 26, the road to the Mount Hood Wilderness Area.

BRIGHTWOOD GUESTHOUSE BED & BREAKFAST

64725 E Barlow Trail Road, Brightwood, OR 97011 503-622-5783
Jan Estep, Innkeeper 888-503-5783
 FAX 503-622-5783

LOCATION	From Portland, take I-84 east to exit 17 (Gresham and Mount Hood Community College). Go right at the second light onto 257th and drive approximately 4.5 miles to the four-way stop (no light). Turn right onto Powell, then left onto Highway 26E, and go 23 miles. Turn left at the Brightwood exit, drive 0.3 mile, turn left at the Y in the road, then right on Barlow Trail Road.
OPEN	All year
DESCRIPTION	A 1935 one-and-a-half-story cedar-shake cottage decorated with cedar paneling, wall hangings, bright oriental art and artifacts, and comfortable upholstered furnishings.

Brightwood Guesthouse Bed & Breakfast, Brightwood

NO. OF ROOMS	One room with a private bathroom.
RATES	Year-round rates are $132.50 for a single or double. Additional guests are $15.90 each. There are multiple-night discounts, a two-night minimum stay during weekends and holidays, and cancellation requires 72 hours' notice.
CREDIT CARDS	No
BREAKFAST	Full breakfast is served in the guesthouse or on the private deck and includes savory brioche or scrapple, homemade cream waffles, berries and whipped cream, maple syrup, muesli, roasted-potato and onion omelet, juice, coffee, and a truffle muffin for dessert.
AMENITIES	The guesthouse is always filled with flowers; coffee brewer with fresh Starbucks coffee; full kitchen with popcorn, teas, condiments, spices and herbs, flatware, dishes, and crystal stemware; two mountain bikes; CD player, clock radio, TV/VCR; kimonos and slippers; maid service. "Special events warrant a special libation or cake."
RESTRICTIONS	No smoking, no pets, children over 13 and under 9 months (non-ambulatory) are welcome. Hedgerow is the resident Siamese cat, and there are koi in the guesthouse pond. Hedgerow is not allowed in the guesthouse.
REVIEWED	*Where to Stay in Oregon; Hot Showers, Soft Beds and Dayhikes in the Central Cascades*

MEMBER	Associated Bed & Breakfasts of Mount Hood and the Northern Willamette Valley
KUDOS/COMMENTS	"A unique guesthouse styled after a Japanese teahouse. It has everything a guest would want and then some."

MAPLE RIVER

20525 East Mountain Country Lane,　　　　　　　503-622-6273
Brightwood, OR 97011
Jim & Barbara Dybvig, Innkeepers
WEBSITE www.moriah.com/inns

BROOKINGS

Brookings enjoys the state's mildest winter temperatures and is encircled by breathtaking beauty. To the north lie Samuel H. Boardman and Harris Beach State Parks; to the east, the verdant Siskiyou Mountains, deeply cut by the Chetco and Winchuck Rivers; and to the south, ancient redwood groves. Because of the favorable climate, most of the Easter lilies sold in North America are grown here. Brookings also boasts the Oregon Coast's safest harbor—and therefore it's a busy port. Just east of Highway 101 is Azalea State Park, where fragrant Western azaleas bloom in May, alongside wild strawberries, fruit trees, and violets; you can picnic amid all this splendor on hand-hewn myrtlewood tables. The Redwood Nature Trail in the Siskiyou National Forest winds through one of the few remaining groves of old-growth coastal redwoods in Oregon.

BROOKINGS SOUTH COAST INN

516 Redwood Street, Brookings, OR 97415　　　541-469-5557
Ken Raith & Keith Pepper, Innkeepers　　　　　800-525-9273
EMAIL scoastin@wave.net　　　　　　　　　　　FAX 541-469-6615

LOCATION	From the north: Take Highway 101 into Brookings. Turn left at the third stoplight onto Oak Street, then left onto Redwood Street. From the south: Take Highway 101 into Brookings and turn right at the first stoplight after crossing the Chetco River onto Oak Street. Then turn left onto Redwood Street.
OPEN	All year
DESCRIPTION	A 1917 two-story Craftsman inn designed by Bernard Maybeck and decorated with turn-of-the-century antiques.

NO. OF ROOMS	Four rooms with private bathrooms. Try the Rose Room.
RATES	Year-round rates are $89-109 for a single or double. There is no minimum stay and cancellation requires seven days' notice.
CREDIT CARDS	American Express, Discover, MasterCard, Visa
BREAKFAST	Full breakfast served in the dining room includes juice and entrées such as spiced waffles with fresh fruit sauces, orange French toast with marionberry Marnier sauce, or deep-dish French toast with cream cheese and brandied blueberry sauce.
AMENITIES	Robes, TV/VCR, ceiling fans in each room; video library; indoor hot tub and sauna; exercise equipment; wraparound porch; strolling garden; large stone fireplace; antique grand piano; antiques throughout.
RESTRICTIONS	No smoking, no pets, children over 12 are welcome. Muffin and Biscuit are the resident golden retrievers. They are on the premises, but not in guest areas unless requested.
REVIEWED	*Frommer's Washington & Oregon, Hidden Pacific Northwest, Northwest Best Places, Oregon Handbook, Lonely Planet*
MEMBER	Professional Association of Inkeepers International, Southern Oregon Coast Bed & Breakfast Association
RATED	AAA 2 Diamonds

CHART HOUSE LODGE, OUTFITTER AND B&B

15833 Pedrioli Drive, Brookings, OR 97415
David & Dorothy Lehton, Innkeepers
WEBSITE *www.virtualcities.com*

541-469-3867
800-290-6208

CHETCO RIVER INN

21202 High Prairie Road, Brookings, OR 97415
Sandra Brugger, Innkeeper
WEBSITE *www.chetcoriverinn.com*

541-670-1645

LOCATION	From Highway 101 in Brookings, go east on North Bank Chetco River Road for 17 miles. Cross the South Fork Bridge and turn left at the T. Go 0.3 mile and turn left at the sign.
OPEN	All year
DESCRIPTION	A 1987 two-story "modern rustic" backcountry inn, an environmentally sensitive lodge, open and spacious with comfortable furnishings, marble floors, and oriental rugs.

NO. OF ROOMS	Five rooms with private bathrooms.
RATES	Year-round rates are $115-135 for a single or double and $500 for the entire inn. There is no minimum stay and cancellation requires seven days' notice.
CREDIT CARDS	American Express, Discover, MasterCard, Visa
BREAKFAST	Full breakfast is served in the dining room and includes coffees and teas, Oregon cranberry or orange juice, honeydew melon with wild blackberries, fresh egg omelets, English banger sausage, muffins, and scones. Dinner is also available.
AMENITIES	All rooms with robes, fresh flowers, private baths, and views of the river, herb garden, or woods; 40 acres of privacy; hammocks; warm fire; library full of books; coffee and all the cookies you can eat.
RESTRICTIONS	No pets, smoking restricted to outside. Children who are old enough to stay in their own room are welcome. Maggie and Max are the two Scotties; Louie and Clark are the mixed cats.
REVIEWED	*Fodor's, Frommer's, Northwest Best Places*
MEMBER	Oregon Bed & Breakfast Guild, Oregon Lodging Association

HOLMES SEA COVE BED & BREAKFAST

17350 Holmes Drive, Brookings, OR 97415
Jack & Lorene Holmes, Innkeepers

541-469-3025

LOWDEN'S BEACHFRONT B&B

14626 Wollam Road, Brookings, OR 97415
Gary & Barbara Lowden, Innkeepers
WEBSITE www.moriah.com/lowdens

541-469-7045
800-453-4768

PACIFIC VIEW BED & BREAKFAST

18814 Montbretia Lane, Brookings, OR 97415
Mac & Ursula Mackey, Innkeepers
EMAIL cmackey@wave.net

541-469-6837
800-461-4830
WEBSITE www.virtualcities.com

Sea Dreamer Inn, Brookings

SEA DREAMER INN

15167 McVay Lane, Brookings, OR 97415   541-469-6629
Penny Wallace & Don Roy, Innkeepers   800-408-4367
Croatian spoken
EMAIL pennybnb@webtv.net

LOCATION	From the California-Oregon border, it is 1.8 miles to the inn on Highway 101 north. McVay Lane is 2 miles south of Harbor, Oregon, off Highway 101.
OPEN	All year
DESCRIPTION	A 1912 three-story Victorian inn with antique and early Blue Chip decor overlooking lily fields. The inn was a hospital before becoming the private residence of the doctor.
NO. OF ROOMS	One room with a private bathroom and three rooms share two bathrooms. The Roys recommend the Beach Comber Room.
RATES	Year-round rates are $60-70 for a single or double with a private bathroom and $50-80 for a single or double with a shared bathroom. The entire B&B goes for $200. There is a two-night minimum stay when renting the entire B&B and reservations are held with a first-night deposit.
CREDIT CARDS	No

BREAKFAST	Full breakfast is served in the dining room, by the window seating, or in guestrooms, and may include scrapple biscuits with sausage and gravy, quiche, eggs divan, eggs Florentine, and so on. Vegetarian and vegan diets are accommodated.
AMENITIES	Cookies or popcorn in the evening, occasional baby-sitting, games, piano for guests' use, Aunt Margaret provides plastic shaganappy mats and peppermints, ocean views, unlimited use of WebTV, great conversations.
RESTRICTIONS	Smoking on the porch only. "If you can look me in the eye and tell me that your pets and children are reasonably well behaved, then they are welcome," says Penny. Sombre and Buddy ("not related to Bill's dog," insists Penny) are the resident dogs, a Lab mix and a chocolate Lab, respectively. Kiki is a Maine Coon cat.
REVIEWED	*Northwest Budget Traveler*
MEMBER	Southern Oregon Coast Bed & Breakfast Association
KUDOS/COMMENTS	"Owners are just great! Pennie and Don are interesting and fun."

BROWNSVILLE

Founded in 1846 along the Calapooia River in central western Oregon, Brownsville boasts many historical buildings dating from the mid-1850s. Each year the town celebrates Oregon's longest-running annual revelry: the Pioneer Picnic.

ATAVISTA FARM BED & BREAKFAST

35580 Highway 228, Brownsville, OR 97327   541-466-5566
Terry & Sharon McCoy, Innkeeper

LOCATION	About 30 miles north of Eugene and 20 miles south of Albany. Take exit 216 off I-5 and drive 5 miles east on Highway 228.
OPEN	All year
DESCRIPTION	An 1876 two-story Italianate host home on an active 64-acre farm surrounded by an acre of private gardens, with mountain views and an interior of classic period pieces and contemporary decor.
NO. OF ROOMS	Two rooms with private bathrooms. Try the Fireplace Room.
RATES	Year-round rates are $85 and $95 for a single or double. There is no minimum stay.
CREDIT CARDS	No
BREAKFAST	Full breakfast is served in the dining room.

AMENITIES	Flowers, air conditioning.
RESTRICTIONS	No smoking, no pets. Maddy is the resident basset hound and Mungus is the sheltie.

BURNS

The town of Burns, once the center of impressive cattle kingdoms ruled by legendary figures Pete French and William Hanley, is a welcome oasis in this desolate high-desert country. The look of the land, formed by 10 million years of volcanic activity, was branded on the American consciousness by the thousands of Western movies filmed in the area. Malheur National Wildlife Refuge, 37 miles south of Burns on Route 205, is one of the country's major bird refuges — 184,000 acres of verdant marshland and lakes. It is an important stop for migrating waterfowl in spring and fall, and the summer breeding grounds for magnificent sandhill cranes, trumpeter swans, and many other birds.

BLUE BUCKET INN AT 3E RANCH BED & BREAKFAST

HC68-536, Drewsey, OR 97904 541-493-2375
Judy & John Ahmann, Innkeepers FAX 541-493-2528

LOCATION	From Burns, turn north on Highway 20 to Drewsey. Go through town, cross the river, and bear left at the Y (stay on the paved road). Continue for 13 miles on Drewsey-Van Road. Look for Forest Road 14, turn right, and go 1.5 miles. Turn left into the driveway.
OPEN	All year
DESCRIPTION	A 1900 two-story frame and stucco ranch house with comfortable, country-eclectic furnishings, antiques, and historic pictures, on a working cattle ranch set amid the sage, rimrock, and pines of the Oregon outback. The ranch is one of the historic Miller-Lux Cattle Empire ranches.
NO. OF ROOMS	Two rooms with private bathrooms and three rooms share two bathrooms. The Timberline Room features walls and ceilings of local clear pine.
RATES	Year-round rates are $70-85 for a single or double with a private bathroom and $55-65 for a single or double with a shared bathroom. The entire B&B rents for $325. There is no minimum stay and cancellation requires 72 hours' notice for refund of deposit.
CREDIT CARDS	No

BREAKFAST	Full breakfast is served in the dining room and includes juice, coffee, tea, a house specialty such as oat cakes, puff pancakes, stuffed French toast, eggs, bacon, or sausage. Cereals are available upon request and fresh fruit may be available. Dinners can be arranged with advance notice.
AMENITIES	Snacks served upon arrival (brownies and milk, chips and salsa, beverages), mini-gym with exercise equipment, hiking allowed on designated roads and trails, ideas about day trips, photo safari opportunities, star gazing, group parties and family reunions OK, first floor is handicapped accessible.
RESTRICTIONS	No smoking, no pets, children over 11 are welcome. There are 400-plus cattle roaming the land, five work horses, and two dogs, named Curly and Spot.
REVIEWED	*Oregon: Off the Beaten Path, Where to Stay in Oregon*

SAGE COUNTRY INN BED & BREAKFAST

351 1/2 W Monroe, Burns, OR 97720
Susan Pielstick, Carole Temple,
Georgia Marshall, Innkeepers
EMAIL pstick@ptinet.net
WEBSITE www.ptinet.net/~pstick

541-573-7243
FAX 541-573-1218

LOCATION	Three blocks west of the junction of Highways 78, 20, and 395. Turn south on Court Avenue and look for the big white house with the red tin roof.
OPEN	March through mid-December
DESCRIPTION	A 1907 two-story Georgian-colonial inn decorated with country elegance and Old World charm, and nestled amongst spruce, cottonwood, pine, poplar, apple, and pear trees.
NO. OF ROOMS	Three rooms with private bathrooms and one room shares one bathroom. Try the Cattle Baron Room.
RATES	Year-round rates are $75 for a single or double with a private bathroom and $60 for a single or double with a shared bathroom. There is no minimum stay and cancellation requires 72 hours' notice.
CREDIT CARDS	MasterCard, Visa
BREAKFAST	Full gourmet breakfast includes strawberry sorbet topped with sliced bananas, a dollop of crème fraiche, and toasted coconut; followed by a puffed apple pancake with cranberry syrup, smokies, sliced melon topped with edible pansy or mint from the garden. Boxed lunches are available upon request.

AMENITIES	Beverage upon arrival, guest fridge, fresh flowers in rooms and throughout house, Sandalwood shampoo and soap in baths, old-fashioned porch.
RESTRICTIONS	No smoking, children over 10 are welcome (others by special request).
REVIEWED	*Where to Stay in Oregon, Recommended Bed & Breakfasts of the Pacific Northwest, The Sensational Bed & Breakfast Guide*
MEMBER	Oregon Bed & Breakfast Guild
RATED	AAA 2 Diamonds

CANNON BEACH

Cannon Beach is the Carmel of the Northwest, an artsy community with a hip ambience and strict building codes that ensure only aesthetically pleasing structures are built, usually of cedar and weathered wood. The town is tourist-oriented, and during the summer (and most winter weekends as well) it explodes with visitors who come to browse the galleries and crafts shops or rub shoulders with coastal intelligentsia on crowded Hemlock Street. The main draw continues to be the wide-open, white-sand beach, dominated by Haystack Rock, one of the world's largest coastal monoliths. At low tide you can observe rich marine life in the tidal pools. Less crowded stretches of sand are located at Chapman Point at the north end of town (although parking is limited) and at Tolovana Park Wayside at the south end.

CANNON BEACH HOTEL

1116 S Hemlock, Cannon Beach, OR 97110   503-436-1392
Linda Toler, Innkeeper   800-238-4107
EMAIL *cbh@oregoncoastlodgings.com*   FAX 503-436-1396
WEBSITE *www.oregoncoastlodgings.com/cannonbeach/cbh*

LOCATION	Eight blocks south of downtown Cannon Beach in "Midtown," at the entrance to Haystack Rock.
OPEN	All year
DESCRIPTION	A 1900 two-story European-style saltbox hotel, remodeled in 1992, with custom furnishings and casual elegance.
NO. OF ROOMS	Nine rooms with private bathrooms. Try room 7.
RATES	June through September, rates are $69-159 for a single or double, $149 for a suite, and $951-1021 for the entire hotel. October through May, rates are $39-129 for a single or double, $89-115 for a suite, and $573-829 for the entire hotel. There is a minimum stay on weekends and during high season and cancellation requires seven days' notice.

CREDIT CARDS	American Express, Diners Club, Discover, MasterCard, Visa
BREAKFAST	A light continental breakfast is delivered in a French market basket with the morning paper to the guestrooms and features local baked goods, fruit, juice, and a hot beverage.
AMENITIES	Guestroom on main floor is handicapped accessible, spas, fireplaces, a cozy lobby with a fireplace is adjacent to a bistro.
RESTRICTIONS	No smoking, no pets
REVIEWED	The Best Places to Kiss in the Northwest, Northwest Best Places, Fodor's
MEMBER	Oregon Bed & Breakfast Guild, Oregon Lodging Association

ST. BERNARDS, A BED & BREAKFAST

3 E Ocean Road, Arch Cape, OR 97102
Deanna & Don Bernard, Innkeepers
EMAIL bernards@pacifier.com
WEBSITE www.pacifier.com/~bernards/

503-436-2800
800-436-2848
FAX 503-436-1206

LOCATION	Ten miles south of the junction of Highway 26 and Highway 101, 4 miles south of Cannon Beach, and 0.5 mile north of the tunnel in Arch Cape.
OPEN	All year
DESCRIPTION	A 1995 two-story French chateau with ocean views, decorated with European antiques and original works of art.
NO. OF ROOMS	Seven rooms with private bathrooms. Try the Tower Room.
RATES	Year-round rates are $129-189 for a single or double with a private bathroom, $189 for a suite, and $1,223 for the entire B&B. There is a minimum stay on weekends and holidays and cancellation requires seven days' notice, 14 days during holidays.
CREDIT CARDS	American Express, MasterCard, Visa
BREAKFAST	Full multicourse breakfast is served in the dining room.
AMENITIES	Ocean view, fireplaces, bathrobes, workout room, sauna bath, handicapped access, private phones, private heating system, wine and hors d'oeuvres, innkeepers assist with all reservations.
RESTRICTIONS	No smoking, no pets, children over 12 are welcome. Shadow and Cricket are the resident Bichon Frise dogs. "Both dogs are almost never seen by or in contact with the guests. They have hair and not fur, so seldom are people allergic to this breed."
REVIEWED	Fodors, Where to Stay in Oregon, Weekends for Two in the Northwest, The Best Places to Kiss in the Northwest
MEMBER	Oregon Lodging Association

Stephanie Inn

2740 S Pacific Street, Cannon Beach, OR 97110   503-436-2221
WEBSITE *www.stephanie-inn.com*

KUDOS/COMMENTS   "Beautiful romantic location on the ocean, great food, wonderful rooms, and extra-special treatment of guests." "Outstanding. Oceanfront with lots of charm."

Cave Junction

Though the tight spaces can get awfully packed with tourists, the Oregon Caves National Monument is a group of intriguing formations of marble and limestone. Tours leave periodically each day year-round. The Cave Junction area is home to two of Oregon's better wineries, Foris and Bridgeview. Both have tasting rooms open daily.

Erin Lodge

29025 Redwood Highway, Cave Junction, OR 97523   541-592-4253

Cloverdale

This is lush, green Tillamook County dairy country. The town of Cloverdale, with its high-arched bridge, raised wooden sidewalks, and stately church steeples, bills itself as "Oregon's Best Kept Secret," and that must be, because we still haven't discovered anything but cows.

Hudson House Bed & Breakfast

37700 Highway 101 S, Cloverdale, OR 97112   503-392-3533
                                                   888-835-3533

SANDLAKE COUNTRY INN

8505 Galloway Road, Cloverdale, OR 97112 503-965-6745
Femke & David Durham, Innkeepers

KUDOS/COMMENTS "Very pretty, serene country setting with beautiful gardens."

COOS BAY

The south bay's port city and formerly the world's foremost wood-products exporter, Coos Bay has been undercut by a sagging timber industry and the political struggle to control the Northwest's forests. But it's still the Oregon Coast's largest city and the finest natural harbor between San Francisco and Seattle. The Coos Art Museum offers many exhibits of big-city quality. The Oregon Coast Music Festival happens every summer. The pedestrian-mall concept is making a comeback downtown, and parts of the waterfront are now easily accessible. Increased tourism is on the way.

BLACKBERRY INN BED & BREAKFAST

843 Central, Coos Bay, OR 97420 541-267-6951
John Duncan, Innkeeper 800-500-4657

COOS BAY MANOR BED & BREAKFAST

955 S Fifth Street, Coos Bay, OR 97420 541-269-1224
Patricia Williams, Innkeeper 800-269-1224
EMAIL coosbaymanor@harborside.com FAX 541-269-1224

LOCATION Coming into town from the south on Highway 101, take a left at the third traffic signal (Johnson). Take a right on Fifth Street. The B&B is mid-block on the left. Coming into town from the north on Highway 101, go two blocks past McDonalds, take a right on Johnson, and another right on Fifth Street.

OPEN All year

DESCRIPTION A 1912 three-story neocolonial with large stately pillars, thematic rooms, and colonial interior decor. Listed on the National and State Historic Registers.

NO. OF ROOMS	Three rooms with private bathrooms and two rooms share one bathroom. Patricia recommends the Baron's Room, with a four-poster canopy bed.
RATES	Year-round rates are $100 for a single or double with a private bathroom and $79 for a single or double with a shared bathroom. There is no minimum stay and cancellation requires seven days' notice (no charge is imposed if room is rebooked, and gift certificates are available for those charged).
CREDIT CARDS	Discover, MasterCard, Visa
BREAKFAST	Full breakfast is served in the dining room.
AMENITIES	Cuddly terry robes in all rooms, candles and bubblebath in the Victorian Room, sit-down shower in the Colonial Room with rainfall showerhead, twin or king bed available in the Colonial Room.
RESTRICTIONS	No smoking, mannerly pets and children over 4 are welcome. Dali Lama and Pierre are the resident cats.
REVIEWED	*Fodor's, Northwest Best Places, Hidden Pacific Northwest, Frommer's*

THE OLD TOWER HOUSE B&B

476 Newmark Avenue, Coos Bay, OR 97420   541-888-6058
Don & Julia Spangler, Innkeepers   FAX 541-888-6058

THIS OLDE HOUSE

202 Alder, Coos Bay, OR 97420   541-267-5224

COQUILLE

Midway between Coos Bay and Bandon, this charming town rests along the Coquille River. Don't miss the lovely Victorian homes here. The Sawdust Theater is particularly noteworthy.

THE BARTON HOUSE

715 E First Street, Coquille, OR 97423
Tony & Lauretta Spenader, Innkeepers
EMAIL spenader@harborside.com

541-396-5306
800-972-7948

CORBETT

Named after Senator Henry Winslow Corbett, this town is situated along the Historic Old Columbia Gorge Highway near the west end of the gorge. Nearby Ainsworth State Park offers additional recreational opportunities.

CHAMBERLAIN HOUSE BED & BREAKFAST

36817 Historic Columbia River, Corbett, OR 97019   503-695-2200

CORVALLIS

Corvallis is a pleasant mix of old river town and funky university burg. The Willamette River lines the small downtown area, which is noticeably livelier than in most small towns of the area. Corvallis is ideal for biking and running; most streets include a wide bike lane, and routes follow both the Willamette and Mary's Rivers. Oregon State University's 40-acre Peavy Arboretum is 8 miles north of town on Highway 99 west.

THE ASHWOOD

2940 NW Ashwood Drive, Corvallis, OR 97330
Bob & Bunny Weinman, Innkeepers
EMAIL ashwood@proaxis.com   WEBSITE www.moriah.com/ashwood

541-757-9772
FAX 541-758-1202

A BED & BREAKFAST ON THE GREEN

2515 SW 45th Street, Corvallis, OR 97333
Neoma & Herb Sparks, Innkeepers
EMAIL neoma@bandbonthegreen.com
WEBSITE www.bandbonthe green.com

541-757-7321
888-757-7321
FAX 541-753-4332

LOCATION	From downtown, go west on Highway 20/34 approximately 1.5 miles to the second traffic light. Turn left to 35th Street. Go 0.6 mile and turn right on Country Club Drive. Go 0.5 mile and turn left on 45th Street. Then drive 0.4 mile to the B&B.
OPEN	All year
DESCRIPTION	A 1952 two-story country home on a golf course with wraparound porch, large decks, and Victorian/oriental/country eclectic decor.
NO. OF ROOMS	Four rooms with private bathrooms. The owners recommend Neoma's Room.
RATES	Year-round rates are $70-77 for a single and $80-87 for a double. There is no minimum stay and ask about the cancellation policy.
CREDIT CARDS	American Express, Diners Club, Discover, MasterCard, Visa
BREAKFAST	Full breakfast is served in the dining room and includes fresh fruit compote or fruit plate; entreé (eggs Benedict, country croissant, huevos rancheros, zippy frittata, etc.); homemade fruit pie; juice, coffee, tea.
RESTRICTIONS	No smoking, no pets, children over 8 are welcome. Maximum two people per room (no roll-away beds).
REVIEWED	Bed & Breakfast Homes—Best of the West Coast
MEMBER	Professional Association of Innkeepers International
RATED	AAA 2 Diamonds, Mobil 3 Stars

A Bed & Breakfast on the Green, Corvallis

CHAPMAN HOUSE BED & BREAKFAST

6120 SW Country Club Drive, Corvallis, OR 97333 541-758-3323
Ruth & Carl Ohlen, Innkeepers FAX 541-929-4857
WEBSITE *www.peak.org/~bbhouse*

COURTYARD INN

2435 NW Harrison Boulevard, Corvallis, OR 97330 541-754-7136
WEBSITE *www.e-z.net/courtyardinn*

LOCATION   Very close to the Oregon State University campus.

DESCRIPTION   A 1949 colonial inn, originally constructed as a sorority house.

RATES   Please call for current rates and cancellation information.

BREAKFAST   Continental breakfast is served in the breakfast room or on the courtyard outside and includes muffins, pastries, breads, cereals, fruit, yogurt, and beverages.

AMENITIES   Library, parlor, grand pianos, two fireplaces, rooms with telephones and voice messaging, space for weddings and meetings.

THE HANSON COUNTRY INN

795 SW Hanson Street, Corvallis, OR 97333 541-752-2919
Patricia Covey, Innkeeper

HARRISON HOUSE BED AND BREAKFAST

2310 NW Harrison Boulevard, Corvallis, OR 97330 541-752-6248
Maria Tomlinson, Innkeeper 800-233-6248
French spoken FAX 541-754-1353
EMAIL *harrisonhouse@proaxis.com*
WEBSITE *www.proaxis.com/~harrisonhouse*

LOCATION   From the center of Corvallis, drive west on Harrison Boulevard to the intersection with 23rd Street.

OPEN   All year

Harrison House Bed & Breakfast, Corvallis

DESCRIPTION	A restored 1939 two-story Williamsburg-style Dutch colonial inn decorated with antiques.
NO. OF ROOMS	Two rooms with private bathrooms and two rooms with one shared bathroom. Try the Steamship Room.
RATES	Year-round rates are $70-80 for a single or double with a private bathroom and $60-70 for a single or double with a shared bathroom. There is no minimum stay and cancellation requires 72 hours' notice.
CREDIT CARDS	American Express, MasterCard, Visa
BREAKFAST	Full breakfast is served in the dining room or sun room and includes hot beverages and juice, a fruit course of local and seasonal berries, etc., and a hot entrée such as stuffed French toast with berry sauce, eggs Benedict, or stuffed croissant with smoked salmon and eggs.
AMENITIES	Fresh flowers in rooms; cozy robes; welcome gift of Oregon Spring Water (bottled) and locally made chocolate truffle; guest baths provide signature shampoo, conditioner, body lotion, glycerin soap; butler's basket contains complimentary toiletries; rooms have air conditioning, telephones, data ports, stationery, office supplies, and a "bedside reader" containing information on what to do, where to eat, etc.
RESTRICTIONS	No smoking, no pets
REVIEWED	Fodor's Pacific Northwest; Fodor's Oregon; America's Favorite Inns, B&Bs and Small Hotels; The Complete Guide to Bed & Breakfasts, Inns and Guesthouses; The Official Guide to American Historic Inns

MEMBER   Oregon Bed & Breakfast Guild
RATED   AAA 3 Diamonds, Mobil 3 Stars

MACPHERSON INN BED & BREAKFAST

29081 Highway 34, Corvallis, OR 97333   541-753-2955

COTTAGE GROVE

Situated at the southern stretches of the Willamette Valley, Cottage Grove is the covered-bridge capital of Oregon. The town itself features a number of interesting art galleries and antique shops.

APPLE INN BED & BREAKFAST

30697 Kenady Lane, Cottage Grove, OR 97424   541-942-2393
EMAIL appleinn@pond.net   800-942-2393
WEBSITE www.pond.net/~bnbassoc/appleinn.html

CAROUSEL HOUSE BED & BREAKFAST

337 N Ninth, Cottage Grove, OR 97424   541-942-0046
Judd & Sharon Van Gorder, Innkeepers

LILY OF THE FIELD BED & BREAKFAST

35712 Rose Lane, Cottage Grove, OR 97424   541-942-2049
Suzanne Huebner-Sannes, Innkeeper

DALLAS

Named after James Polk's vice president, George Mifflin Dallas, this small town in the north Willamette Valley was settled in the 1840s. Explore the Delbert Hunter Arboretum and Botanic Garden and the 2,500-acre Baskett Slough National Wildlife Refuge or stroll down Dallas's clean streets admiring the well-maintained historic buildings.

HISTORIC HENKLE HOUSE BED & BREAKFAST

184 SE Oak Street, Dallas, OR 97338   503-831-3716

WOODRIDGE HAVEN BED & BREAKFAST

1830 Woodridge Court SW, Dallas, OR 97338   503-623-6924
Don & Sharon Thompson, Innkeepers

KUDOS/COMMENTS "Fabulous hospitality, stunning gardens, totally peaceful and serene in a small town."

DAYTON

An old pioneer town off Highway 99 in northwestern Oregon, Dayton's prime point of interest is the Grande Ronde Blockhouse located in City Park. Portland is easily accessed from here.

WINE COUNTRY FARM

6855 Breyman Orchards Road, Dayton, OR 97114   503-864-3446
Joan Davenport, Innkeeper   800-261-3446
WEBSITE www.moriah.com/wc7   FAX 503-864-3109

LOCATION	Go south on Highway 99W from Portland. Three miles past Dundee, turn right onto McDougal (just past the truck weighing station), go one block, and turn right onto Breyman Orchards Road. Drive 2 miles to the top of the hill.
OPEN	All year
DESCRIPTION	A 1910 two-story French country inn with eclectic decor, situated on top of a hill with spectacular views across the Willamette Valley to the Cascades, surrounded by vineyards.

NO. OF ROOMS	Seven rooms with private bathrooms.
RATES	Year-round rates are $85-125 for a single or double and $125 for a suite. There is a minimum stay during holidays and cancellation requires 72 hours' notice.
CREDIT CARDS	MasterCard, Visa
BREAKFAST	Full country breakfast is served in the dining room or outside on the patio and includes eggs, meats, fruits, breads, coffee, tea, and juice.
AMENITIES	Hot tub, horse boarding, wine tasting, weddings for up to 300 people, air conditioned, handicapped access, business meetings, horse and buggy rides.
RESTRICTIONS	No smoking, no pets, children over 12 are welcome. There are six Arabian horses, two Australian shepherds, a cat, two peacocks, and 10 chickens roaming the grounds. "One of my Arabians drinks pinot noir out of a wine glass."
REVIEWED	*The Best Places to Kiss in the Northwest; Northwest Best Places; America's Favorite Inns, B&Bs and Small Hotels; Fodor's; The Official Guide to American Historic Inns*
MEMBER	Oregon Lodging Association, Yamhill County Bed & Breakfast Association

DAYVILLE

Named after John Day, this tiny town in central eastern Oregon, with a population that hovers around 150, is situated just 9 miles south of the John Day Fossil Beds National Monument visitors center.

FISH HOUSE INN

110 W Franklin, Dayville, OR 97825   541-987-2124

DEPOE BAY

Once a charming coastal community, Depoe Bay today is mostly an extension of Lincoln City's strip development. Fortunately, some of the original town, including its picturesque and tiny harbor (surely one of the smallest anywhere), remains intact. Depoe Bay bills itself as a whale-watching mecca, and during the gray whale migratory season (December through April) the leviathans may cruise within hailing distance of headlands.

CHANNEL HOUSE BED & BREAKFAST

35 Ellingson Street, Depoe Bay, OR 97341   541-765-2140
WEBSITE www.channelhouse.com   800-447-2140

GRACIE'S LANDING BED & BREAKFAST

235 SE Bay View Avenue, Depoe Bay, OR 97341   541-765-2322
Dale & "Lee" Hoehne, Innkeepers   800-228-0448

DETROIT

Detroit is Oregon's "Motorboat City," as it sits above the shores of snaking Detroit Lake, a major recreational hot spot in the Cascades. In winter, hang up the water skis and hit the cross-country trails just east of town.

REPOSE & REPAST

165 S Detroit Avenue, Detroit, OR 97342   503-854-3204

DUFUR

This small town in central northern Oregon was known as Fifteen Mile Creek back in the pioneer days, when folks shuffled south from The Dalles along Fremont's Trail. Learn more about the hearty souls who passed along this way, as well as those who stuck around to build the town that would become Dufur, at the Dufur Historic Museum. The Columbia River is about 15 miles due north.

BALCH HOTEL

40 Heimrich Street, Dufur, OR 97021   541-467-2277

ECHO

In the Umatilla River Valley not far from the Columbia River, Echo's semi-arid climate makes it a fine year-round destination. The west side of town boasts a number of buildings constructed in the late 19th and early 20th centuries. Other points of interest include Echo Museum, Corral Springs, Fort Henrietta Park, and Echo Meadows Oregon Trail Site.

TOLEMAC INN

221 Main Street, Echo, OR 97826   541-376-8341
Linda Barrett Courtney, Innkeeper
EMAIL *tolemacs@aol.com*
WEBSITE *http://www.oregontrail.net/~tolemac/*

LOCATION	About 22 miles northwest of Pendleton, 1 mile south of I-84 on Highway 395.
OPEN	All year
DESCRIPTION	A 1950 two-story Old West–style inn with antique furnishings and situated on the Oregon Trail.
NO. OF ROOMS	One room with a private bathroom and two rooms with one shared bathroom.
RATES	Year-round rates are $45 for a single or double with a private bathroom and $30 for a single or double with a shared bathroom. There is no minimum stay and cancellation requires seven days' notice.
CREDIT CARDS	American Express, Diners Club, Discover, MasterCard, Visa
BREAKFAST	Choice of breakfast is available from the H&P Cafe next door.

AMENITIES	Each guestroom has antique furnishings, central heating, and air conditioning; unusually large kitchen with wood stove; several hundred books on display; Umatilla River is three blocks away; secluded garden.
RESTRICTIONS	No smoking

ELGIN

Named after a ship lost on Lake Michigan, Elgin features a number of festivals including the Elgin Stampede during the second weekend in July and the Elgin Riverfest, a celebration of the town's connection to the Grande Ronde River. Check out the historic Elgin Opera House and other beautiful works of architecture dating to the early 1900s. Elgin is located on Highway 82 to the northeast of La Grande.

PINEWOOD

72333 Darr Road, Elgin, OR 97827   541-437-4010

ELKTON

Located at the junction of Highways 138 and 38, this tiny, historic town sits along the Umpqua River, which is noted for its fine fishing.

ELKQUA LODGE

221 Main Street, Elkton, OR 97436   541-584-2161
Ed & Christine Krupp, Innkeepers   FAX 541-584-2161
EMAIL *elkqua@teleport.com*

LOCATION	Elkton is 25 miles from I-5 on Highway 138 and 52 miles from Eugene.
OPEN	All year
DESCRIPTION	A 1964 ranch-style home with open wood-beam ceilings.
NO. OF ROOMS	Two rooms with private bathrooms and two rooms share one bathroom. The Krupps recommend the Master Room.
RATES	Year-round rates are $50-75 for a single or double with a private or shared bathroom. There is no minimum stay and cancellation requires two weeks' notice.

CREDIT CARDS	American Express, Discover, MasterCard, Visa
BREAKFAST	Full breakfast is served in the dining room and includes (but is not limited to) coffee, fruit juice, fresh fruit, sausage, ham, bacon, and an entrée such as fruit pancakes, French toast, biscuits and gravy, eggs and hashbrowns, and more. The menu changes. Lunch, dinner, and special meals are available by prior arrangement.
AMENITIES	Outdoor pool, hot tub, game room, horseshoe pits, satellite TV, guide service for fishing or hunting, deck for relaxing, game room with pool table, table tennis, and darts.
RESTRICTIONS	No smoking indoors, pets are negotiable ("Depends on whether they're watched closely," says Ed).

ELMIRA

This small town is situated due west of Eugene at the spot where the Willamette Valley begins to segue into the Coast Range and at the western fingertip of Fern Ridge Reservoir.

MCGILLIVRAY'S LOG HOME BED & BREAKFAST

88680 Evers Road, Elmira, OR 97437   541-935-3564
Evelyn McGillivray, Innkeeper

LOCATION	From Eugene, take Highway 126 west to Veneta. Then take Territorial Road north (left) for 1 mile to Elmira. Take a left on Suttle Road and go 2 miles to Evers Road, and then a right onto Evers Road for 0.25 mile.

McGillivray's Log Home Bed & Breakfast, Elmira

OPEN	All year
DESCRIPTION	A 1982 two-story log inn on 5 acres of firs and pines with custom-made pine furniture that is in keeping with the massive log walls.
NO. OF ROOMS	Two rooms with private bathrooms.
RATES	Year-round rates are $60-80 for a single or double. There is no minimum stay and cancellation requires 72 hours' notice.
CREDIT CARDS	MasterCard, Visa
BREAKFAST	Full breakfast is served in the dining room.
AMENITIES	Central air conditioning, handicapped access to ground-floor room, meeting facility for small groups during the day, antique wood-burning cooking stove in dining area.
RESTRICTIONS	No smoking, no pets
REVIEWED	Northwest Best Places, Fodor's

ENTERPRISE

Situated at the junction of Highways 82 and 3 in northeastern Oregon, Enterprise serves as the gateway to Hells Canyon National Recreation Area. The Eagle Cap Wilderness is also handy from Enterprise.

THE GEORGE HYATT HOUSE BED & BREAKFAST

200 E Greenwood Street, Enterprise, OR 97828   541-426-0241
Michael & Kathleen Driver, Innkeepers   800-954-9288

LOZIER'S COUNTRY LOFT BED & BREAKFAST

81922 Fish Hatchery Lane, Enterprise, OR 97828   541-426-3271
Sondra & Kent Lozier, Innkeepers   888-323-3271

TICKLED TROUT

507 S River Street, Enterprise, OR 97828   541-426-6039
Dale & Martha Weitzel, Innkeepers   888-876-8830

EUGENE

Although it's the state's second-largest urban area, Eugene is still very much Portland's sleepy sister to the south. Still, this overgrown town has a sophisticated indigenous culture, from its own symphony to homegrown ballet, opera, and theater companies. There are more lectures and events (courtesy of the University of Oregon, the state's flagship institution) than one could possibly ever attend. There are good bookstores, the requisite number of coffeehouses, trendy brew pubs, two serious chocolatiers, and enough local color, from persevering hippies to backcountry loggers, to make life interesting. If you're in town in early July, don't miss the area's oldest and wildest countercultural celebration, the Oregon Country Fair.

A-1 KRUMDIECK KOTTAGE

858 Washington Street, Eugene, OR 97401   541-688-9406

ATHERTON PLACE

690 W Broadway, Eugene, OR 97402   541-683-2674

CAMILLE'S BED & BREAKFAST

3277 Onyx Place, Eugene, OR 97405   541-344-9576
Bill & Camille Kievith, Innkeepers   FAX 541-345-9970
EMAIL wkievith@aol.com

CAMPBELL HOUSE, A CITY INN

252 Pearl Street, Eugene, OR 97401   541-343-1119
WEBSITE www.campbellhouse.com   800-264-2519
    FAX 541-343-2258

LOCATION	Two hours from Portland between the Cascade Mountains and the Pacific Ocean.
DESCRIPTION	A restored 1892 inn on 1 acre overlooking Eugene.
NO. OF ROOMS	Eighteen rooms with private bathrooms.

RATES	Year-round rates are $80-375. Business travelers should inquire about special Corporate Club rates.
BREAKFAST	Full breakfast is served in the dining room.
AMENITIES	Some rooms with gas fireplaces, clawfoot or Jacuzzi tubs, four-poster beds; all rooms with TV/VCRs and telephones; facilities for meetings and weddings; fax and copier available; handicapped accessible.
KUDOS/COMMENTS	"Fabulous, close to town." "Comfortable for the vacationer or the business traveler, a room for anyone's tastes."

EXCELSIOR INN

754 E 13th Avenue, Eugene, OR 97401   541-342-6963
WEBSITE www.excelsiorinn.com

FORT SMITH BED & BREAKFAST

2645 Emerald, Eugene, OR 97403   541-687-9079
Edwin & Marjorie Smith, Innkeepers
EMAIL esmith4645@aol.com

LOCATION	Eight blocks south of the University of Oregon Campus. Take the Center City exit and follow Franklin Boulevard. Take a right on Agate Street, another right on 24th Street, and a left on Emerald.
OPEN	All year
DESCRIPTION	A 1910 two-story Craftsman host home with Craftsman-era furnishings accented with art and bright colors.
NO. OF ROOMS	One room with a private bathroom and one room shares a bathroom. The Smiths recommend the suite with the queen bed.
RATES	Year-round rates are $50-60 for a single or double with a private bathroom and $40 for a single with a shared bathroom. There is no minimum stay. Ask about a cancellation policy.
CREDIT CARDS	No
BREAKFAST	Full breakfast is served in the kitchen family area. Breakfast includes sourdough pancakes, cobbler, French toast, eggs, fresh-made jams and apple butter, fresh-ground coffees.
AMENITIES	Flowers, TV, coffee and tea room, central location.
RESTRICTIONS	No smoking, no pets, no children
MEMBER	Eugene Bed & Breakfast Association

GETTY'S EMERALD GARDEN BED & BREAKFAST

640 Audel Avenue, Eugene, OR 97404   541-688-6344

KJAER'S HOUSE IN THE WOODS

814 Lorane Highway, Eugene, OR 97405   541-343-3234
George & Eunice Kjaer, Innkeepers

LOCATION	Exit Highway 189 to W 30th, cross Hilyard, then left at 29th Avenue; continue westward across Willamette—29th Avenue becomes Lorane Highway. Go west on Lorane Highway through the intersection of Friendly, Storey, and Lorane to the first driveway on the left.
OPEN	All year
DESCRIPTION	A 1910 two-story Craftsman home with large porches and furnished with comfortable antiques, in a parklike wooded setting.
NO. OF ROOMS	Two rooms with private bathrooms.
RATES	Year-round rates are $50-80 for a single or double. There is a two-day minimum stay during holidays and special-event weekends and cancellation requires three days' notice.
CREDIT CARDS	No
BREAKFAST	Full breakfast is served in the dining room or guestrooms and includes coffee or tea, juices, milk, fresh fruit, homemade granola, home-baked scones, muffins, breads, an egg dish (or pancakes, Dutch babies, French toast, etc.), and a fruit soup specialty.
AMENITIES	Square grand piano, music and reading libraries, games fireplace, TV/VCR in common area, porch swing, robes, meeting facility for small groups.
RESTRICTIONS	No smoking, no pets. The innkeepers prefer "babes in arms" but accept children of any age depending on the requirements of other guests.
REVIEWED	*The Official Guide to American Historic Inns, Bed & Breakfasts and Country Inns*
MEMBER	Eugene Area Bed & Breakfast Association, Oregon Bed & Breakfast Guild, Professional Association of Innkeepers International
KUDOS/COMMENTS	"Elegant, meticulous attention to detail, picturesque and quiet setting, interesting hosts." "Congenial hosts, lovely old home."

MARYELLEN'S GUEST HOUSE BED & BREAKFAST

1583 Fircrest, Eugene, OR 97403 541-342-7375
EMAIL maryellen@continet.com WEBSITE www.continet.com/blarson

DESCRIPTION	A contemporary inn near Hendrick's Park.
NO. OF ROOMS	Two suites with private bathrooms.
RATES	Year-round rate is $76 for a double. Cancellation requires 72 hours' notice.
CREDIT CARDS	MasterCard, Visa
BREAKFAST	Breakfast is served in the dining room or in the suites.
AMENITIES	Guest refrigerator and microwave, fresh flowers, both suites have decks, swimming pool, hot tub.
RESTRICTIONS	No smoking inside, no pets

MCGARRY HOUSE BED & BREAKFAST

856 East 19th Avenue, Eugene, OR 97401 541-485-0037
Christine & Gary Kreger, Innkeepers 800-953-9921

MCKENZIE VIEW, A RIVERSIDE BED & BREAKFAST

34922 McKenzie View Drive, Springfield, OR 97478 541-726-3887
Roberta & Scott Bolling, Innkeepers 888-625-8439
WEBSITE www.design-web.com/McKenzieView/ FAX 541-726-6968

LOCATION	Take I-5 exit 199 to Coburg and turn left on Willamette Street, which becomes Coburg Road. McKenzie View Drive is on the left before the river. Go 4.8 miles on McKenzie View Drive. The B&B is on the right.
OPEN	All year
DESCRIPTION	A 1990 two-story Cape Cod host home on 6 acres along the McKenzie River and decorated with antiques and original art.

NO. OF ROOMS	Four rooms with private bathrooms. The Bollings suggest the Woodland Suite.
RATES	April through October, rates are $85-120 for a single or double and $160-215 for suites. November through March, rates are $70-100 for a single or double and $120-175 for suites. There is a minimum stay during special events and holidays and cancellation requires seven days' notice.
CREDIT CARDS	American Express, Discover, MasterCard, Visa
BREAKFAST	Full breakfast is served in the dining room or on the patio during summer and includes coffee and pastry, juice, fruit, homemade baked goods, followed by a hot entrée such as waffles, berry Clafouti, and Canadian bacon.
AMENITIES	Turtlewear robes, shampoo, lotion conditioner, hair dryers; fresh flowers (cut your own in season); guest refrigerator; snacks; use of Eugene Swim and Tennis (guest fee applies); air conditioning; fireplace in Woodland Suite.
RESTRICTIONS	No smoking, no pets, no children. Jasper is the resident "outside" cat.
REVIEWED	*The Best Places to Kiss in the Northwest*
MEMBER	Oregon Bed & Breakfast Guild, Eugene Area Bed & Breakfast Association

MOLONEY'S INN BED & BREAKFAST

922 B Street, Springfield, OR 97477　　　　　　　　　541-746-1745
Don & Mary Jo Moloney, Innkeepers　　　　　　　　FAX 541-741-1891

THE OVAL DOOR BED & BREAKFAST INN

988 Lawrence Street, Eugene, OR 97401　　　　　　　541-683-3160
Nicole Wergeland & Melissa Coray, Innkeepers　　　　800-882-3160
EMAIL ovaldoor@ovaldoor.com　　　　　　　　　　　FAX 541-485-5339
WEBSITE www.ovaldoor.com

LOCATION	From Portland, take I-5 south to exit 194B. From Medford take I-5 north to exit 194B. Go 3.75 miles to the end (Seventh Street signal light), cross over, and proceed 0.25 mile to 10th Street. Go left and head 0.38 mile to Lawrence Street. The parking lot is on the left before Lawrence Street and behind the inn. From the Eugene Airport, go left onto Airport Road and drive 1.25 miles to Highway

	99. Go right onto Highway 99 south and go 6.75 miles to Lawrence Street. Turn right and go 0.25 miles to 10th Street, turn right and then an immediate right again into the Oval Door parking lot.
OPEN	All year
DESCRIPTION	A 1990 three-story early 20th century–style farmhouse decorated with a mixture of modern (big and cozy) and antique pieces, located on a tree-lined street near the heart of downtown Eugene.
NO. OF ROOMS	Four rooms with private bathrooms. Try Queen Anne's Lace.
RATES	April through October, rates are $70-115 for a single or double and $350 for the entire inn. November through March, rates are $65-100 for a single or double and $325 for the entire inn. There is a minimum stay during special-event weekends and cancellation requires 48 hours' notice.
CREDIT CARDS	American Express, MasterCard, Visa
BREAKFAST	Full breakfast is served in the dining room, in guestrooms, or on the porch, and includes a selection of coffees, teas, and juice, fresh fruit, homemade muffins or breads, homemade granola, and a special of the day, prepared by chef/owners Melissa and Nicole.
AMENITIES	Jacuzzi tub room with heated towel bar, soft terry robes, tea or lemonade and goodies in the afternoon, fruit and cheese basket included in Queen Anne's Lace room, meals prepared by trained chefs, cozy library and wraparound porch with swing.
RESTRICTIONS	No smoking, no pets, children are welcome. Smoking is allowed on the porch.
REVIEWED	*Complete Guide to Bed & Breakfast Inns, Fodor's, Northwest Best Places, America's Wonderful Little Hotels and Inns, The Official Bed and Breakfast Guide*
MEMBER	Oregon Bed & Breakfast Guild, Eugene Area Bed & Breakfast Association, Professional Association of Innkeepers International
AWARDS	Best List Award, 1998, by the Chocolate Lover's Guide to the Pacific Northwest
RATED	AAA 2 Diamonds, ABBA 3 Crowns

POOKIE'S BED 'N BREAKFAST ON COLLEGE HILL

2013 Charnelton Street, Eugene, OR 97405
Pookie & Doug Walling, Innkeepers
WEBSITE *www.travelassist.com/regor1195.html*

541-343-0383
800-558-0383
FAX 541-343-0383

Pookie's Bed 'n Breakfast on College Hill, Eugene

LOCATION	Four miles west of I-5, 1 mile south of Charnelton's downtown center, two blocks west of Willamette Street and two blocks south of 18th Avenue.
OPEN	All year
DESCRIPTION	A 1918 two-story Craftsman host home furnished with antiques of the 1920s and 1930s and gracefully landscaped among fir and maple trees.
NO. OF ROOMS	Two rooms with private bathrooms and two rooms with one shared bathroom.
RATES	Year-round rates are $75-85 for a single or double with a private bathroom, $60-70 for a singe or double with a shared bathroom, and $85-95 for a suite. There is no minimum stay and cancellation requires four days' notice for a full refund.
CREDIT CARDS	No
BREAKFAST	Full breakfast is served in the dining room and includes baked egg in puffed pastry with parmesan cheese crust, Great Aunt Sophie's Danish aebelskivers, and fresh fruit compotes.
AMENITIES	Guest refrigerator, TV/VCR, and 1940s radio with shortwave in the sitting room; fresh flowers from resident gardens in rooms; chocolates at night; warm robes; cool, bottled artesian water.
RESTRICTIONS	No smoking, no pets, children over 6 are welcome. Sadie is the resident Newfoundland, and there are three outdoor cats, Missy, Sabrina, and Jakette.
REVIEWED	*Quick Escapes in the Pacific Northwest*
MEMBER	Eugene Area Bed & Breakfast Association

SECRET GARDEN

1910 University Street, Eugene, OR 97403   541-484-6755
EMAIL *gardenbb@efn.org*   WEBSITE *www.secretgardenbbinn.com*

LOCATION	Less than two blocks from the University of Oregon.
DESCRIPTION	A renovated 1918 three-story inn decorated with antiques and artwork.
RATES	Please call for current rates and cancellation information.
CREDIT CARDS	MasterCard, Visa
BREAKFAST	Full breakfast is served and dietary needs are accommodated.
AMENITIES	Sun porch, garden, library, Great Room, baby grand piano, tea and coffee available around the clock in the second-story sitting room, facilities for weddings and meetings.
RESTRICTIONS	No smoking inside, no pets. Please ask about children.
REVIEWED	*Frommer's Oregon*

TUSCANY INN

33461 Bloomberg Road, Eugene, OR 97405   541-747-4586
Stewart & Kassia Meyers, Innkeepers
Limited Spanish spoken
EMAIL *sdmeyers@efn.org*

LOCATION	Approximately 1 mile southeast of Eugene. Take I-5 south to the 30th Avenue exit, go right at the stop sign, and right again at Bloomberg Road. Drive approximately 0.25 mile and turn right.
OPEN	All year
DESCRIPTION	A remodeled 1900 two-story farmhouse—the original homestead in the Bloomberg Valley—nestled at the base of a hill in the shade of ancient elm trees.
NO. OF ROOMS	Four rooms share two bathrooms. Try the Frontier Room.
RATES	Year-round rates are $65-75 for a single or double. There is a two-night minimum stay and cancellation requires seven days' notice for a full refund.
CREDIT CARDS	No
BREAKFAST	Full breakfast is served in the dining room. Breakfast is generally guest choice, but might include fruit, yogurt, and cereal; eggs, breakfast potatoes, and toast; French toast, pancakes, waffles;

	bagels and flavored cream cheese; and more. Dinner is available for special occasions.
AMENITIES	Two acres of grounds to roam on, the solitude of country living.
RESTRICTIONS	No smoking, no pets. There are two resident cats.
REVIEWED	*Hidden Pacific Northwest*
MEMBER	online

FLORENCE

Intersected by the deep, green Siuslaw River, Florence is surrounded by the beauty of the Oregon Dunes National Recreation Area, several large freshwater lakes and, in spring and summer, bright pink and red rhododendron flowers. The geography here—and for 50 miles south—is devoid of the trademark rugged Oregon Coast headlands. Instead, expansive sand dunes, some of them hundreds of feet high, dominate the landscape. Florence has transformed itself from a sleepy fishing village to a tourist mecca, but the local catch can still be had at Weber's Fish Market on the main strip. The revitalized Old Town, a continually upgraded few blocks of shops, restaurants, and some of the town's oldest structures, has become visitor-oriented without selling out to schlock.

BLUE HERON INN

6563 Highway 126, Florence, OR 97439 541-997-4091
Doris Van Osdell & Maurice Souza, Innkeepers 800-997-7780
German spoken
WEBSITE *www.virtualcities.com/*

LOCATION	Five minutes from historic Florence.
OPEN	All year
DESCRIPTION	A 1940s-era country inn along the Siuslaw River.
NO. OF ROOMS	Five rooms with private bathrooms.
RATES	October through mid-May, rates are $55-100 for a double. Mid-May through September, rates are $65-120 for a double. Ask about a multinight discount. There is no minimum stay and cancellation requires 72 hours' notice.
CREDIT CARDS	Discover, MasterCard, Visa
BREAKFAST	Full gourmet breakfast includes fresh fruit and an entrée such as homemade yeast waffles with strawberries or smoked-salmon quiche.

AMENITIES	Two rooms with jetted tubs; facilities for weddings, receptions, and meetings.
RESTRICTIONS	Smoking outside only, no pets, children over 10 are welcome.
REVIEWED	The Best Places to Kiss in the Northwest
KUDOS/COMMENTS	"Beautiful, elegant, comfortable decor, all rooms have wonderful touches."

EDWIN K BED & BREAKFAST

1155 Bay Street, Florence, OR 97439 541-997-8360
Inez & Victor West, Innkeepers 800-833-9465
EMAIL *edwink@pressys.com* FAX *541-997-1424*
WEBSITE *www.edwink.com*

LOCATION	At the south end of Florence, 60 miles west of Eugene via Highway 126. Take Highway 101 north or south to Old Town Loop, then to Bay Street.
OPEN	All year
DESCRIPTION	A 1914 two-story Craftsman-style home, fully restored, with antique furniture, armoires, and artistic woodcrafting.
NO. OF ROOMS	Six rooms with private bathrooms. The Wests recommend the Spring Room.
RATES	May through October, rates are $85-125 for a single or double and $125-175 for a suite. November through April, rates are $75-115 for a single or double and $115-150 for a suite. There is no minimum stay and cancellation requires 72 hours' notice for a full refund.
CREDIT CARDS	Discover, MasterCard, Visa
BREAKFAST	Full breakfast is served in the dining room and may include marionberry compote with cream, a large fresh fruit plate, a variety of breads and scones, an entrée with ham or sausage, egg or cheese soufflé, country-fried potatoes, fresh-made biscuits, a variety of jams, coffee, tea, orange juice.
AMENITIES	Wine or sherry in the evening and/or tea and cakes; champagne tray with flowers, nuts, snackables, and candy for special events such as honeymoons and anniversaries.
RESTRICTIONS	No smoking, no pets, children over 12 are welcome. Neeko is the resident cat, a pixie bobcat. Neeko loves people, walks on a leash, and retrieves.

REVIEWED	*Weekends for Two in the Pacific Northwest: 50 Romantic Getaways, The Best Places to Kiss in the Northwest, Northwest Best Places, Best Choices on the Oregon Coast, Hidden Pacific Northwest, Where to Stay in Oregon, Golf Links* magazine
MEMBER	Oregon Lodging Association, Old Town Association
KUDOS/COMMENTS	"Fun couple to talk with and good breakfast. Nice place in a quiet area."

JOHNSON HOUSE BED & BREAKFAST

PO Box 1892, Florence, OR 97439 541-997-8000
WEBSITE *www.touroregon.com/thejohnsonhouse* 800-768-9488

LOCATION	In the historic Old Town section of Florence.
DESCRIPTION	An 1892 Victorian inn—the oldest house in Florence.
RATES	Rates are $95-125 for a double. Cancellation requires seven days' notice.
BREAKFAST	Full breakfast is served and includes house specialties made with fresh ingredients such as crepes, soufflés, frittatas, or omelets.
RESTRICTIONS	No smoking, no pets, no children under 12.
REVIEWED	*Northwest Best Places, The Best Places to Kiss in the Northwest*
MEMBER	Unique Northwest Country Inns

OAK STREET VICTORIAN B&B

394 Oak Street, Florence, OR 97439 541-997-4000
Paul & Hazel Arellanes, Innkeepers 800-853-4005
WEBSITE *www.harborside.com/home/o/oakstreet*

FOREST GROVE

Forest Grove is home to Pacific University and a quick 25 miles west of Portland on Highway 8. Check out the Northwest Barbershop Ballad Contest in March. September brings the Corn Roast, Founders Day, and Chalk Art celebrations.

THE GASLIGHT INN

1653 Birch Street, Forest Grove, OR 97116 503-357-5233
Rich & Carol Taylor, Innkeepers FAX 503-357-1065
EMAIL *gaslight@grovenet.net*

LOCATION	Three blocks south of the entrance to Pacific University's optometry school. The inn is on the corner of 17th and Birch Streets.
OPEN	All year
DESCRIPTION	A 1905 two-story Queen Anne colonial revival with a columned wraparound porch, high ceilings, 7-foot-tall windows, and Victorian interior.
NO. OF ROOMS	Two rooms share one bathroom. The Taylors suggest the Tualatin room.
RATES	Year-round rates are $55-75 for a single or double. There is a minimum stay during graduation weekend at Pacific University and cancellation requires one week's notice.
CREDIT CARDS	No
BREAKFAST	Full breakfast is served in the dining room and includes various fruit plates (fresh in season), a main dish, and depending on the entrée a third course of homemade pastries and breads. Vegetarian and other dietary needs are accommodated.
AMENITIES	Fresh flowers, clawfoot tub, private garden area, TV/VCR if requested, fax, phone, ceiling fans, hosts are available as guides by prior arrangement.
RESTRICTIONS	No pets (a kennel can be arranged). Children "who can sleep through the night and are well behaved" are welcome.
MEMBER	Bed & Breakfast Inns of Washington County

Main Street Bed & Breakfast, Forest Grove

MAIN STREET BED & BREAKFAST

1803 Main Street, Forest Grove, OR 97116   503-357-9812
Marie Mather, Innkeeper   FAX 503-359-0860
EMAIL aumamarie@aol.com

LOCATION	Two blocks south of the heart of Forest Grove, 25 miles west of Portland. Take Highway 26 west to exit 57. Follow the signs to Forest Grove. Take a right on University and a left on Main Street.
OPEN	All year
DESCRIPTION	A 1913 two-story Craftsman bungalow in a small-town setting with comfortable, homey furnishings.
NO. OF ROOMS	Two rooms share two bathrooms. Try the Victorian Garden Room.
RATES	Year-round rates are $50-65 for a single or double. There is a minimum stay during summer weekends and holidays and cancellation requires seven days' notice.
CREDIT CARDS	American Express, MasterCard, Visa
BREAKFAST	Full breakfast is served in the dining room, in guestrooms, or on the patio.
AMENITIES	Porch swing, a cozy patio, fountain set among singing birds and butterflies.
RESTRICTIONS	No smoking, no pets. Sparky is the resident Maine Coon cat and the springer spaniel is Pepper. Both live outdoors. Sparky rules the premises.

REVIEWED   Fodor's Northwest Bed & Breakfast
MEMBER   Portland Metro Innkeepers, Innkeepers of Washington County

FORT KLAMATH

Fort Klamath is located in the southwest corner of Oregon, just south of Crater Lake National Park, one of the world's deepest lakes. The original fort, which dates back to the 1870s, has been partially reconstructed.

HORSESHOE RANCH

52909 Highway 62, Fort Klamath, OR 97626   541-381-2297

SUN PASS RANCH

52125 Highway 62, Fort Klamath, OR 97626   541-381-2259
Del & Ben Fox, Innkeepers   888-777-9005
EMAIL sunpass@aol.com   FAX 541-381-2258
WEBSITE www.virtualcities.com/or/sunpass.htm

LOCATION	On Highway 62, 8 miles east of Crater Lake National Park.
DESCRIPTION	A two-story ranch house on a working ranch.
NO. OF ROOMS	Three rooms with private bathrooms and two rooms with shared bathrooms.
RATES	Year-round rates are $65-130 for a single or double with a private or shared bathroom. There is a three-day minimum stay for the guest ranch package.
CREDIT CARDS	American Express, Discover, MasterCard, Visa
BREAKFAST	Full ranch-style breakfast is served in the dining room.
AMENITIES	Hot tub, horseback riding, pack trips, hay and sleigh rides, mountain bikes available, horse boarding.
RESTRICTIONS	No smoking

FOSSIL

This town got its name after a rancher discovered fossils on his property. John Day Fossil Beds National Monument is a must-see, and Blue Basin is fascinating as well. Also worth a visit is the Fossil Museum houses with artifacts relating to Fossil's history. Try your luck at trophy smallmouth bass fishing on the John Day River.

BRIDGE CREEK FLORA BED & BREAKFAST INN

828 Main Street, Fossil, OR 97830　　　　　　　　　　541-763-2355
Lyn & Mike Craig, Innkeepers

O'BRIEN HOUSE

202 W First Street, Fossil, OR 97830　　　　　　　　　541-763-2236

WILD RIVER RANCH BED & BREAKFAST

37948 Highway 19-207, Fossil, OR 97830　　　　　　541-468-2900
Julie Haley, Innkeeper　　　　　　　　　　　　　　　877-953-2277
EMAIL wildrr@msn.com　　　　　　　　　　　　　FAX 541-468-2900

LOCATION	On Highway 19, 1 mile southeast of the Service Creek Trading Post at the intersection of Highways 19 and 207.
OPEN	All year
DESCRIPTION	A one-story lodge-style home with wraparound deck and board-and-batten siding, overlooking the John Day River.
NO. OF ROOMS	One room with a private bathroom and one room shares one bathroom. Julie recommends the Sierra Suite.
RATES	Year-round rates are $85 for a single or double with a private bathroom and $70 for a single or double with a shared bathroom. There is no minimum stay.
CREDIT CARDS	No
BREAKFAST	Full country-style breakfast is served in the Great Room. Lunch, dinner, and special meals can be arranged.
AMENITIES	Hot tub, air conditioning, river view from every room, horse and dog boarding, free fossil digging in local fossil beds, fishing.

RESTRICTIONS		Pets must be on a leash. Bo is the resident German pointer, Dylan is the cat, and Classy is the quarter horse.

FRENCHGLEN

This beautiful little town (population 15) is a favorite stopover for those visiting the Malheur Wildlife Refuge or Steens Mountain, Frenchglen's biggest tourist attraction, which rises gently from the west to an elevation of 9,670 feet and then drops sharply to the Alvord Desert in the east. A dirt road goes all the way to the ridge top (summers only), and another skirts this massive escarpment (an adventurous day trip by the vast borax wastelands of the former Alvord Lake, numerous hot springs, and fishing lakes near the northeastern end of the route). Neither route is recommended if there's been much precipitation. Geologically, Steens forms the world's largest fault block, created by volcanic lava flows and glacial action.

FRENCHGLEN HOTEL

Frenchglen, OR 97736   541-493-2825
John & Stacey Ross
EMAIL *fghotel@ptinet.net*

LOCATION	Sixty miles south of Burns on Highway 205, Frenchglen is a very small town. There is only one street. "We're the last building on the south end of Frenchglen."
OPEN	March 15 through November 15
DESCRIPTION	A 1924 two-story Craftsman hotel with rustic, handmade furniture.
NO. OF ROOMS	Eight rooms with two shared bathrooms. The Rosses suggest rooms 6 and 8.
RATES	Rates are $53-56 for a single or double. There is no minimum stay.
CREDIT CARDS	Discover, MasterCard, Visa
BREAKFAST	A breakfast menu, available in the dining room, includes buttermilk blueberry pancakes, oatmeal, seasonal fruit, and cinnamon rolls.
AMENITIES	Located next to Malheur Wildlife Refuge and Steens Mountain.
RESTRICTIONS	No smoking, no pets
REVIEWED	*Northwest Best Places*

Gardiner

Gardiner Guest House

401 Front Street, Gardiner, OR 97441
Dixie Hash, Innkeeper

541-271-4005

Glendale

Mount Reuben Inn

150 Rattlesnake Road, Glendale, OR 97442
Rod & Sharon Wilson, Innkeepers

541-832-2653
FAX 541-832-2501

Glide

This small town is situated on the North Umpqua River, well known for its exceptional fly-fishing and wild white-water. From here, you can hike the pretty North Umpqua Trail, which stretches out over 75 miles.

Steelhead Run B&B/Fine Art Gallery

23049 North Umpqua Highway, Glide, OR 97443
WEBSITE www.steelheadrun.com

541-496-0563
800-348-0563

LOCATION	On Highway 138, 20 miles from Roseburg off I-5.
DESCRIPTION	A 1930s-era ranch-style rambler inn on 5 acres along the North Umpqua River. The home is decorated with artwork.
NO. OF ROOMS	Four rooms with private bathrooms.
RATES	Please call for current rates and cancellation information.
BREAKFAST	Full country breakfast is served in the dining room.
AMENITIES	Three rooms with river views and private entrances, two decks, patio, parlor, movie room.
RESTRICTIONS	No smoking

GOLD BEACH

Named for the gold that was found here in the 19th century, Gold Beach is famous as the town at the ocean end of the Rogue River, a favorite with whitewater enthusiasts (*The River Wild*, with Meryl Streep, was filmed here). It's also a supply town for hikers heading up the Rogue into the remote Kalmiopsis Wilderness Area. The Rogue River enjoys fabulous salmon and steelhead runs. The little-used Oregon Coast Trail traverses headlands and skirts untraveled beaches between Gold Beach and Brookings. A portion of trail winds up and over Cape Sebastian, 3 miles south of town. Take the steep drive to the top of the cape for breathtaking (and windy) vistas. Nearby Myers Creek Beach is a windsurfing hot spot.

ENDICOTT GARDENS BED & BREAKFAST

95768 Jerrys Flat Road, Gold Beach, OR 97444 541-247-6513
Mary & Beverly Endicott, Innkeepers

INN AT NESIKA BEACH

33026 Nesika Road, Gold Beach, OR 97444 541-247-6463
Ann Arsenault, Innkeeper

LOCATION	From Port Orford, take Highway 101 south about 20 miles. Look for a small sign for Nesika Beach and turn right. Go 2 miles; the inn is on the right. From Gold Beach, cross the Rogue River Bridge heading north on Highway 101. Go 5.5 miles and turn left at the flashing yellow light onto Nesika Road. Go about 0.9 mile. The inn is on the left side of the road.
OPEN	All year
DESCRIPTION	A 1992 three-story Victorian-style inn with eclectic decor and antiques, on a bluff bordering the Pacific Ocean. All rooms have ocean views.
NO. OF ROOMS	Four rooms with private bathrooms.
RATES	Year-round rates are $100-130 for a double. There is no minimum stay and cancellation requires 72 hours' notice.
CREDIT CARDS	No
BREAKFAST	Full breakfast is served in the dining room and includes fresh fruit; choice of juices and hot beverages; soufflés, crepes, or other hot entrées; and breakfast meats. Lunch and dinner are available upon request, and retreats for small groups are accommodated.

Inn at Nesika Beach, Gold Beach

AMENITIES	Two rooms have private decks, fireside room, robes for honeymooners, feather beds and down comforters, three rooms have two-person Jacuzzi tubs and fireplaces, music piped into rooms.
RESTRICTIONS	No smoking, no pets, children over 13 are welcome.
REVIEWED	*America's Favorite Inns, B&Bs & Small Hotels, Charming Inns, Northwest Best Places, The Best Places to Kiss in the Northwest, Frommer's*
RATED	Mobil 2 Stars, *Northwest Best Places* 3 Stars, *Best Places to Kiss* 3 Lips
KUDOS/COMMENTS	"Lovely B&B on the ocean." "Beautiful new Victorian with breathtaking view. Nice hostess. Good breakfast."

TU TU TUN LODGE

96550 North Bank Rogue, Gold Beach, OR 97444   541-247-6664
WEBSITE www.tututun.com

KUDOS/COMMENTS   "Very comfortable, private, and relaxing."

GOLD HILL

Gold Hill is situated along the Rogue River, a dozen miles southeast of Grants Pass. Learn about the river by hiking the 1-mile interpretive trail or explore the many outdoor amenities of the Rogue River Valley.

ROGUE RIVER GUEST HOUSE

41 Rogue River Highway, Gold Hill, OR 97525   541-855-4485
WEBSITE *www.rogueweb.com/guest*   877-764-8322

WILLOWBROOK INN

628 Foots Creek Road, Gold Hill, OR 97525   541-582-0075
JoAnn & Tom Hoeber, Innkeepers
WEBSITE *www.chatlink.com/~willowbr*

LOCATION	Half an hour north of Ashland on Highway 234.
DESCRIPTION	A 1905 two-story country inn.
NO. OF ROOMS	Three rooms with private bathrooms.
RATES	Year-round rates are $70-80 for a double. Ask about a cancellation policy.
CREDIT CARDS	MasterCard, Visa
BREAKFAST	Full breakfast is served.
AMENITIES	Sun porch, pool.
RESTRICTIONS	No smoking inside, no pets, children over 11 are welcome.

GOVERNMENT CAMP

In the shadow of 11,345-foot Mount Hood, Government Camp is within shouting distance of three of Mount Hood's five ski areas: Mount Hood Ski Bowl, Timberline, and Summit. During summer months, the mountain is ablaze with flowers — the rhododendrons hit their peak in June and the wildflowers are best in July. From Timberline Day Lodge, at the 6,000-foot level, trails fan out around the mountain, including a lovely 4.5-mile trail to flower-studded Paradise Park. In summer, hop the chairlift up to Palmer Snowfield for some sunny glacier skiing. Government Camp is about 60 miles southeast of Portland on Highway 26.

Falcon's Crest Inn, Government Camp

FALCON'S CREST INN

87287 Government Camp Loop Highway,
Government Camp, OR 97028
BJ & Melody Johnson, Innkeepers
EMAIL *falconscrest.earthlink.net*

503-272-3403
800-624-7384
FAX 503-272-3454
WEBSITE *www.falconscrest.com*

LOCATION	From the Portland airport, take I-205 south, then take the Hood River exit to I-84 east. From I-84, take the 181st Avenue exit, turn right, and go south to Burnside. Get in the left-hand turn lane, turn left onto Burnside, and follow until it turns into Highway 26 east. Follow Highway 26 east through the Mount Hood corridor villages, the last one being Rhododendron. When approaching Government Camp, turn left onto the Business Loop. The driveway is across from the Mount Hood Brew Pub.
OPEN	All year
DESCRIPTION	A 1983 three-story Cascadian chalet with a glass front, located in the heart of the Mount Hood National Forest and recreational areas. Each room is decorated in theme styles such as Southwest and French country.

NO. OF ROOMS	Five rooms with private bathrooms. Try the master suite.
RATES	Year-round rates are $95-179 for a single or double, $169-179 for a suite. There is a minimum stay during major holidays and cancellation requires three days' notice.
CREDIT CARDS	American Express, Discover, MasterCard, Visa
BREAKFAST	Full breakfast is served in the dining room and includes unlimited orange juice, coffee, and tea; creamy scrambled eggs; ham slices baked with maple syrup; BJ's special pancakes, and warm maple syrup. A breakfast tray is delivered to each room in the morning with coffee, tea, and a basket of the inn's signature minimuffins. Six-course gourmet dinners are served nightly, with advance reservations required. Catered group lunches are also available.
AMENITIES	Each room with phone and robes; the inn has a full liquor license, so guests may order a favorite libation; wedding and reception facility with on-site coordinator; meeting facilitator for business/corporate retreats, dinners, and small conferences.
RESTRICTIONS	No smoking, no pets, children over are 6 are welcome.
MEMBER	Associated Bed & Breakfasts of Mount Hood/Northern Willamette Valley

MOUNT HOOD MANOR

88900 E Government Camp Loop, Government Camp, OR 503-272-3440

GRAND RONDE

This sleepy little town lies between McMinnville and the spectacular Oregon Coast on Highway 18. Try your luck at the Spirit Mountain Casino; and when the well runs dry, drown your sorrows at the local wineries or take to the hills for some hunting or fishing.

GRANNY FRANNY'S FARM

50730 SW Hebo Road, Grand Ronde, OR 97347
Kip & Teresa Smith, Innkeepers
EMAIL smithte@macnet.com
WEBSITE www.macnet.com/home/smithte

503-879-5002
800-553-9002
FAX 503-879-5513

LOCATION	From the Spirit Mountain Casino, drive 1.4 miles west and turn right onto Grand Ronde Road. Go 1.4 miles north to the stop sign and turn left onto Highway 22 (Hebo Road). Go 1 mile west, slowing down when the road curves to the right, and turn right into the driveway when you see the big green mailbox.
OPEN	All year
DESCRIPTION	A 1983 two-story farm-style host home nestled among Douglas fir trees on a family farm and decorated with period furniture and antiques.
NO. OF ROOMS	Two rooms share two bathrooms.
RATES	Year-round rates are $55-65 for a single or double. There is no minimum stay. Ask about a cancellation policy.
CREDIT CARDS	MasterCard, Visa
BREAKFAST	Full breakfast is served in the dining room and includes homemade breads, juice, coffee or tea, local fruits in season, an egg and meat dish, waffles, crepes, French toast, and breakfast desserts. Coffee in bed is available upon request.
AMENITIES	Soaps; shampoos; fruit-and-bread brown bags for wine tasters; flowers while in season; candies at bedtime; bathrobes; feeding and spoiling the animals of the farm; shuttle to and from casino by prior arrangement.
RESTRICTIONS	No smoking. Liesel is the resident golden retriever, Sinbad is the black tabby, Shatzi is the gold, long-haired tabby, Simon is the Siamese, and there are two horses.
MEMBER	Yamhill County Bed & Breakfast Association, Mid-Valley Bed & Breakfast Association

GRANTS PASS

The Rogue River is one of Oregon's most beautiful rivers, chiseled into the coastal mountains from Grants Pass to Gold Beach, protected by the million-acre Siskiyou National Forest, flecked with abandoned gold-mining sites, and inhabited by splendid steelhead and roaming Californians.

FLERY MANOR

2000 Jumpoff Joe Creek Road, Grants Pass, OR 97526   541-476-3591
Marla & John Vidrinskas, Innkeepers
Some Lithuanian, German, and Russian spoken   FAX 541-471-2303
EMAIL *flery@flerymanor.com*   WEBSITE *www.flerymanor.com*

Flery Manor, Grants Pass

LOCATION	Ten miles north of Grants Pass. Take exit 66 off I-5, turn east on Jumpoff Joe Creek Road, and go 1.7 miles. Turn left onto Shorthorn Gulch and drive 300 feet to the manor.
OPEN	All year
DESCRIPTION	A secluded 1992 three-story contemporary inn decorated with family antiques and original artwork, situated near the Rogue River on 7 acres with mountain views.
NO. OF ROOMS	Three rooms with private bathrooms and one room shares one bathroom.
RATES	March to October, rates are $75-125 for a single or double with a private bathroom, $75 for a single or double with a shared bathroom, and $125 for a suite. Low-season rates are $67.50-112.50 for a single or double with a private bathroom, $67.50 for a single or double with a shared bathroom, and $112.50 for a suite. There is no minimum stay and cancellation requires 15 days' notice for one to two rooms, 30 days' notice for three to four rooms, with a $15-per-room fee.
CREDIT CARDS	MasterCard, Visa
BREAKFAST	Full three-course breakfast is served in the dining room and includes healthy gourmet dishes, all original and developed for the Flery Manor. Breakfast might feature "egg on a cloud" with hollandaise sauce, orange blossom French toast, wild apple and blackberry crepes with Grand Marnier cream, peach yogurt and pecan scones, baked potato pancakes, and more. The menu includes dishes designed especially for guests with special dietary needs.

AMENITIES	Two-story fireplace in living room, library with old and new books, games; huge wraparound balcony with wicker furniture and umbrella tables; ponds, paths, gazebo, waterfall, stream, and flower gardens; barbecue grill; suite with fireplace, Jacuzzi, large sitting room, and French doors to private balcony; beds have uniquely designed canopies; robes and fresh flowers in rooms; central air conditioning; turndown service with homemade truffles and flowers; bathroom amenities; coffee and tea set up in hall outside rooms; evening hors d'oeuvres; access to private health club and pool; space for meetings, weddings, and other events; TV/VCR in common room; fax and other business services for guests in the library and parlor.
RESTRICTIONS	No smoking, no pets, children over 10 are welcome. There are black swans and lots of deer, wild ducks, and other waterfowl on the property—over 50 species of birds in the spring.
REVIEWED	*The Best Places to Kiss in the Northwest; Fodor's; Best Places to Stay in the Pacific Northwest; Frommer's; America's Favorite Inns, B&Bs, & Small Hotels; Bed & Breakfast Homes: Best of the West Coast; Where to Stay in Oregon*
MEMBER	Professional Association of Innkeepers International, Oregon Lodging Association, Oregon Bed & Breakfast Guild

HOME FARM

157 Savage Creek Road, Grants Pass, OR 97527   800-522-7967
Cheri & Bill Murray, Innkeepers

THE IVY HOUSE

139 SW I Street, Grants Pass, OR 97526   541-474-7363
Doreen Pontius, Innkeeper

LOCATION	In the historic district of Grants Pass, one block off 6th Street (the main drag through town).
OPEN	All year
DESCRIPTION	A 1908 two-story English arts and crafts brick host home with "early miscellaneous," comfortable furnishings. Listed on the National and State Historic Registers.
NO. OF ROOMS	One room with a private bathroom and four rooms share four bathrooms. Doreen suggests the Master Bedroom.

The Ivy House, Grants Pass

RATES	Year-round rates are $80 for a single or double with a private bathroom and $55-75 for a single or double with a shared bathroom. There is no minimum stay and cancellation requires 24 hours' notice.
CREDIT CARDS	American Express, Discover, MasterCard, Visa
BREAKFAST	Full English breakfast is served in the dining room and includes fruit, juice, tea or coffee, a hot main entrée with bangers, bacon, tomatoes, mushrooms, and eggs, plus crumpets, muffins, banana bread, marmalade, and jam.
AMENITIES	Jacuzzi bathtub in master bedroom, robes, flowers on table at breakfast, cups of tea on demand, modern heating and air conditioning.
RESTRICTIONS	No smoking

LAWNRIDGE HOUSE

1304 NW Lawnridge, Grants Pass, OR 97526 541-476-8518
Barbara Head, Innkeeper

PINE MEADOW INN BED & BREAKFAST

1000 Crow Road, Grants Pass, OR 97532 541-471-6277
Nancy & Maloy Murdock, Innkeepers 800-554-0806
EMAIL pmi@pinemeadowinn.com FAX 541-471-6277
WEBSITE www.pinemeadowinn.com

LOCATION	Take exit 61 off I-5 and go west 5 miles to Crow Road. Turn right and go up 1 mile. Pine Meadow Inn is on the left at the juncture of Crow Road and E Crow Road.
OPEN	All year
DESCRIPTION	A 1991 two-story Midwestern farmhouse on 9 acres of meadow and woods near the Rogue River, with casually elegant decor and turn-of-the-century antiques.
NO. OF ROOMS	Four rooms with private bathrooms. Try the Willow Room.
RATES	April through September, rates are $80-100 for a double and $342 for the entire B&B. October through March, rates are $65-88 for a double and $305 for the entire B&B. Cancellation requires 15 days when one or two rooms are booked, 30 days when three or four are booked, with a $15 charge per room.
CREDIT CARDS	American Express, MasterCard, Visa
BREAKFAST	Three-course healthy gourmet breakfast is served in the dining room and includes seasonal fruits and veggies from the gardens; specialties include Granny Smith waffles, fresh veggie dilled frittata, raspberries on a cloud, and tangy cheese blintzes. Special dietary needs are accommodated.
AMENITIES	Extensive library; rooms exceptionally well-lit for reading, in or out of bed; fresh flowers; turndown service; cookies by the bedside; in-room phones; full baths; hair dryers; iron/ironing board in each room; hot tub under towering pines; koi pond with gentle waterfall; paths and benches in private woods; wicker furniture on wraparound porch; hammock under pines and oaks; central air conditioning and ceiling fans.
RESTRICTIONS	No smoking, no pets, children over 10 are welcome.
REVIEWED	*Northwest Best Places; Fodor's; The Best Places to Kiss in the Northwest; Best Places to Stay in the Pacific Northwest; Special Places for the Discerning Traveler; Frommer's; Oregon Handbook; Oregon: Off the Beaten Path; America's Favorite Inns, B&Bs and Small Hotels; Hidden Pacific Northwest; Oregon Discovery Guide*
MEMBER	Oregon Bed & Breakfast Guild, Professional Association of International Innkeepers, Oregon Lodging Association, Grants Pass Chamber of Commerce, Grants Pass Bed & Breakfast Association
RATED	AAA 3 Diamonds, Mobil 2 Stars
AWARDS	Selected one of the Top Five inns in Oregon in 1997 by Fred Nystrom, author of *Special Places for the Discerning Traveler*.

Weasku Inn, Grants Pass

WEASKU INN

5560 Rogue River Highway, Grants Pass, OR 97527　　541-471-8000
Carl Johnson, Innkeeper　　800-493-2758
EMAIL info@weasku.com　　WEBSITE www.weasku.com

LOCATION	Take I-5 to exit 48/Rogue River. Take a left and go over the bridge. Take a right on Old Rogue River Highway. Go 3 miles. The B&B is on the right side past Savage Rapids Dam.
OPEN	All year
DESCRIPTION	A 1924 two-story log cabin with Pacific Northwest furnishings.
NO. OF ROOMS	Seventeen rooms with private bathrooms. Dayle recommends the River Suite Cabin.
RATES	Year-round rates are $85-295 for a single or double and $195-295 for the river cabin. There is no minimum stay and cancellation requires 24 hours' notice.
CREDIT CARDS	American Express, Diners Club, Discover, MasterCard, Visa
BREAKFAST	Continental-plus is served in the dining room and includes fruit, pastries, juice, cereal, coffee, and tea.
AMENITIES	Evening wine and cheese reception, river access, whirlpool tubs, robes, air-conditioning, meeting facilities, fireplaces, gift store, refrigerators.
RESTRICTIONS	No smoking, no pets
REVIEWED	Lanier Travel Guide

HALFWAY

Once just a midway stop between two bustling mining towns, Halfway is now the quiet centerpiece of Pine Valley—stashed between the fruitful southern slopes of the Wallowa Mountains and the steep cliffs of Hells Canyon. The continent's deepest gorge, Hell's Canyon, begins at Oxbow Dam, 16 miles east of Halfway.

CLEAR CREEK BED & BREAKFAST

RR 1, Box 737, Halfway, OR 97834 541-742-2238
WEBSITE www.neoregon.com/ccgg

HAMMOND

Hammond is situated at the northwestern tip of Oregon, where the Columbia River pours into the Pacific Ocean. From here, the coast and Fort Stevens State Park are handy.

OFFICERS INN BED & BREAKFAST

540 Russell Place, Hammond, OR 97121 503-861-0884
WEBSITE www.moriah.com/officersinn 800-377-2524

HOOD RIVER

Fruit orchards are everywhere. Hood River is ideally located on the climatic cusp between the wetter west side and the drier east side of the Cascades, alongside the mighty Columbia, so it gets the sun and enough moisture (about 31 inches annually) to keep the creeks flowing and the orchards bearing. Thirty miles to the south, 11,245-foot Mount Hood dominates the horizon; however, from the town itself, the views are of Washington's Mount Adams, the Columbia, and its ubiquitous windsurfers. Visitors come to hike, fish, climb, and ski on Mount Hood and Mount Adams. And the area has some of the best mountain biking in the Northwest.

AVALON BED & BREAKFAST

3444 Avalon Drive, Hood River, OR 97031 541-386-2560
Jim & Dorothy Tollen, Innkeepers 888-386-3941
EMAIL avalon@moriah.com WEBSITE www.moriah.com/avalon

LOCATION	Take the first Hood River exit (exit 62 from the west) and travel east on Cascade to 13th (first traffic light); turn right and go up the hill to Belmont Drive. Turn right and go west about five blocks, turn left (south) onto Avalon, go to the stop sign, and turn right. Travel west about two city blocks.
OPEN	All year
DESCRIPTION	A 1906 two-story farmhouse with country decor adjacent to an orchard on 0.5 acre of lawn, flowers, and gardens.
NO. OF ROOMS	Three rooms with one shared bathroom. "The west room has a view of Mount Adams and is very cozy."
RATES	High season rates are $50-65 for a single or double. Regular season rates are $45-55 for a single or double. There is no minimum stay and cancellation requires 48 hours' notice.
CREDIT CARDS	Discover, MasterCard, Visa
BREAKFAST	Full country breakfast is served in the dining room and includes coffee, tea, hot chocolate, juice, fruit, and a main entrée such as almond pancakes or eggs Benedict. Vegetarian meals are also available. "You won't go away hungry."
AMENITIES	Robes in rooms; hot tub on deck; hair dryer; coffee, soft drinks, and fruit (in season) available near rooms; flowers; special packages, romance packages (chocolates, flowers, dinner); fishing, windsurfing, reduced ski-lift tickets.
RESTRICTIONS	No smoking
MEMBER	Oregon Bed & Breakfast Guild, Bed & Breakfast Guild of Oregon, Bed & Breakfast Association of Oregon, Hood River Bed & Breakfast Association

BERYL HOUSE BED & BREAKFAST

4079 Barrett Drive, Hood River, OR 97031 541-386-5567
Kim Pfautz & John Lovell, Innkeepers

KUDOS/COMMENTS "An older home on the outskirts of Hood River."

BROWN'S BED & BREAKFAST

3000 Reed Road, Hood River, OR 97031 541-386-1545
Al & Marion Brown, Innkeepers

LOCATION	Take exit 62 off I-84, travel 4 miles on Country Club Road to Reed Road, then 3 miles to Brown's Road, which ends at Brown's B&B.

OPEN	All year
DESCRIPTION	A 1930 two-story farmhouse with country-style decor.
NO. OF ROOMS	Two rooms with one shared bathroom. The best room has a view of Mount Hood.
RATES	Please call for current rates and cancellation information.
CREDIT CARDS	MasterCard, Visa
BREAKFAST	Full farm-style breakfast is served in the kitchen and includes fresh fruit juice, fruit cup, sourdough pancakes, eggs, meat, coffee, tea, and milk.
AMENITIES	Each bedroom has a king-size bed that can be broken down into twin beds. The B&B backs up to a forest with trails and an orchard.
RESTRICTIONS	No smoking, no pets, children over 3 are welcome. Luke is the resident golden Lab.
REVIEWED	Where to Stay in Oregon
MEMBER	Hood River Bed & Breakfast Association

COTTONWOOD BED & BREAKFAST

224 13th Street, Hood River, OR 97031   541-386-1390
EMAIL droll@gorge.net

GORGE VIEW BED & BREAKFAST

1009 Columbia Street, Hood River, OR 97031   541-386-5770
Pat & Ann Frodel, Innkeepers
EMAIL gorgeview@gorge.net
WEBSITE www.gorge.net/gorgeview

LOCATION	From I-84, take the Hood River city center exit (63). Cross the overpass toward town and take the first right at Cascade Street. Follow Cascade west eight blocks and turn right on 10th Street. Go one block, then turn left on Columbia Street. The B&B is the second house on the left.
OPEN	May 15 through October 15
DESCRIPTION	A 1917 two-story Victorian bungalow with an oversize, wraparound front porch with panoramic views of the Columbia River and Mount Adams.

NO. OF ROOMS	One room with a private bathroom and three rooms share two bathrooms. There is also a bunkroom with four beds.
RATES	Mid-May through mid-October, rates are $70-80 for a single or double with a private bathroom, $65-75 for a single or double with a shared bathroom, and $35 per person for the bunkroom. There is a two-night minimum stay during weekends in the summer and cancellation requires seven days' notice.
CREDIT CARDS	MasterCard, Visa
BREAKFAST	Full breakfast is served in the dining room and includes Dutch babies, huevos Gorge View, blueberry cakes, French toast, omelets, homemade muffins, and fresh fruit.
AMENITIES	Hot tub, outdoor shower, home-cooked breakfasts, refrigerator and barbecue for guest use, air conditioning, equipment storage for sports equipment, friendly and relaxed environment.
RESTRICTIONS	No smoking, no pets, children are welcome.
REVIEWED	*Cheap Sleeps*
MEMBER	Oregon Bed & Breakfast Guild

HACKETT HOUSE

922 State Street, Hood River, OR 97031   541-386-1014
Sherry Dobo & Pat Barnett, Innkeepers

HOOD RIVER HOTEL AND PASQUALE'S RISTORANTE

102 Oak Avenue, Hood River, OR 97031   541-386-1900
Pasquale & Jacquie Barone, Innkeepers   800-386-1859
EMAIL HRHotel@gorge.net   541-386-6090
WEBSITE www.HoodRiver Hotel.com

LOCATION	Take exit 63 off of I-84 (approximately 63 miles from the Portland International Airport). Go two blocks south to Oak Avenue and turn left. The hotel is one block down on the left.
OPEN	All year
DESCRIPTION	Fully restored 1913 National Historic Landmark hotel.
NO. OF ROOMS	Forty-one rooms with private bathrooms. Pasquale recommends room 310.

Hood River Hotel and Pasquale's Ristorante, Hood River

RATES   March 15 through November 15, rates are $59-145 for a single or double and $89-145 for a suite. November 15 through March 15, rates are $49-135 for a single or double and $85-135 for a suite. There is no minimum stay. Cancellation requires five days' notice during high season, 48 hours in low season.

CREDIT CARDS   American Express, Diners Club, Discover, MasterCard, Visa

BREAKFAST   Continental breakfast is served, or guests can use coupons toward items on the restaurant's full breakfast menu.

AMENITIES   Jacuzzi, sauna, exercise facility, air conditioning, handicapped access, meeting rooms.

RESTRICTIONS   Smoking in designated areas only.

REVIEWED   *Weekends for two in the Pacific Northwest: 50 Romantic Getaways; Northwest Best Places; The Definitive Guide—Selected Hotels & Inns, North America; Fodor's; Best Places to Stay in the Northwest; Frommer's; Hot Showers, Soft Beds and Dayhikes in the Central Cascades; Doin' the Northwest with your Pooch*

INN AT THE GORGE—BED & BREAKFAST

1113 Eugene Street, Hood River, OR 97031   541-386-4429

LAKECLIFF ESTATE BED & BREAKFAST

3820 Westcliff Drive, Hood River, OR 97031   541-386-7000
Bruce & Judy Thesenga, Innkeepers   FAX 541-386-1803
EMAIL lakecliff@hotmail.com

LOCATION	Take exit 62 off I-84, go right on Westcliff Drive, and the B&B is the first driveway on the left.
OPEN	Mid-may through mid-September
DESCRIPTION	A 1908 three-story shingled lodge with beamed ceilings and five native-stone fireplaces, with elegant, lodge-style decor, on 11 acres with a view of the Columbia River. Listed on the National Historic Register.
NO. OF ROOMS	Two rooms with private bathrooms and two rooms share two bathrooms. Try Emily's Room.
RATES	May through September, rates are $110 for a single or double with a private bathroom, $90 for a single or double with a shared bathroom, and $125 for the guesthouse. There is no minimum stay and cancellation requires 14 days' notice.
CREDIT CARDS	No
BREAKFAST	Full breakfast is served in the dining room and includes coffee and biscotti (available at 7 a.m. on the second floor), orange juice, fresh fruit compote, a hot entrée with breakfast meat, and sweets.
AMENITIES	Bottled water, afternoon snack, deck with rocking chairs overlooking the Columbia River, shuffleboard court, sweets before bed, rooms with robes, large selection of books and magazines.
RESTRICTIONS	No smoking, no pets, children over 12 are welcome. Truman is the resident yellow Lab, and Muffy and Parker are the cats. The cats are great molers—and all pets are outside only.
REVIEWED	*Northwest Best Places*, *Fodor's Bed & Breakfast & Country Inns*, *The Best Places to Kiss in the Northwest*, *Best Places to Stay in the Northwest*, *Where to Stay in Oregon*, *Fodor's America's Best Bed & Breakfasts*
MEMBER	Oregon Bed & Breakfast Guild

Panorama Lodge B&B

2290 Old Dalles Drive, Hood River, OR 97031   541-387-2687
Lee Jenkins, Innkeeper

LOCATION	From I-84, take exit 64 and follow Highway 35 south. Go 0.25 mile past the China Gorge restaurant and turn left on Eastside Road toward Panorama Point County Park. Go 2 miles and turn left on Old Dalles Road.
OPEN	Memorial Day weekend until sometime in October
DESCRIPTION	A 1978 three-story log lodge with a gambrel roof and an interior of cedar and wood logs.
NO. OF ROOMS	Five rooms share two bathrooms. Lee recommends room B.
RATES	Rates are $45-85 for a single or double with a shared bathroom. The entire B&B rents for between $245-295. There is a minimum stay required to rent the entire B&B during weekends in July and August.
CREDIT CARDS	No
BREAKFAST	Continental or full breakfast is served in the dining room and includes fresh-baked breads, fresh fruits, and juices; sometimes eggs, omelets, potatoes, bacon, and ham. Special meals are also available.
AMENITIES	Barbecue, limited kitchen use for dinners, flowers and gardens, relaxing atmosphere.
RESTRICTIONS	No smoking inside, no pets. "Good place for children," says Lee.
MEMBER	Hood River Bed & Breakfast Association

State Street Inn

1005 State Street, Hood River, OR 97031   541-386-1899

IONE

Ione is prime Oregon wheat country. Local festivals include a big barbecue bash in June and a Fourth of July celebration.

WOOLERY HOUSE BED & BREAKFAST

170 E Second, Ione, OR 97843   541-422-7218

JACKSONVILLE

The town started with a boom when gold was discovered in Rich Gulch in 1851. Then the railroad bypassed it, and the tidy little city struggled to avoid becoming a ghost town. Much of the 19th-century city has been restored. The strip of authentic Gold Rush–era shops, hotels, and saloons along California Street has become a popular stage set for films. Jacksonville is renowned for antique shops. Britt Festival, an outdoor music and arts series, runs from late June through September. Listeners gather on the grass to enjoy open-stage performances of jazz, bluegrass, folk, country, classical music, musical theater, and dance. The Jacksonville Museum, housed in the stately 1883 courthouse, follows the history of the Rogue Valley with plenty of photos and artifacts.

HISTORIC ORTH HOUSE B&B
"THE TEDDY BEAR INN"

105 W Main Street, Jacksonville, OR 97530   541-899-8665
Lee & Marilyn Lewis, Innkeepers   800-700-7301
EMAIL historicorthhousebnb@medford.net   FAX 541-899-9146
WEBSITE www.historicorthhousebnb.com

LOCATION	Exit I-5 at exit 30 (Highway 62), go 0.5 mile to old Highway 99 (Court Street). Go south about 1 mile to Highway 238 (Main Street in Medford), turn right, and follow signs to Jacksonville. Take a right on California Street and go two blocks to Third Street. Take a left (south) and go one block to Main Street. The B&B is on the corner.
OPEN	All year
DESCRIPTION	An 1880 two-story Italianate villa with Victorian decor, antique toys, and teddy bears. Listed on the National and State Historic Registers.

Historic Orth House B&B "The Teddy Bear Inn", Jacksonville

NO. OF ROOMS	Three rooms with private bathrooms and one room shares a bathroom. Try Josie's Room, which has a clawfoot tub.
RATES	May through October, rates are $120-135 for a single or double with a private bathroom and $85-110 for a single or double with a shared bathroom; suites go for $150 for two and $190 for four, and the entire B&B goes for $400 for eight. November through April, rates are $85-100 for a single or double with a private bathroom and $65-85 for a single or double with a shared bathroom; suites go for $125 for two and $150 for four, and the entire B&B goes for $300 for eight. There is no minimum stay, a credit card number or 50 percent deposit holds room, and cancellation requires seven days' notice.
CREDIT CARDS	MasterCard, Visa
BREAKFAST	Full breakfast is served in the dining room and includes seasonal fruit, assorted breakfast breads, juice, cereals, and a hot dish such as French toast, waffles, or various types of egg casseroles.
AMENITIES	Afternoon and evening tea and treats, robes and candy in rooms, gift teddy bears for special occasions, air conditioning in rooms, two porches and garden swing.
RESTRICTIONS	No smoking inside, no pets, children are welcome.
REVIEWED	*Frommer's Oregon*
MEMBER	Oregon Bed & Breakfast Guild
RATED	AAA 2 Diamonds
AWARDS	Best Look of Christmas, 1996, and Best Victorian Building, 1997, selected by the Jacksonville Chamber of Commerce

JACKSONVILLE INN

175 E California Street, Jacksonville, OR 97530　　541-899-1900
Linda & Jerry Evans, Innkeepers　　800-321-9344
Greek, Italian, and Spanish spoken　　FAX 541-899-1373
EMAIL jvinn@mind.net　　WEBSITE jacksonvilleinn.com

LOCATION	Located in the center of the historic town of Jacksonville, which is 7 miles from Medford.
OPEN	All year
DESCRIPTION	Elegantly restored 1861 two-story brick inn and three honeymoon cottages, and an award-winning gourmet restaurant. Listed on the National and State Historic Registers.
NO. OF ROOMS	Eleven rooms with private bathrooms.
RATES	Year-round rates are $112 for a single or double, $115-245 for a suite, and $150-245 for a honeymoon cottage. There is no minimum stay and cancellation requires 72 hours' notice.
CREDIT CARDS	American Express, Diners Club, Discover, MasterCard, Visa
BREAKFAST	Full breakfast is served in the dining room. Guests can order from a full-service menu in the award-winning restaurant. A special Sunday brunch is available, as are lunch, winemaker dinners, and picnic dinners during the Peter Britt Summer Music Festival.
AMENITIES	Complimentary guest robes; flowers in rooms; whirlpool tubs and steam showers; wine tastings upon arrival; connoisseurs' wine cellar with over 2,000 selections; entertainment systems, fireplaces, and private patios in cottages; small conference/meeting facilities; small wedding facilities; entirely air-conditioned; nonsmoking establishment except for patio dining after 9 p.m.
RESTRICTIONS	No smoking, no pets, children are welcome.
MEMBER	International Innkeepers Association, Oregon Bed & Breakfast Guild, Unique Inns of the Pacific Northwest, Oregon Bed & Breakfast Association
RATED	AAA 3 Diamonds, Mobil 3 Stars
AWARDS	5 Star Diamond Academy Restaurant Industry Award,1991, for the Top Continental Restaurant in the United States; Award of Excellence given by *Wine Spectator* 1993, 1994, 1995. Outstanding Wine List, *Wine Spectator*
KUDOS/COMMENTS	"Historic building with restaurant. Tastefully furnished with a friendly and efficient staff."

THE MCCULLY HOUSE INN

240 E California Street, Jacksonville, OR 97530
Mary Ann & Dennis Ramsden, Innkeepers
WEBSITE www.mccullyhouseinn.com

541-899-1942
800-367-1942
FAX 541-899-1560

THE TOUVELLE HOUSE

455 N Oregon Street, Jacksonville, OR 97530
WEBSITE www.wave.net/upg/touvelle

800-846-8422

KUDOS/COMMENTS "Wonderful hospitality and food, beautifully decorated."

THE WELLS RANCH HOUSE BED & BREAKFAST

126 Hamilton Road, Jacksonville, OR 97530
The Wells Family, Innkeepers
EMAIL glwsound@aol.com   WEBSITE www.bbonline.com/or/wellsranch/

541-899-1472
FAX 541-899-7829

LOCATION	Take I-5 to Medford, then take Highway 238 to the center of Jacksonville. Go 8 miles and take a left onto Upper Applegate Road. Drive 2 miles, turn right on Hamilton Road, and go to the second driveway on the right.
OPEN	All year
DESCRIPTION	A 1974 two-story country ranch house with a blue pine interior and antique wood cookstove.
NO. OF ROOMS	One room with a private bathroom.
RATES	Year-round rates are $95 for a single or double. There is no minimum stay. Call about the cancellation policy.
CREDIT CARDS	No
BREAKFAST	Full breakfast is served in the dining room or kitchen and includes homemade jams, fresh-baked breads, gourmet pastries, bagels, Belgian waffles, muffins, Danish, fruit, juice, and coffee.
AMENITIES	Horse and livestock; llama ranch tour; cattle ranch tour; fireplaces; TV/VCR, phone and fax; air conditioning; toiletries; clawfoot tub bath upon request; complimentary jar of homemade jam; views from the kitchen of mountains, pasture, and the red barn.
RESTRICTIONS	No smoking, no children. Puppers is the resident hound and Big Kitty keeps him company. There are cattle and a horse named Oscar on the property.

JOHN DAY

You are in the midst of dry cattle country in an area loaded with history: John Day is just off the old Oregon Trail, and the whole region was once bulging with gold (during the height of the Gold Rush in 1862, $26 million in gold was mined in the neighboring town of Canyon City). Kam Wah Chung Museum, next to the city park, was the stone-walled home of two Chinese herbal doctors at the turn of the century. A tour makes for an interesting glimpse of the Chinese settlement in the West: opium-stained walls, Chinese shrines, and herbal medicines are on display, as well as a small general store. John Day Fossil Beds National Monument lies to the west: the banded Painted Hills, extremely ancient fossils, and fascinating geological layers.

SONSHINE B&B

210 NW Canton, John Day, OR 97845   541-575-1827
Carolyn & Carl Stout, Innkeepers
EMAIL *cstout@orednet.org*

LOCATION	Two blocks north of Main Street on Canton across from the Kam Wah Chung Museum and City Park.
OPEN	All year
DESCRIPTION	A 1945 host home with comfortable, regional decor.
NO. OF ROOMS	Two rooms share one bathroom.
RATES	April through October, rates are $55 for a single or double. November through March, rates are $35 for a single or double. There is no minimum stay and cancellation requires 24 hours' notice for a full refund.
CREDIT CARDS	No
BREAKFAST	Full breakfast is served in the kitchen and includes French toast with apricot glaze, oatmeal buttermilk hotcakes with fruit syrup, elk steak, venison sausage, rhubarb-nut muffins, fresh fruit, rice pudding, fresh juice, homemade bread, and frittatas.
AMENITIES	Air-conditioned rooms, queen beds, local information and advice about seeing the area from hosts who enjoy visiting with guests and seeing to their comfort.
RESTRICTIONS	No smoking. Fred is the resident cat.

JOSEPH

This is the fabled land of the Wallowas, ancestral home of Chief Joseph, from which he fled with a band of Nez Perce warriors to his last stand near the Canadian border. The town itself is becoming something of an art colony. David Manuel, State of Oregon official sculptor for the Oregon Trail Celebration, runs the Manuel Museum and Studio on Main Street. Valley Bronze of Oregon has built a foundry and a showroom in Joseph. Wallowa Lake State Park lies on the edge of the Wallowa-Whitman National Forest and Eagle Cap Wilderness. An Alpenfest with music, dancing, and Bavarian feasts happens every September, but the peak season is still midsummer, when pristine Wallowa Lake and its shores are abuzz with go-carts, sailboats, and windsurfers. In winter the attraction is miles and miles of unpeopled cross-country trails throughout the lovely Wallowa highlands.

CHANDLERS' BED, BREAD & TRAIL INN

700 S Main, Joseph, OR 97846 541-432-9765
Jim & Ethel Chandler, Innkeepers 800-452-3781
EMAIL chanbbti @ eoni.com WEBSITE www.eoni.com/~chanbbti

LOCATION	From Portland, take I-84 to Ontario. Exit onto Highway 82 and proceed 85 miles to Joseph. The inn is on the left just as you leave Joseph toward Wallowa Lake.
OPEN	All year
DESCRIPTION	A 1983 two-story post-and-beam lodge with rustic decor.
NO. OF ROOMS	Three rooms with private bathrooms and two rooms share 1½ bathrooms.
RATES	High-season rates are $85 for a double with a private bathroom and $60 for a double with a shared bathroom. Regular-season rates are $70 for a double with a private bathroom and $50 for a double with a shared bathroom. There is a minimum stay and cancellation requires one week's notice.
CREDIT CARDS	American Express, MasterCard, Visa
BREAKFAST	Full three-course breakfast includes fresh fruit, hot cereal, and a main course. Dinner is also available for large groups.
RESTRICTIONS	No smoking, no pets, children over 12 are welcome.
REVIEWED	*Country Inns of the Far West: Pacific Northwest, Northwest Budget Traveler, Where to Find the Oregon in Oregon*
MEMBER	American & Canadian Bed & Breakfast Association

TAMARACK PINES INN

60073 Wallowa Lake Highway, Joseph, OR 97846   541-432-2920

JUNCTION CITY

A former railroad hub, Junction City buzzes with year-round festivals including Springfest in May and several celebrations that honor the city's rich Scandinavian history. Check out the pretty "Daffodil Drive" in midspring.

BLACK BART BED & BREAKFAST

94125 Love Lake Road, Junction City, OR 97448   541-998-1904
Irma & Don Mode, Innkeepers

KUDOS/COMMENTS   "This is a lovely, well-kept home and grounds. Happy host and hostess. Furnishings are of excellent quality."

KERBY

Kerby rests along the Illinois River in southwest Oregon, about 40 miles southwest of Grants Pass on scenic Highway 199. From here, you are within striking distance of Oregon Caves National Monument, the Siskiyou National Forest, and the Kalmiopsis Wilderness Area.

KERBYVILLE INN

24304 Redwood Highway, Kerby, OR 97531   541-592-4689
Lelo Kerivan, Innkeeper

OPEN	March through December
DESCRIPTION	A 1990 inn and guesthouse.
NO. OF ROOMS	Five rooms with private bathrooms. Lelo recommends the Chardonnay Suite.
RATES	Year-round rates are $59 for a single or double and $79-89 for a suite.
CREDIT CARDS	MasterCard, Visa

BREAKFAST	Continental breakfast is served.
RESTRICTIONS	No smoking
MEMBER	Oregon Bed & Breakfast Association

KIMBERLY

LAND'S INN BED & BREAKFAST

HC 1, Box 117, Kimberly, OR 97848　　　　　　541-934-2333

KLAMATH FALLS

This city of 17,000 people, the largest for 70 miles around, is so isolated that it once led a movement to secede from Oregon and become the state of Jefferson. Now its residents happily welcome tourists, bird-watchers, and sportspersons from both Oregon and California (just 25 miles south). It's a pretty drive through the high desert from Bend, or over the mountain passes from Medford or Ashland. Take Highway 139 a few miles south to the Lava Beds National Monument Visitor Center in Tulelake, California. Upper Klamath Lake, 143 square miles, lies on the remains of a larger ancient lake system and is the largest lake in Oregon; it's fine for fishing and serves as the nesting grounds for many birds, including white pelicans. The Williamson River, which flows into the lake, yields plenty of trout.

BOARDING HOUSE INN

1800 Esplanade Avenue, Klamath Falls, OR 97601　　　　541-883-8584

IRON GATE ESTATE BED & BREAKFAST

2035 Portland Street, Klamath Falls, OR 97601　　　541-884-1308
Joanne & Ron Smith, Innkeepers　　　　　　　　　　888-884-4184

LOCATION	East on Portland Street. At the yellow blinking light, take (Business) Highway 97.
OPEN	All year

DESCRIPTION	A 1912 two-story host home with Old English decor and a landscape that includes over 250 flower varieties.
NO. OF ROOMS	Two rooms with private bathrooms. Try the Blue Room.
RATES	Year-round rates are $55-85 for a single or double. There is no minimum stay and cancellation requires 10 days' notice.
CREDIT CARDS	Discover, MasterCard, Visa
BREAKFAST	Full breakfast is served in the dining room and includes fresh fruit, juice, coffee, tea, home-baked breads, muffins, egg dishes, meats, yogurt, and granola.
AMENITIES	Wine and hors d'oeuvres at check-in, hot tub, heated pool June through October, unlimited hot water from geothermal well, shuttle to Amtrak and airport, robes, gym.
RESTRICTIONS	No smoking, no pets. Martini is the resident poodle.
MEMBER	American Bed & Breakfast Association

THOMPSONS' BED & BREAKFAST

1420 Wild Plum Court, Klamath Falls, OR 97601   541-882-7938
Mary Pohll, Innkeeper
EMAIL tompohll@aol.com

LOCATION	Take the Lakeshore/Oregon Avenue exit off Highway 97 and go west on Lakeshore for 1.5 miles. Turn left on Lynnewood, another left on Vista Way, and drive to the dead end. Go right, then take a quick left onto Wild Plum Court.
OPEN	All year
DESCRIPTION	A 1987 two-story cedar host home with Victorian interior, overlooking Upper Klamath Lake.
NO. OF ROOMS	Four rooms with private bathrooms. Try the Sunset Room.
RATES	Year-round rates are $65-80 for a single or double and $250 rents the entire B&B. There is no minimum stay.
CREDIT CARDS	No
BREAKFAST	Full breakfast is served in the dining room and includes Belgian waffles, bacon, fresh fruit, orange juice, coffee, and tea.
AMENITIES	Complimentary drinks, coffee, tea, soft drinks, wine, and popcorn; common room with refrigerator and microwave; next door to Moore Park, which features a marina, tennis courts, and hiking trails; spectacular views; private entrance.
RESTRICTIONS	No smoking, no pets
REVIEWED	*Northwest Best Places, The Country Inn Guide, American Historic Inns*

LA GRANDE

Situated in the Grande Ronde Valley between the Wallowa and Blue Mountains, La Grande offers exceptional access to outdoor adventures of all shapes and sizes. Sprawling Wallowa-Whitman National Forest is a great place to begin your adventures. Check out the Oregon Trail Interpretive Park at Blue Mountain Crossing and grab a relaxing soak at the Lehman Hot Springs west of town.

COUNTRYSIDE INN BED & BREAKFAST

62528 Jay Bird Drive, La Grande, OR 97850 541-963-3329
EMAIL *jlouderm@orednet.org* FAX 541-963-3329

STANG MANOR INN

1612 Walnut, La Grande, OR 97850 541-963-2400
Marjorie & Pat McClure, Innkeepers 888-286-9463
EMAIL *stang@eoni.com* WEBSITE *www.eoni.com/stang*

LOCATION	Leave I-84 at exit 261, turn left, and proceed west on Island Avenue for approximately 0.75 mile to the first stop sign. Proceed directly across the intersection onto "N" Avenue. Go 15 blocks, turn right onto Walnut, and go three blocks.
OPEN	All year
DESCRIPTION	A fully restored 1923 two-story Georgian colonial inn, a former timber baron's mansion, with period furnishings. Listed on the National and State Historic Registers.
NO. OF ROOMS	Four rooms with private bathrooms. Try the Suite.
RATES	Year-round rates are $75-95 for a single or double, $95 for a suite, and $335 for the entire inn. There is no minimum stay and cancellation requires notice by 6 p.m. the day before arrival.
CREDIT CARDS	American Express, MasterCard, Visa
BREAKFAST	Full breakfast is served in the dining room and includes coffee, tea, and juice; fruit plate; a breakfast meat; and a main dish, which may be strada, eggs and croissants, French toast, etc.
AMENITIES	Pleasant patio, acre of lawns and roses, large birdbath suitable for extroverts.
RESTRICTIONS	No smoking, no pets, children over 9 are welcome. Elsie is the resident cat.
REVIEWED	*Northwest Best Places*, *Fodor's*
RATED	AAA 2 Diamonds, ABBA 4 Crowns, Mobil 3 Stars

LA PINE

This is rural Oregon at its finest, with sprawling cattle ranches and alfalfa farms set alongside state and federal forests. The nearby Deschutes and Little Deschutes Rivers are prized for their white-water rafting and fine trout fishing, and there are numerous lakes dotting the landscape. Don't miss the Newberry Crater National Volcanic Monument. Local festivals include Last Frontier Days over July 4th and the Winter Festival in January.

DIAMOND STONE GUEST LODGE & GALLERY

PO Box 4584, La Pine, OR 97709
Doug & Gloria Watt, Innkeepers
EMAIL *mortuplink@aol.com*
WEBSITE *www.diamondstone.com*

541-536-6263
800-600-6263
FAX 541-536-9711

LOCATION	Twenty-five miles south of Bend, 8 miles south of Sunriver, 8 miles north of La Pine, and 3 miles west of the turnoff to Newberry Crater National Volcanic Monument and Paulina and East Lakes.
OPEN	All year
DESCRIPTION	A 1960 two-story lodge decorated with paintings and sculptures of western and wildlife themes. The lodge is situated on 5 acres adjacent to Quail Run Golf Course, with Mount Bachelor and the Cascade Mountains as a backdrop.
NO. OF ROOMS	Three rooms with private bathrooms. Try the luxurious Green Room.
RATES	Year-round rates are $80 for a single or double and $110-120 for a suite. There is a two-night minimum stay on weekends in the summer or winter and during holidays.
CREDIT CARDS	American Express, MasterCard, Visa
BREAKFAST	Full breakfast is served in the dining room or in the guestrooms by prior arrangement. Breakfast features Scandinavian delicacies known as aebelskivers, with fresh fruit, juices, western-style pepper bacon, and fresh-brewed coffee. "This breakfast provides a wonderful start to your day."
AMENITIES	Robes and towels for running back and forth to the outdoor hot tub, telephones, TV/VCRs, over 200 videos, library, lots of interesting art to view, complimentary beverage upon arrival.
RESTRICTIONS	None. Resident pets are Kala the Corgi dog, and an outdoor cat named Franklin.
REVIEWED	*Northwest Best Places*

LAFAYETTE

Named after the town in Indiana of the same name, Oregon's Lafayette features a splendid historic district with plenty of antique shops to browse. Check out the Yamhill County Historical Museum and Barn with its wonderful collection of pioneer memorabilia featuring quilts and pioneer arts and crafts. The barn houses early tools and farm machinery.

KELTY ESTATE BED & BREAKFAST

675 Third Street, Lafayette, OR 97127   503-864-3740
Ron & Jo Ann Ross, Innkeepers   800-867-3740

LAKEVIEW

At an elevation of nearly 4,300 feet, Lakeview calls itself "Oregon's Tallest Town." It's better known for its geyser, Old Perpetual—which doesn't exactly rival Yellowstone's Old Faithful, but is Oregon's only geyser. It's located in a pond at Hunter's Hot Springs, a 47-acre property dotted by hot-springs pools, on the west side of Highway 395 about 2 miles north of town. Abert Lake, 20 miles north of Lakeview, is a stark, shallow body of water over which looms Abert Rim, a massive fault scarp. One of the highest exposed geologic faults in North America, the rim towers 2,000 feet above the lake.

HERYFORD HOUSE BED & BREAKFAST

108 S "F" Street, Lakeview, OR 97630   541-947-4727

LANGLOIS

This agricultural community offers access to Floras Lake and Boice Park. Langlois marks the northern boundary of "Little New Zealand," so named because of the multitudinous sheep that dot the hillsides.

FLORAS LAKE HOUSE BY THE SEA

92870 Boice Cope Road, Langlois, OR 97450   541-348-2573
Liz & Will Brady, Innkeepers
WEBSITE www.floraslake.com

LEABURG

Leaburg is situated along the McKenzie River, 25 miles east of Eugene on Highway 126.

MARJON BED & BREAKFAST INN

44975 Leaburg Dam Road, Leaburg, OR 97489   541-896-3145
Marguerite Haas, Innkeeper
WEBSITE www.virtualcities.com

LOCATION	From the center of Eugene, go east on McKenzie Highway (126) to milepost 24. Turn right onto Leaburg Dam Road and go 1 mile to the end of the road. The inn is on the left.
OPEN	All year
DESCRIPTION	A 1971 one-story Swiss chalet with cedar exterior and French provincial and Asian interior, with furnishings from all over the world, located 50 feet from the river on 2 landscaped acres.
NO. OF ROOMS	Two rooms with private bathrooms. Marguerite recommends the French Provincial suite.
RATES	Year-round rates are $95 for a single or double and $125 for a suite. The living room is available for conferences for $175. There is no minimum stay and cancellation requires seven days' notice less a $5 fee.
CREDIT CARDS	No
BREAKFAST	Full five-course gourmet breakfast is served in the dining room or outside on the covered terrace and includes juice, sculptured fruit served under glass, crumbled-bacon soufflé, fruit-filled muffins, coffee, and tea. Special breakfasts are available for those with health concerns.
AMENITIES	Complimentary wine or soft drink on arrival; waterfall, grotto, and dock; suite with whirlpool bathtub, mirrored walls, dressing table, sewing kit, TV, reading lamps, sofa, private deck, large bed, crystal chandelier, hand-painted gold accents on French provincial furniture.
RESTRICTIONS	No pets, no children, smoking on the terrace only. Pearl is the resident cat. Pearl will sit and stay on command.

LINCOLN

SPYGLASS INN

2510 SW Dune, Lincoln, OR 97367 541-994-2785
Jim Murphy & Diane Disse, Innkeepers

LINCOLN CITY

There is no off-season here. Every weekend is crowded, courtesy in part to a slew of factory outlets located halfway through town and gaming casinos (to the north and east). Whether you come for summer sun or winter storms, be prepared to move slowly through these parts. The good news is that the restaurant, lodging, and activity choices have never been so favorable. You can seek some solitude on the 7 miles of continuous sandy beach that begin at Roads End (at the north end of town) and continue south all the way to Siletz Bay.

BREY HOUSE "OCEAN VIEW" BED & BREAKFAST INN

3725 NW Keel Avenue, Lincoln City, OR 97367 541-994-7123
Milt & Shirley Brey, Innkeepers
WEBSITE www.moriah.com/breyhouse

LOCATION	At the north end of town off Highway 101, turn onto N 39th and head toward the ocean at the BP gas station. Go to Jetty, turn left, and drive to the sign.
OPEN	All year
DESCRIPTION	A 1941 three-story Cape Cod with ocean views and modern but comfortable furnishings.
NO. OF ROOMS	Four rooms with private bathrooms. Try the Admiral's Room.
RATES	Year-round rates are $75-160 for a single or double and $115 for a suite. There is no minimum stay and cancellation requires seven days' notice.
CREDIT CARDS	Discover, MasterCard, Visa
BREAKFAST	Full breakfast is served in the dining room and includes tea, coffee, milk, juice, fruit, breads or scones, a hot dish such as crab quiche, and cheesecake for dessert.

AMENITIES	Flannel sheets, electric blankets, and quilts; some rooms have gas fireplaces.
RESTRICTIONS	No smoking, no pets, children over 14 are welcome.

ENCHANTED COTTAGE

4507 SW Coast Avenue, Lincoln City, OR 97367   541-996-4101
EMAIL *daythia@wcn.net*

OCEAN MEMORIES—A TOUCH OF ELEGANCE ON THE OREGON COAST

2003 SW Coast Avenue, Lincoln City, OR 97367   541-994-8183
LaMonte & Ella Mae Urban, Innkeepers   FAX 541-994-8183
EMAIL *oceanmemories@wcn.net*

LOCATION	Turn west off Highway 101 at the 12th Street SW traffic light. Go 0.4 mile to Fleet, turn right, and go 0.1 mile to 11th Street. Go west on 11th Street to the ocean. Turn left on Coast Avenue and go 0.5 mile. The B&B is on the ocean side of the street.
OPEN	All year
DESCRIPTION	A 1995 three-story traditional host home with luxurious decor.
NO. OF ROOMS	Two rooms with private bathrooms. The Urbans recommend the Penthouse Room.
RATES	Year-round rates are $110-150 for a single or double. There is no minimum stay.
CREDIT CARDS	No
BREAKFAST	Full breakfast or continental-plus is served in the dining room or the guestrooms.
AMENITIES	Flowers, robes, evening refreshment, coffee in room, candlelight breakfast.
RESTRICTIONS	No smoking, no pets, no children.

PACIFIC REST BED & BREAKFAST

1611 NE 11th, Lincoln City, OR 97367
Ray & Judy Waetjen, Resident Owners

541-994-2337
888-405-7378

YOUNG'S B&B—TASTES OF YESTERDAY

3848 NW Lee, Lincoln City, OR 97367
Dean & Claire Young, Innkeepers

541-994-6575

LOCATION	Two blocks from the ocean; call for directions.
OPEN	All year
DESCRIPTION	A 1952 one-story beach cottage with a knotty pine living room and kitchen, decorated with antiques, early American quilts, and handmade braided rugs.
NO. OF ROOMS	Two rooms with private bathrooms. Try the Iowa Suite.
RATES	Year-round rates are $60-70 for a single or double. There is no minimum stay. Ask about a reservation/cancellation policy.
CREDIT CARDS	No
BREAKFAST	Full breakfast is served in the kitchen area and includes beverages, an entrée, pastry, and fruit.
AMENITIES	Fresh flowers, hot beverages delivered to rooms before breakfast and in the evenings.
RESTRICTIONS	No smoking. Jessie is the resident dachshund.
REVIEWED	*One Coast* magazine

MANZANITA

Resting mostly on a sandy peninsula with undulating dunes covered in beach grass, shore pine, and Scotch broom, Manzanita is a lazy but growing community that is gaining popularity as a coastal getaway for in-the-know urbanites. The adjacent beach and nearby Nehalem Bay have become windsurfing hot spots. Nehalem Bay State Park, just south of town, offers hiking and biking trails as well as miles of little-used beaches. There's beachcombing galore on either the ocean side or the Nehalem Bay side of the Manzanita peninsula, and resident sea lions bask on the sand near the mouth of the Nehalem River. Overlooking it all is nearby Neahkahnie Mountain, with a steep, switchbacked trail leading to its 1,600-foot summit—the best viewpoint on the northern Oregon Coast.

THE ARBORS BED & BREAKFAST

78 Idaho Avenue, Manzanita, OR 97130
Judd & Lee Burrow, Innkeepers
EMAIL arbors@doormat.com
WEBSITE www.doormat.com/lodging/arbors.htm

503-368-7566
888-664-9587
FAX 503-368-7400

LOCATION	At the Manzanita junction with Highway 101 (amber signal light), turn west onto Laneda Avenue and travel about 0.5 mile to the ocean. At the ocean, the street turns right and becomes Ocean Road. Continue one block to Idaho Avenue and turn right. The Arbors is 200 feet ahead on the right.
OPEN	All year
DESCRIPTION	A 1922 two-story English cottage with Craftsman influences surrounded by white picket fences with arbors over the gates. The house is situated within extensive country-style gardens that blaze with color from early spring through fall.
NO. OF ROOMS	Three rooms with private bathrooms. Try Henrietta's Room.
RATES	Year-round rates are $100-110 for a single or double, $110 for a suite, and $330 for the entire B&B. There is a two-night minimum stay, three nights during holiday weekends, and cancellation requires seven days' notice with $10 charge.
CREDIT CARDS	American Express, Discover, MasterCard, Visa
BREAKFAST	Full breakfast is served family style and includes a fruit plate or compote followed by either a baked entrée or specialty pancakes, plus homemade scones, jams, salsas, biscuits, muffins, juice, coffee, and tea.
AMENITIES	Fresh flowers; fresh-baked cookies with selection of teas, cocoas, etc. in the afternoon; sunny outdoor seating areas in gardens; veranda porch for sheltered seating; first-floor suite is handicapped accessible via ramp.
RESTRICTIONS	No smoking, no pets, children over 8 are welcome. Rosebud and Cosmos are the resident cats. "Rosebud will escort you to your bathroom sink, where she expects you to turn on the water for her drink."
REVIEWED	*Best Places to Kiss in the Northwest*, *Lonely Planet*
MEMBER	Oregon Bed & Breakfast Guild

MAUPIN

C&J LODGE BED & BREAKFAST

PO Box 130, Maupin, OR 97037
Carrol & Judy White, Innkeepers
WEBSITE *www.deschutesriver.com*

800-395-3903

MCMINNVILLE

McMinnville is growing up: The feed stores and steel mill are still here, but so are the high-tech companies and espresso hangouts. And the growing wine industry has had a positive effect, especially on the food scene: There's a better concentration of interesting places to eat here than elsewhere in this region's wine country. Along with its central location, that makes this town a good headquarters for wine touring. Serious wine lovers can OD on great wine and food while hobnobbing with wine celebrities (including some of France's hot young winemakers) at the three-day International Pinot Noir Celebration in late July or early August on the grounds of gracious old Linfield College.

BAKER STREET BED & BREAKFAST

129 SE Baker Street, McMinnville, OR 97128
Cheryl Collins, Resident Owner
EMAIL *cheryl@bakerstreetinn.com*
WEBSITE *www.bakerstreetinn.com*

503-472-5575
800-870-5575

LOCATION	Downtown, two doors south of First Street on Baker.
OPEN	All year
DESCRIPTION	A 1914 two-story Craftsman inn with antiques and fine china throughout the house.
NO. OF ROOMS	Five rooms with private bathrooms. Cheryl recommends The Golden Oak or the Burgundy Rose.
RATES	Year-round rates are $75-95 for a single or double. There is a two-night minimum stay required over Saturdays, and some local event weekends require three nights minimum stay. Cancellation requires 14 days' notice.
CREDIT CARDS	American Express, Carte Blanche, Diners Club, Discover, MasterCard, Visa

Baker Street Bed & Breakfast, Mc Minnville

BREAKFAST	Full breakfast is served in the dining room and may include fruit, eggs, breakfast meat, waffles, quiche, croissants, French toast, strata, or an egg puff with bacon. Vegetarian and restricted diets can be accommodated.
AMENITIES	Fresh flowers; air conditioning; jetted tub for two; cottage with living room, kitchen, and dinette; facilities for small meetings and weddings.
RESTRICTIONS	No smoking, no pets, children are welcome in the cottage.
REVIEWED	*The Complete Guide to Bed & Breakfasts, Inns & Guesthouses; Where to Stay in Oregon*
MEMBER	Professional Association of Innkeepers International, Oregon Bed & Breakfast Guild, American Bed & Breakfast Association
RATED	ABBA 3 Crowns
AWARDS	1993 Beautification Award, McMinnville Chamber of Commerce

GAHR FARM B&B COTTAGE

18605 SW Masonville Road, McMinnville, OR 97128   503-472-6960
Harriet & Ted Gahr, Innkeepers

MATTEY HOUSE BED & BREAKFAST

10221 NE Mattey Lane, McMinnville, OR 97128 *503-434-5058*
Jack & Denise Seed, Innkeepers
WEBSITE *www.fodors.com*

ORCHARD VIEW INN BED & BREAKFAST

16540 NW Orchard View Road, McMinnville, OR 97128 *503-472-0165*
Wayne & Marrayne Schatter, Innkeepers

LOCATION	Five miles west off Highway 99 from downtown McMinnville and 2.6 miles off Baker Creek Road.
OPEN	All year
DESCRIPTION	A 1975 one-story contemporary redwood octagon with contemporary furnishings and Chinese antiques, and a large deck overlooking a forest and meadow.
NO. OF ROOMS	Two rooms with private bathrooms and two rooms share one bathroom. Try the Iris Room.
RATES	Year-round rates are $80 for a double with a private bathroom, $75 for a double with a shared bathroom, and $290 for the entire B&B (requires a two-day minimum stay). There is a three-day minimum stay during the Pinot Noir Festival at the end of July. Cancellation requires five days' notice.
CREDIT CARDS	No
BREAKFAST	Full breakfast is served in the dining room and includes juice, fresh fruit, entrée, regular or decaf coffee, tea, and hot chocolate.
AMENITIES	Robes for rooms with shared baths; all rooms with air conditioning; kitchen open for guests to use ice maker, microwave, and to make tea or coffee.
RESTRICTIONS	No smoking inside, no pets, no children. Duffer, Monday, and Coco are the resident dogs. They are not permitted inside the inn.
REVIEWED	*Fodor's, The Best Places to Kiss in the Northwest, Best Places to Stay in the Northwest*
MEMBER	Yamhill County Bed & Breakfast Association

Steiger Haus Bed and Breakfast, McMinnville

STEIGER HAUS BED AND BREAKFAST

360 SE Wilson Street, McMinnville, OR 97128　　503-472-0821
Susan & Dale DuRette, Innkeepers　　FAX 503-472-0100

LOCATION	From Highway 99 west, turn east on Third Street (historic downtown). Travel north 0.1 mile and turn south on Davis Street. Travel 0.25 mile. Turn west on Wilson; the B&B is on the corner of Davis and Wilson.
OPEN	All year
DESCRIPTION	A 1983 three-story European-style inn nestled in a beautiful parklike setting.
NO. OF ROOMS	Five rooms with private bathrooms.
RATES	Year-round rates are $60-95 for a single or double and $90-130 for a suite. Corporate rates for a single person in room are $60-110. Inquire about the minimum stay on holidays, and cancellation requires one week's notice.
CREDIT CARDS	Discover, MasterCard, Visa
BREAKFAST	Full breakfast is served in the dining room and includes seasonal foods, fresh orange juice, melon with lemon sauce, blueberry muffins, and Belgian waffles with marscapone and berry medley.

AMENITIES	Garden; horseshoes and badminton in summer; large decks; one suite with jetted tub, VCR/TV, and refrigerator; one suite with fireplace.
RESTRICTIONS	No smoking, no pets, children over 10 are welcome. Speck is the resident (outside) cat. Often have deer in the yard and occasionally pheasants in the summer.
REVIEWED	Recommended Country Inns, Northwest Best Places, The Best Places to Kiss in the Northwest, Sunset magazine, Fodor's West Coast Bed & Breakfasts
MEMBER	Professional Association of Innkeepers International
RATED	AAA 2 Diamonds

WILLIAMS HOUSE BED & BREAKFAST

809 NE Evans, McMinnville, OR 97128   503-434-9016
Carol Jones, Innkeeper   800-441-2214
WEBSITE www.mytown.com (look under Oregon and McMinnville)

YOUNGBERG HILL VINEYARD & INN

10660 SW Youngberg Hill Road, McMinnville, OR 97128   503-472-0727
Kevin & Tasha Byrd, Innkeepers   888-657-8668
EMAIL tasha.byrd@intel.com   FAX 503-472-1313
WEBSITE www.youngberghill.com

LOCATION	From Portland, take I-5 south to Highway 99 west and drive through McMinnville, turning right at the junction with Route 18 onto Old Sheridan. Go 1 mile, turn right onto Peavine Road, go 2 miles, and turn left onto Youngberg Hill Road. After 1 mile, look for the sign on the right.
OPEN	All year
DESCRIPTION	A 1989 three-story modern Craftsman-style farmhouse perched high atop a hill overlooking its own private vineyard and farmland, with French country decor.
NO. OF ROOMS	Five rooms with private bathrooms.
RATES	High-season rates are $130-150 for a single or double. Regular-season rates are $99-199 for a single or double. There is a minimum stay during holidays and cancellation requires seven days' notice. No charge is imposed if the room is rebooked.

Youngberg Hill Vineyard & Inn, McMinnville

CREDIT CARDS	American Express, MasterCard, Visa
BREAKFAST	Full three-course breakfast is served in the dining room or on the porch, and includes fresh fruit, bread or muffins, and a three-item entrée. Winemaker dinners are also available.
AMENITIES	Afternoon appetizers, honor bar, conference room for up to 30 people, air conditioning, limited handicapped access, flowers, turndown service, nighttime chocolates, fruit bowl, fresh-baked cookies.
RESTRICTIONS	No smoking, no pets, children over 12 are welcome. Pantaloons is the resident cat, Tav is the horse, and Gracie is the peahen.
REVIEWED	*Northwest Best Places, Best Places to Kiss in the Northwest, Fodor's, Frommer's*
MEMBER	Professional Association of International Innkeepers

MEDFORD

Southern Oregon's largest city is well known across the nation, due to the marketing efforts of Harry and David's, the mail-order giant known for its pears, other fruit, and condiments. The Craterian Ginger Rogers Theater is a downtown performing arts center with a 742-seat theater that opened in 1997. The former Craterian movie theater dated back to the 1920s. Why Ginger Rogers? The actress owned a ranch on the nearby Rogue River for many years, once danced on the Craterian stage, and in the last couple of years before her death helped raise money for the theater's $5.3-million renovation.

CARPENTER HILL INN

846 Carpenter Hill Road, Medford, OR 97501   541-535-4147

UNDER THE GREENWOOD TREE BED & BREAKFAST

3045 Bellinger Lane, Medford, OR 97501   541-776-0000
French and German spoken
WEBSITE *www.greenwoodtree.com*

DESCRIPTION	A two-story country inn decorated with Persian rugs, wallpaper, and antiques and set on 10 acres.
NO. OF ROOMS	Five rooms with private bathrooms.
RATES	Please call for current rates and cancellation information.
CREDIT CARDS	Visa
BREAKFAST	Three-course gourmet breakfast is served.
AMENITIES	Flower gardens, afternoon tea, turndown service with chocolate truffles.
RESTRICTIONS	No smoking inside. Please call about children.

WHISPERING PINES

305 N Grape, Medford, OR 97501   541-582-1757
Lorna & Karen, Innkeepers   800-788-1757

MILL CITY

Mill City is situated southeast of Salem on Highway 22. The town stretches across the North Santiam River, and its two sides are joined by an old wrought-iron railroad bridge that has been converted into a pedestrian-only viaduct.

IVY CREEK BED & BREAKFAST

525 NE Alder Street, Mill City, OR 97360   503-897-2001
Cathy Robertson, Innkeeper

MORRISON COTTAGE

418 NE Alder Street, Mill City, OR 97360   503-897-3371

MILWAUKIE

Situated along the Willamette River, Milwaukie is known as the City of the Dogwoods. It also throws a good party to celebrate the Bing cherry. Big-city doings are minutes away in Portland.

HISTORIC BROETJE HOUSE

3101 SE Courtney, Milwaukie, OR 97222   503-659-8860
Lois Bain & Lorraine Hubbard, Innkeepers

LOCATION	Six miles south of Ross Island Bridge off McLoughlin Boulevard (99E), turn left onto Courtney Road. Go to the stop sign and turn left on Oatfield. The B&B is the first house on the left.
OPEN	All year
DESCRIPTION	An 1889 four-story Queen Anne country inn with elegant country furnishings, and a four-story water tower, nestled beneath redwoods in a quiet residential neighborhood. Listed on the National and State Historical Registers.
NO. OF ROOMS	One room with private a bathroom and two rooms share one bathroom. Lorraine suggests the Queen Anne Room.
RATES	Year-round rates are $95 for a single or double with a private bathroom and $55-70 for a single or double with a shared

Historic Broetje House, Milwaukie

	bathroom. The entire B&B rents for $220. There is no minimum stay and cancellation requires three days' notice.
CREDIT CARDS	American Express, MasterCard, Visa
BREAKFAST	Full breakfast is served in the dining room and includes fresh fruit, muffins, an entrée, coffee, and tea. Special meals are also available.
AMENITIES	Robes, air conditioning, gardens and gazebo, space for weddings and receptions for up to 150, meeting facilities.
RESTRICTIONS	No smoking inside
REVIEWED	Romantic America
MEMBER	Portland Metro Innkeepers Association

MITCHELL

HISTORIC OREGON HOTEL BED & BREAKFAST

104 Main Street, Mitchell, OR 97750   541-462-3027
Dan & Cherie Hopper, Innkeepers

MONMOUTH

In the Willamette Valley southwest of Salem, this community offers access to Sara Helmick State Park on the Luckiamute River.

HOWELL'S BED & BREAKFAST

212 N Knox Street, Monmouth, OR 97361 503-838-2085
Clint & Sandra Boylan, Innkeepers 800-368-2085
EMAIL *howell@moriah.com* WEBSITE *www.moriah.com/howell*

LOCATION	Four blocks west of Highway 99, west at Jackson Street.
OPEN	All year
DESCRIPTION	An 1891 three-story Queen Anne inn located in the midst of wine country with original woodwork, wallpapers, and rooms filled with museum-quality antiques.
NO. OF ROOMS	Three rooms with private bathrooms and two rooms with one shared bathroom. The Boylans recommend the Housemother's Suite.
RATES	Year-round rates are $59-110 for a single or double with a private bathroom and $59-79 for a single or double with a shared

Howell's Bed & Breakfast, Monmouth

	bathroom. There is no minimum stay and cancellation requires 10 days' notice.
CREDIT CARDS	Discover, MasterCard, Visa
BREAKFAST	Full breakfast is served in the dining room and includes a choice of entrées such as honey hazelnut waffles, blackberry pancakes, blueberry French toast, or quiche, omelets, and other baked egg delights. Allergy and other dietary needs are easily accommodated.
AMENITIES	Outdoor spa with Japanese-style covering surrounded by many large flower baskets, gazebo, beautiful gardens with 80 varieties of heirloom and modern roses, collection of vintage fashions and antique cars, hostess is a classical pianist who enjoys playing for guests.
RESTRICTIONS	No smoking, children over 12 are welcome. "This is a haven for people with allergies," says Sandra. "It's dust and animal free."
REVIEWED	*Northwest Budget Traveler, Fodor's Pacific Northwest's Best Bed & Breakfasts*
MEMBER	Oregon Bed & Breakfast Guild, Oregon Lodging Association

MOSIER

Mosier is situated along the Columbia River, about 20 miles west of The Dalles on I-84.

CHERRY HILL FARM

1550 Carroll Road, Mosier, OR 97040   541-478-4455

THE MOSIER HOUSE BED & BREAKFAST

704 Third Avenue, Mosier, OR 97040   541-478-3640
The Koerner Family, Innkeepers   FAX 541-478-3640

LOCATION	Mosier is located 5 miles east of Hood River and 17 miles west of The Dalles on I-84. Take exit 69 and drive south into town. Turn right on Washington Street and left on Third Avenue. Drive 0.1 mile and turn right (south) up the driveway to off-street parking.
OPEN	All year
DESCRIPTION	A 1896 two-story Victorian inn listed on both the State and National Historic Registers.

NO. OF ROOMS	One room with a private bathroom and four rooms with shared bathrooms (all bedrooms with shared baths have sinks in bedrooms). The Koerners recommend the Master Suite.
RATES	May through September, rates are $100 for a single or double with a private bathroom and $85 for a single or double with a shared bathroom. The entire B&B rents for $440 per night. October through April, rates are $90 for a single or double with a private bathroom and $77.50 for a single or double with a shared bathroom. The entire B&B rents for $440 per night. There is no minimum stay and cancellation requires four days' notice.
CREDIT CARDS	MasterCard, Visa
BREAKFAST	Full breakfast is served in the dining room. Special meals can be arranged.
AMENITIES	Afternoon tea; robes; house and grounds can be rented for special events, weddings, and small meetings.
RESTRICTIONS	No smoking, no pets
MEMBER	Hood River Bed & Breakfast Association
KUDOS/COMMENTS	"Beautifully restored Victorian home."

MOUNT HOOD

At 11,245 feet, Hood may not be the highest in the chain of volcanoes in the Cascades, but it is one of the best developed, with five ski areas on its base. The lower parts are ablaze with rhododendrons (peaking in June) and wildflowers (peaking in July). One of the best local trails leads 4.5 miles west from Timberline Lodge to flower-studded Paradise Park. Like Rainier, the mountain is girded by a long trail (called Timberline Trail), a 40-mile circuit of the entire peak that traverses snowfields as well as ancient forests.

MOUNT HOOD BED & BREAKFAST

8885 Cooper Spur Road, Mount Hood-Parkdale, OR 97041   541-352-6885
EMAIL mthoodbnb@linkport.com   800-557-8885
WEBSITE www.mthoodbnb.com

KUDOS/COMMENTS	"Beautiful location, great hosts, nice rooms—especially the romantic cabin, beautiful location for weddings and reunions." "Lovely old working farm with great view of Mount Hood."

MOUNT HOOD HAMLET

6741 Highway 35, Mount Hood, OR 97041   800-407-0570
Diane & Paul Romans, Innkeepers
WEBSITE www.mthoodhamlet.com

KUDOS/COMMENTS   "Beautiful view of Mount Hood."

THE OLD PARKDALE INN BED & BREAKFAST

4932 Baseline Road, Mount Hood-Parkdale, OR 97041   541-352-5551
Heidi McIsaac Shuford, Innkeeper
EMAIL parkdaleinn@gorge.net
WEBSITE www.gorge.net/Lodging/parkdaleinn

LOCATION	Fifteen miles south of Hood River, in the town of Parkdale.
OPEN	All year
DESCRIPTION	A 1912 two-story Craftsman inn.
NO. OF ROOMS	Three rooms with private bathrooms. Heidi recommends the Monet Room.
RATES	April 15 through November 15, rates are $95-115 for a single or double and $115-135 for a suite. November 15 through April 15, rates are $85-105 for a single or double and $105-125 for a suite. There is no minimum stay and 10 days' cancellation notice for refund of first-night deposit.
CREDIT CARDS	MasterCard, Visa
BREAKFAST	Full breakfast is served in the guestrooms and includes smoked salmon, fresh fruit, and homemade baked goods.
AMENITIES	Fireplaces, balconies, mountain views, fresh flowers in rooms, monogrammed robes, meeting and wedding facilities.
RESTRICTIONS	No pets
REVIEWED	The Gorge Guide
MEMBER	Hood River Bed & Breakfast Association

NEHALEM

On Highway 101 just south of Manzanita, Nehalam is great for antiquing. The Nehalem River flows past here before emptying into the Pacific.

NEHALEM RIVER INN

34910 Highway 53, Nehalem, OR 97131	503-368-7708

REDWOOD INN

Route 1, Box 270, Nehalem, OR 97131 Judy Gregoire, Innkeeper EMAIL searosebb@oregoncoast.com	503-368-6715

NEW PINE CREEK

HONKER INN BED & BREAKFAST

Snow Goose Lane, New Pine Creek, OR 97635	530-946-4179

NEWBERG

This is a peaceful old Quaker town and also home to some of Oregon's most established wineries. Explore the wine country and along the way stop off at charming Champoeg State Park just 5 miles to the southwest. From Newberg, Portland is an easy 30 minutes to the north on Highway 99 west.

ENTHEOS ESTATE

36280 NE Wilsonville Road, Newberg, OR 97132 Donna Lee Dennis, Innkeeper EMAIL entheos@turbomgmt.com	503-625-1390 FAX 503-625-2699

LOCATION	Take I-5 south from Portland to the Wilsonville exit (283). Turn right (west) onto Wilsonville Road and drive 6.7 miles. Turn left onto the tree-lined driveway.
OPEN	All year
DESCRIPTION	A 1981 French country estate on 4.5 acres on the Willamette River, a chateau-style host home with hardwood floors and oriental carpets.
NO. OF ROOMS	Four rooms with private bathrooms.
RATES	Year-round rates are $125 for a queen or king room.
CREDIT CARDS	MasterCard, Visa
BREAKFAST	Full breakfast is served in the dining room or in summer on the patio overlooking the river and includes Starbucks coffee, juice, yogurt, fresh fruit, an entrée such as eggs, omelets, fancy French toast, banana-pecan whole-grain pancakes, garden sausage or fresh salmon, and a variety of muffins, rolls, oatmeal, and granola.
AMENITIES	Small bar area with coffee, tea, soft drinks, juice, bottled water, and a cookie jar; fruit bowl; roses from the garden; baby grand piano; TV/VCR and videos; wood-burning fireplace; down comforters; leather game table with cards, backgammon, puzzles, etc.; six sitting benches around property; hammock and "porch" swing down by the river; canoe; yard games (horseshoes, croquet, etc.); weddings and receptions, corporate parties, and miniretreats accommodated.
RESTRICTIONS	No smoking, no pets. Sharon is the resident outside cat.

PARTRIDGE FARM

4300 Portland Road, Newberg, OR 97132   503-538-2050

SMITH HOUSE BED & BREAKFAST

415 N College Street, Newberg, OR 97132   503-538-1995

SPRINGBROOK HAZELNUT FARM BED & BREAKFAST

30295 N Highway 99 West, Newberg, OR 97132 503-538-4606
Chuck & Ellen McClure, Innkeepers 800-793-8528
Some Spanish spoken FAX 503-537-4004
EMAIL Ellen@nutfarm.com WEBSITE www.nutfarm.com

LOCATION	Located at milepost 21 on the north side of Highway 99 west, 20 miles from Portland. Take the next driveway after passing the Rex Hill winery.
OPEN	All year
DESCRIPTION	A 1912 two-story Craftsman country inn, cottage, and carriage house, a historic and authentic farm ensemble consisting of four matching buildings, each decorated with antiques, art, and Turkish rugs, and situated on a 60-acre orchard with 10 acres of gardens. Listed on the National Historic Register.
NO. OF ROOMS	Four rooms with private bathrooms and two rooms share two bathrooms. Ellen recommends the Honeymoon Cottage.
RATES	Year-round rates are $95-175 for a single or double with a private bathroom and $95 for a single or double with a shared bathroom. The cottage rents for $175. There is a minimum stay during the summer and cancellation requires one week's notice.
CREDIT CARDS	No
BREAKFAST	Full breakfast is served in the dining room (or in the cottage or carriage house) and includes homemade hazelnut granola; fresh fruit; pastries; a main course such as crepes or frittata; sausage, bacon, or ham; fresh juice; eggs; yogurt; coffee, tea, hot chocolate, and more.
AMENITIES	Pool; pond with canoe; tennis court; orchard for walking; vegetable and flower gardens; meadow; bike routes; hosts make dinner reservations; private-label soaps, shampoos, and lotions; hazelnuts in rooms; air conditioning; piano; two cute dogs that love guests.
RESTRICTIONS	No smoking inside, no pets, children over 16 are welcome. The resident springers are named Duffy and Ghillie. They both eat apples. Ghillie loves playing fetch and soccer.
REVIEWED	*Northwest Best Places; The Best Places to Kiss in the Northwest; Fodor's Northwest; Frommer's Northwest; Lonely Planet Guide to the Northwest; America's Wonderful Little Hotels & Inns; National Trust Guide to Historic Bed & Breakfasts*
MEMBER	Oregon Bed & Breakfast Guild, Yamhill County Bed & Breakfast Association, Oregon Lodging Association

NEWPORT

The most popular tourist destination on the Oregon Coast, Newport blends tasteful development (the Performing Arts Center, for example) with unending shopping-center sprawl. To discover all that Newport has to offer, head for the bay front, a working harbor going full tilt, where fishing boats of all types—trollers, trawlers, shrimpers, and crabbers—berth year-round. The Nye Beach area, on the ocean side of the highway, has fewer tourists and more of an arts-community feel, housing a potpourri of tourists, writers, artists, and fishermen. North of town above Agate Beach, Yaquina Head Outstanding Natural Area features the restored Yaquina Lighthouse (circa 1873 and open to the public), hiking trails, and fantastic cliff-front panoramas.

GREEN GABLES BED & BREAKFAST

156 SW Coast Street, Newport, OR 97365　　　541-265-9141
Sue Hardesty & Nel Ward, Innkeepers　　　　800-515-9065
EMAIL gables@netbridge.net　　WEBSITE www.netbridge.net/gables

LOCATION	Six blocks west and one block south of the intersection of Highways 101 and 20.
OPEN	All year
DESCRIPTION	A 1981 four-story Victorian Queen Anne inn with decks, bay windows, and contemporary furnishings.
NO. OF ROOMS	Two rooms with private bathrooms. Try the Turret Room.

Green Gables Bed & Breakfast, Newport

RATES	Year-round rates are $85-95 for a single or double and $170 for the entire B&B. There is no minimum stay and cancellation requires 48 hours' notice.
CREDIT CARDS	Discover, MasterCard, Visa
BREAKFAST	Full breakfast is served in the dining room or guestrooms.
AMENITIES	Two-person whirlpools, refrigerator, microwave, TV/VCR in each room; robes; coffee delivered to rooms "as early as you wish"; hot pot with teas, coffee, cider, and hot chocolate in room; bookstore on bottom level; 4 miles of beach; woodstove in common area.
RESTRICTIONS	No smoking, children over 15 are welcome. Beaujolais and Merlot are the resident poodles, and Charlie is the black cat.

NEWPORT BELLE BED & BREAKFAST

Newport, OR 541-265-6940
WEBSITE *www.newportbelle.com*

LOCATION	Across from downtown Newport in the South Beach Marina.
DESCRIPTION	A sternwheel riverboat with three decks.
NO. OF ROOMS	Five rooms with private bathrooms.
RATES	Year-round rates are $125-145 for a double. Cancellation requires five days' notice for a refund of deposit.
BREAKFAST	Gourmet breakfast is served in the salon.
RESTRICTIONS	No smoking, no pets, no children. Soft-soled shoes should be worn.

OAR HOUSE BED & BREAKFAST

520 SW Second Street, Newport, OR 97365 541-265-9571
Jan LeBrun, Innkeeper 800-252-2358
EMAIL *oarhouse@newportnet.com*
WEBSITE *www.newportnet.com/oarhouse*

LOCATION	From Highway 101 and Hurbert Street (in the city center), go west three blocks to the second stop sign where Hurbert intersects SW Second. The B&B is across the street.
OPEN	All year
DESCRIPTION	A 1900 2½-story Craftsman inn furnished with international art, Persian carpets, and antiques. This Lincoln County Historic Site also has a lighthouse tower.

NO. OF ROOMS	Five rooms with private bathrooms.
RATES	Memorial Day weekend through October, rates are $100-130 (one-night stays) or $90-120 (for two or more nights) for a single or double. November through Memorial Day weekend, rates are $90-120 (weekends) or $80-110 (Monday through Thursday) for a single or double. There is a minimum stay during holidays and special events. Cancellation requires 72 hours' notice.
CREDIT CARDS	Discover, MasterCard, Visa
BREAKFAST	Full breakfast is served in the morning room and includes coffee or tea, juice, fruit plate, and a hot entreé with meat.
AMENITIES	Guest amenity bar stocked with soft drinks, teas, candies, and nuts; guest sitting room with fireplace and DMX music system; the innkeepers also provide three newspapers and numerous periodicals, and games.
RESTRICTIONS	No smoking, no pets, no children.
REVIEWED	*Lonely Planet*
MEMBER	Oregon Bed & Breakfast Guild, Professional Association of Innkeepers International, Oregon Lodging Association
KUDOS/COMMENTS	"Innkeeper is very knowledgable about growing wine industry and an advocate for her community—great breakfasts!"

OCEAN HOUSE

4920 NW Woody Way, Newport, OR 97365　　　541-265-6158
Marie & Bob Garrard, Innkeepers　　　800-56-B-and-B
EMAIL *garrard@oceanhouse.com*　　　WEBSITE *www.oceanhouse.com*

LOCATION	Half a mile south of Newport's north city limits on Highway 101.
OPEN	All year
DESCRIPTION	An oceanfront, 1940 two-story Cape Cod inn with stunning views of miles of beach, rocky headlands, and 0.5 acre of gardens.
NO. OF ROOMS	Five rooms with private bathrooms.
RATES	Year-round rates are $90-165 for a single or double. There is a minimum stay during weekends and holidays and cancellation requires seven days' notice with a $15 charge.
CREDIT CARDS	Discover, MasterCard, Visa
BREAKFAST	Full four-course breakfast is served in the dining room and includes fruit, juice, baked goods, a hot entrée, and meat. Specials diets are always accommodated.

AMENITIES	Rooms with double Jacuzzi spas, fireplaces, king-size beds or four-poster queen beds, private decks or sitting rooms; round-the-clock guest bar with hot beverages and baked goods; Oregon Coast art gallery.
RESTRICTIONS	No smoking, no pets, children over 17 are welcome. Pancho is the resident parrot.
REVIEWED	*The Best Places to Kiss in the Northwest, Northwest Best Places, Best Places to Stay in the Northwest*
MEMBER	Oregon Lodging Association, Professional Association of International Innkeepers, Oregon Bed & Breakfast Guild

SEA CLIFF BED & BREAKFAST

749 NW Third Street, Newport, OR 97365   541-265-6664
                                              888-858-6660

SOLACE BY THE SEA BED & BREAKFAST

9602 S Coast Highway 101, South Beach, OR 97366   541-867-3566
Todd & Lisa Whear, Innkeepers   888-476-5223
Some Spanish and Swedish spoken   FAX 541-867-3599
EMAIL solace@newportnet.com   WEBSITE www.solacebythesea.com

LOCATION	Three and a half miles south of Newport's Yaquina Bay bridge on Highway 101 between mile markers 145 and 146.
OPEN	All year
DESCRIPTION	A 1997 three-story cedar-sided host home facing the ocean and nestled among the coastal shore pines, with contemporary furnishings. The B&B is 80 yards from a cliff with stairway access to the beach.
NO. OF ROOMS	Three rooms with private bathrooms. The Whears recommend Neptune's Garden.
RATES	Year-round rates are $135-175 for a single or double and $175 for a suite. The entire B&B rents for $445. There is a two-night minimum stay during weekends and cancellation requires two weeks' notice.
CREDIT CARDS	American Express, Discover, MasterCard, Visa (3.5 percent charge added with credit card payment)

Solace by the Sea Bed & Breakfast, South Beach

BREAKFAST	Full four-course breakfast is served in the dining room and includes fresh-ground coffees, fresh-squeezed orange juice, gourmet teas, fresh-baked breads and muffins, fresh fruit dishes, and an entrée.
AMENITIES	Fresh flowers around the house, feather beds, robes, Jacuzzi on semi-enclosed tile deck, on-site massage therapist, complimentary coffee and tea bar, library with TV, telephone, and guest refrigerator stocked with soft drinks. Ask Todd about mountain biking and kayaking adventures.
RESTRICTIONS	No smoking, no pets, children over 13 are welcome. A dog kennel is available for $10 per evening. Bailey is the resident purebred Labrador retriever, with a fondness for escorting guests to the beach (and chasing her own tail.)
REVIEWED	*Country Living* magazine
MEMBER	Professional Association of Innkeepers International, Oregon Bed & Breakfast Guild, Newport Bed & Breakfast Association

SYLVIA BEACH HOTEL

267 NW Cliff Street, Newport, OR 97365   541-265-5428

Tyee Lodge Oceanfront Bed & Breakfast, Newport

TYEE LODGE OCEANFRONT BED & BREAKFAST

4925 NW Woody Way, Newport, OR 97365   541-265-8953
Mark & Cindy McConnell, Innkeepers   888-553-8933
Fluent Spanish, decent German, and passable French spoken
EMAIL mcconn@teleport.com
WEBSITE www.newportnet.com/tyee

LOCATION	From Highway 101, turn left into the parking lot on the west side of the highway just south of Lighthouse Road.
OPEN	All year
DESCRIPTION	A 1995 two-story modern ranch-style lodge with Northwest decor on a secluded 0.5 acre with trails leading to tide pools and the beach.
NO. OF ROOMS	Five rooms with private bathrooms. Try the Chinook Room.
RATES	Year-round rates are $100-120 for a single or double. There is no minimum stay and cancellation requires seven days' notice, 14 days during holidays and special events.
CREDIT CARDS	American Express, Discover, MasterCard, Visa
BREAKFAST	Full breakfast is served family style in the dining room and includes a fruit appetizer and fresh breads, followed by main dishes that celebrate the Northwest. Early morning breakfast is available upon request.

AMENITIES	Complimentary beverage bar in the lounge with coffee, teas, soft drinks, and wine; gardens, tended and natural; fire pit in the yard overlooking the beach.
RESTRICTIONS	No smoking, no pets, children over 12 are welcome.
REVIEWED	*The Best Places to Kiss in the Northwest; Frommer's Oregon; Fodor's Northwest; America's Favorite Inns, B&Bs & Small Hotels*
MEMBER	Oregon Bed & Breakfast Guild, Newport Bed & Breakfast Association
RATED	AAA 3 Diamonds, *Best Places to Kiss in the Northwest* 2.5 Lips

NORTH BEND

Named after the large bend in the Coos River on which it was built, North Bend has sustained itself by means of the fishing and lumber industries. It is the gateway to the Bay Area and the Oregon Dunes National Recreation Area. The Annual Southcoast Dixieland Clambake Jazz Festival gets underway in the spring.

2310 LOMBARD BED & BREAKFAST

2310 Lombard Street, North Bend, OR 97459   541-756-3857
Charlotte Skinner, Innkeeper

ITTY BITTY INN MOTEL BED & BREAKFAST

1504 Sherman Ave, North Bend, OR 97459   541-756-6398
Terra Jenett, Resident Owner   888-276-9253

LOCATION	Entering North Bend southbound on Highway 101, the B&B located on the west side, 0.9 mile from the McCullogh Bridge.
OPEN	All year
DESCRIPTION	A one-story 1952 stucco inn with Southwestern decor.
NO. OF ROOMS	Four rooms with private bathrooms. Try room 1.
RATES	May through August rates are $37-42 for a single or double. September through April, rates are $35-40 for a single or double. There is no minimum stay and cancellation requires 48 hours' notice.
CREDIT CARDS	American Express, Discover, MasterCard, Visa
BREAKFAST	Full breakfast is served in the restaurant.

OAKLAND

A great town for viewing historic structures, Oakland boasts a large district of well-preserved structures, dating back to the 1890s, listed on the National Register of Historic Places. Wine enthusiasts should take time to tour the area's thriving wineries. Oakland is situated in the Umpqua Valley, just 20 miles north of Roseburg on Highway 99.

BECKLEY HOUSE BED & BREAKFAST

338 SE Second Street, Oakland, OR 97462 541-488-0338
Karene & Rich Neuharth, Innkeepers FAX 541-459-9320

OCEANSIDE

A tiny seaside resort that defines "quaint," Oceanside lies 8 miles west of Tillamook along the 22-mile Three Capes Scenic Drive. Tracing one of Oregon's most beautiful stretches of coastline, the narrow, winding Three Capes road skirts the outline of Tillamook Bay, climbs over Cape Meares (where you can walk up to, and inside, the Cape Meares lighthouse), then traverses the shores of Netarts Bay before reaching Cape Lookout State Park, another jewel in Oregon's park system. The park offers headland-hugging trails and a huge stretch of little-used beach. The scenic drive scales Cape Lookout, the westernmost headland on the northern Oregon Coast. Back at sea level lies a desertlike landscape of thousands of acres of sandy dunes, a favorite area for off-road recreational vehicles (which are required to stay in designated areas). The road to Pacific City and the route's third cape, Kiwanda, runs through lush, green dairy country.

SEA ROSE BED & BREAKFAST

1685 Maxwell Mountain Road, Oceanside, OR 97134 503-842-6126
Judith Gregoire, Innkeeper
German spoken
EMAIL searosebb@oregoncoast.com
WEBSITE www.bbchanel.com

LOCATION From Tillamook, drive 9 miles west on the Three Capes Scenic Drive to Oceanside. At the stop sign, turn right onto Maxwell Mountain Road and drive up the hill to the first driveway. Please park in the garage.

OPEN All year

DESCRIPTION	A 1938 three-story Cape Cod inn with French country decor, set on a hillside overlooking the sea.
NO. OF ROOMS	Two rooms with private bathrooms.
RATES	Year-round rates are $85-95 for a single or double. There is no minimum stay and cancellation requires two days' notice.
CREDIT CARDS	MasterCard, Visa
BREAKFAST	Full breakfast is served in the dining room and includes fresh fruit, yogurt, homemade granola, muffins or scones, entrée of apfelpfannkuchen and bacon, quiche or eggs, coffeecake or Danish, coffee, and tea.
AMENITIES	Common area with coffee, tea, cookies, popcorn, Tillamook ice cream, evening port, and chocolate; library with books, current magazines, and games; microwave and refrigerator for guests' use.
RESTRICTIONS	No smoking, no pets, children over 14 are welcome.
REVIEWED	*The Best Places to Kiss in the Northwest*, Frommer's

OREGON CITY

This lumber mill town on the Willamette River was founded in 1829 and later became Oregon's territorial capital. Many of the historic buildings are well preserved. Don't miss the informative Clackamas County Historical Society Museum and the End of the Oregon Trail Interpretive Center.

AINSWORTH HOUSE BED & BREAKFAST

19130 S Lot Whitcomb Drive, Oregon City, OR 97045   503-655-5172

TOLLE HOUSE

15921 S Hunter Avenue, Oregon City, OR 97045   503-655-4325

OTIS

Just east of the junction of Highways 101 and 18, Otis is a mere stone's throw from miles of ocean beach and within five miles of Lincoln City. In spring and fall, be mindful of whales steaming along the coast. The sand castle-building contest in July always impresses.

THE LAKE HOUSE BED & BREAKFAST

2165 NE East Devils Lake Road, Otis, OR 97368   541-996-8938
Mary Sell, Innkeeper   888-996-8938
WEBSITE www.lcchamber.com/lakehs.htm

LOCATION	Please call for directions.
OPEN	All year
DESCRIPTION	Two-story cedar home and guest cottage decorated with antiques and country classic decor.
NO. OF ROOMS	Two rooms with private bathrooms. Try the Lake Side Room.
RATES	May through October, rates are $105 for a suite and $95 for the guesthouse. Low-season rates are $85 for a suite and $85 for the guesthouse. The second night is $10 less. There is a two-night minimum stay on weekends and holidays for the Lake Side Room. Ask about a cancellation policy.
CREDIT CARDS	No
BREAKFAST	Full breakfast is served in the dining room and includes fruit, rolls or muffins, juice, smoothies, coffee, tea, milk, and a main dish such as buttermilk pancakes, an egg dish, or apple French toast, always accompanied by bacon or sausage.

The Lake House Bed & Breakfast, Otis

AMENITIES Robes, cable TV in each room; private entrances; early morning coffee; rowboat with life jackets. Fireplace, refrigerator, microwave in the cottage. The Lake Side Room features a private hot tub on balcony overlooking the lake.

RESTRICTIONS No smoking, no pets. Pixie is the resident pooch. She loves to play ball and is well behaved.

SALMON RIVER BED & BREAKFAST

5622 Salmon River Highway, Otis, OR 97368   541-994-2639
Marvin & Pawnee Pegg, Innkeepers

OXBOW

HELL'S CANYON BED & BREAKFAST

1/4 Mile Homestead Road, Oxbow, OR 97840   541-785-3373
WEBSITE www.neoregon.net/hellscanyonbandb

PACIFIC CITY

Pacific City is the home of the dory fleet, Oregon's classic fishing boats. The vessels enter the ocean in the south lee of Cape Kiwanda, sometimes competing with sea lions, surfers, and kayakers for water space. Up above, hang gliders swoop off the slopes of the cape and land on the sandy expanses below. The region's second Haystack Rock (Cannon Beach has the other) sits 0.5 mile offshore. Robert Straub State Park is situated at the south end of town and occupies most of the Nestucca beach sandspit. Fishing enthusiasts flock to the Pacific City area—the Nestucca and Little Nestucca Rivers are known as two of the finest salmon and steelhead streams in the state.

EAGLE'S VIEW BED & BREAKFAST

37975 Brooten Road, Pacific City, OR 97135   503-965-7600
Mike & Kathy Lewis, Innkeepers   888-846-3292
EMAIL eagle@wcn.net   WEBSITE www.moriah.com/eaglesview/

Eagle's View Bed & Breakfast, Pacific City

LOCATION	Seven miles north of Neskowin on Highway 101, turn west toward Pacific City and go exactly 0.5 mile.
OPEN	All year
DESCRIPTION	A 1995 custom-built two-story country cottage carved high on a hill overlooking the Nestucca Bay and River with comfortable country decor, vaulted pine ceilings, rocking chairs, and many homemade quilts and dolls.
NO. OF ROOMS	Five rooms with private bathrooms.
RATES	May through October, rates are $95-115 for a single or double. November through April, rates are $75-115 for a single or double. There is a minimum stay during holiday weekends and cancellation requires seven days' notice.
CREDIT CARDS	MasterCard, Visa
BREAKFAST	Full breakfast is served in the dining room and includes fruit juice, granola, homemade muffins, fresh fruit, and a main entrée (such as Nestucca eggs with smoked salmon). Retreat guests are given all three meals.

AMENITIES	Cookies or brownies in the evening with hot or cold beverages, 4 acres with walking trails and benches, handicapped access, TV/VCR and CD players in all rooms, video and CD library available, queen-size beds.
RESTRICTIONS	No smoking, no pets, children over 15 are welcome. Nikee is the resident panther-black outdoor cat.
REVIEWED	*Northwest Best Places, The Best Places to Kiss in the Northwest, Recommended Country Inns*
MEMBER	Oregon Lodging Association

PENDLETON

In these parts, the name of this town is synonymous with the Wild West. Each September the Pendleton Round-up rolls around—a big event ever since 1910 that features a dandy rodeo. Pendleton Underground Tours provides a 90-minute walk through Pendleton's history—most of it underground—to view the remains of businesses that date back to the turn of the century: bordellos, opium dens, and Chinese jails. The Umatilla tribe's $13-million Tamustalik (pronounced ta-MUST-ah-luck) Cultural Institute sits on 640 acres behind the Wildhorse Gaming Resort. For the first time ever, the institute will tell the story of the Oregon Trail—one of the greatest mass migrations in human history, which had an indelible impact on the Indians of the West—from the Indian point of view.

DORIE'S INN

203 NW Despain Avenue, Pendleton, OR 97801   541-276-1519

THE PARKER HOUSE BED & BREAKFAST

311 N Main Street, Pendleton, OR 97801   541-276-8581
Sandy Parker, Innkeeper   800-700-8581

LOCATION	One block north of the center of downtown Pendleton.
OPEN	All year
DESCRIPTION	A 1917 three-story Italian Renaissance inn, authentic to the period with hardwood floors throughout, original imported Chinese silk wallpaper and draperies, ornate plaster cove ceiling, and a dramatic, curved entry staircase. Listed on the State Historic Register.

NO. OF ROOMS	One room with a private bathroom and four rooms share one bathroom. Sandy suggests the Gwendolyn Room.
RATES	Year-round rates are $85 for a single or double with a private bathroom and $75 for a single or double with a shared bathroom. There is no minimum stay and cancellation requires 72 hours' notice.
CREDIT CARDS	American Express, MasterCard, Visa
BREAKFAST	Full breakfast is served in the dining room or on the front porch and includes fresh seasonal fruits with smoked-salmon eggs Benedict on homemade biscuits, winter berry French toast, cheese and shallot quiche, Dutch babies with rhubarb banana sauce, farmers' omelet with cilantro, fresh fruit crepes filled with seasoned cream cheese, and more. Breakfast is garnished with herbs from Sandy's extensive garden.
AMENITIES	All rooms have French double doors to outside balconies, freshly cut flowers, and fluffy thick robes; a bag of baked treats awaits each guest; an elevator will take guests upstairs to their rooms.
RESTRICTIONS	No smoking, no children. Roffy and Cody are the resident dogs, a springer and king collie, respectively, and Tippi Toes is the cat. "They love being with guests," says Sandy.
REVIEWED	*Northwest Best Places, Fodor's, Hidden Oregon, Oregon Handbook*
MEMBER	Oregon Lodging Association, Bed & Breakfast Association of Oregon

A PLACE APART BED & BREAKFAST INN

711 SE Byers, Pendleton, OR 97801   541-276-0573
Phil & Sharon Kline, Innkeepers   888-441-8932
EMAIL skline@oregontrail.net

LOCATION	From I-84, take exit 210 north to Isaac. Turn left and go to S Main and take a right. Head through town to SE Byers and turn right. The B&B is seven blocks down.
OPEN	All year
DESCRIPTION	A 1901 two-story colonial revival inn with balconies, Doric columns, beadwork cornices, and colonial and Victorian interior, along the Umatilla River. Listed on the National and State Historic Registers.
NO. OF ROOMS	Two rooms share one bathroom. The Klines suggest the Andrew Room.

A Place Apart Bed & Breakfast Inn, Pendleton

RATES	Year-round rates are $55-95 for a single or double. There is no minimum stay and cancellation requires 48 hours' notice.
CREDIT CARDS	Discover, MasterCard, Visa
BREAKFAST	Full gourmet breakfast is served in the dining room and includes fresh-ground coffee and an entrée accompanied by an array of seasonal fruits.
AMENITIES	Complimentary beverage/wine and snacks, garden with gazebo, access to paved walking trail that winds along the river, air conditioning, soft down comforters, cozy flannel robes, locally made scented soaps, fireplace, flowers for special occasions, dinner reservations arranged at one of Oregon's finest restaurants.
RESTRICTIONS	No smoking, no pets, children over 12 are welcome. Bud is the resident outdoor cat that tries to talk guests into letting him inside.
REVIEWED	*Where to Stay in Oregon*

PORT ORFORD

The southern Oregon Coast's oldest town, Port Orford is a premier whale-watching location (occasionally an individual or pod of whales spends all year in its quiet, kelp-protected coves). It's a town far removed from big-city nuances—sheep ranching, fishing, sea-urchin harvesting, and cranberries dominate town life. Yet it's hip in its own way, especially considering the seasonal proliferation of surfers and board sailors, who head for Battle Rock and Hubbard's Creek beaches and the windy waters of Floras Lake. Fishing fanatics should visit the Elk and Sixes Rivers for the salmon and steelhead runs. And—bonus of bonuses—Port Orford marks the beginning of Oregon's coastal "banana belt," which stretches to the California border and means warmer winter temperatures, an earlier spring, and more sunshine than other coastal areas.

HOME BY THE SEA BED & BREAKFAST

444 Jackson Street, Port Orford, OR 97465   541-332-2855
Alan & Brenda Mitchell, Innkeepers
WEBSITE www.homebythesea.com/

LOCATION	About one hour north of the Oregon–California border.
DESCRIPTION	A contemporary host home on the beach.
NO. OF ROOMS	Two rooms with private bathrooms.
RATES	Year-round rates are $85-95 for a double. Cancellation requires 72 hours' notice.
CREDIT CARDS	MasterCard, Visa
BREAKFAST	Full breakfast is served.
AMENITIES	Direct beach access, cable TV, email, shuttle service for hikers of the Coast Trail.
RESTRICTIONS	No smoking, no pets
MEMBER	Oregon Bed & Breakfast Association

STEELBLUE CHAMELEON LODGE

94893 Elk River Road, Port Orford, OR 97465   541-332-3140

PORTLAND

For decades, Portlanders worked hard to make the Rose City a great place to live, and by almost every measure they've succeeded. With its plethora of parks, its charming downtown core, its splendid westside riverfront, and its proximity to so many of Oregon's finest diversions, Portland is a gem. Now the secret's out, and Portlanders are bracing for dramatic population growth. Still, there's every reason to think that this city can hold on to those ideals that have made it such a sought-after place. What Portlanders prize about their town is not its per capita income but its rivers, its neighborhoods, its bookstores, its microbreweries, and, most of the time, its Trail Blazers. Like any city, Portland has its flaws but, better than most, it's able to meet them head-on.

ABERNATHY'S BED & BREAKFAST

0333 SW Flower Street, Portland, OR 97201 503-243-7616
David Hickerson, Innkeeper FAX 503-316-9118

CENTURY GARDEN BED & BREAKFAST

1960 SE Larch Avenue, Portland, OR 97214 503-235-6846
Dennis & Carol Olpin, Innkeepers

LOCATION	Across the Hawthorne Bridge from downtown to SE 11th, turn right and go about 5 blocks to Harrison. Turn left, go past 12th, and take the next left at Larch. Century Garden is the second house on the right.
OPEN	All year
DESCRIPTION	A 1909 two-story American Four Square host home located in Portland's historic district, decorated with "grandmother's treasures and linens."
NO. OF ROOMS	One suite with private bathroom and two rooms share a bathroom.
RATES	Year-round rates are $99 for a single or double with a private bathroom, $59-79 for a single or double with a shared bathroom, and $99-120 for a suite. There is no minimum stay and cancellation requires two weeks' notice.
CREDIT CARDS	Discover, MasterCard, Visa
BREAKFAST	Full breakfast is served in the common room or on the balcony. Select your breakfast from a menu that includes eggs cooked to order, fresh fruit plate, bacon, sausage, hot gingerbread muffins,

AMENITIES	buttermilk pancakes, waffles, Carol's B&B retreat sandwich, bagels, English muffins, cereal, and yogurt. Picnic baskets and box breakfasts (for guests leaving early) are also available. Rose on plate, gift closet full of handmade items from Oregon, maps marking local points of interest, four rose gardens and one circle garden to enjoy while strolling, common room with TV, microwave, refrigerator, eating area, and access to balcony.
RESTRICTIONS	No smoking, no pets, no children

CLINKERBRICK HOUSE

2311 NE Schuyler, Portland, OR 97212　　　　503-281-2533
Peggie & Bob Irvine, Innkeepers

KUDOS/COMMENTS　"Charming, homelike atmosphere in a historic area. Lovely house and grounds. Warm and friendly innkeepers."

GEDNEY GARDENS

2651 NW Cornell Road, Portland, OR 97210　　　　503-226-6514
　　　　　　　　　　　　　　　　　　　　　　　FAX 503-228-8134

GENERAL HOOKER'S BED & BREAKFAST

125 SW Hooker Street, Portland, OR 97201　　　503-222-4435
Lori Hall, Innkeeper　　　　　　　　　　　　　800-745-4135
EMAIL lori@generalhookers.com　　　　　　　FAX 503-295-6410
WEBSITE www.generalhookers.com

LOCATION	In the downtown area between SW First and Second Avenues on Hooker Street, 1½ blocks east of Barbur Boulevard.
OPEN	All year
DESCRIPTION	An 1888 two-story, midsize Queen Anne Victorian inn with eclectic, comfortable decor, high ceilings, skylights, and "nary a ruffle in sight." Located in the Lair Hill historic district and listed on the National and State Historic Registers.
NO. OF ROOMS	Two rooms with private bathrooms and two rooms share one bathroom. Lori recommends the Rose Room.

RATES	July through October 15th, rates are $95-125 for a single or double with a private bathroom and $85-95 for a single or double with a shared bathroom. October 16th through June, rates are $85-115 for a single or double with a private bathroom and $75-85 for a single or double with a shared bathroom. Rates are subject to change. There is a two-night minimum stay most of the year and cancellation requires one week's notice.
CREDIT CARDS	American Express, MasterCard, Visa
BREAKFAST	Vegetarian and heart-healthy breakfast is served in the dining room and usually is planned around seasonal fruit, with juice, granola and other cereals, coffee, herb teas, and brewed English tea.
AMENITIES	Air conditioning; the whole house has electronic filtration (the owner has asthma); central sound system plays baroque and chamber music (mostly); robes; large travel, music, and film libraries; in-room phones, TV/VCRs with premium channels; all rooms have access to roof deck with tables and chairs with views of downtown; guest refrigerator with wine or beer (first glass is on the house); half-priced day pass to the new Metro YMCA facilities.
RESTRICTIONS	No smoking, no pets, children over 10 are welcome. "Happy" Hooker is the resident Abyssinian cat. She's 13 now and not as active as before when she was the greeter.
REVIEWED	*Recommended Country Inns, Portland's Best Places, Fodor's Bed & Breakfast and Country Inns*
MEMBER	Oregon Bed & Breakfast Guild, Portland Metro Innkeepers
RATED	AAA 2 Diamonds, Mobil 2 Stars
KUDOS/COMMENTS	"This B&B has all the amenities one could want along with a heart-healthy breakfast. My personal experience was to spend several post-operative days here and felt as well cared for as if I had been in my own home."

Georgian House Bed & Breakfast

1828 NE Siskiyou, Portland, OR 97212 503-281-2250
Willie Ackley, Innkeeper 888-282-2250
FAX 503-281-3301

LOCATION	Five miles from Portland's business district, very close to the convention center and Lloyd Center Mall in historic Irvington.
OPEN	All year
DESCRIPTION	A 1922 three-story, red-brick Georgian colonial inn with dark blue shutters and a wrought-iron gate.

NO. OF ROOMS	Two rooms with private bathrooms and two rooms share 1½ bathrooms. Willie recommends the Captain Irving Suite.
RATES	Year-round rates are $85-100 for a single or double with a private bathroom, $65-75 for a single or double with a shared bathroom, and $85 for a suite. There is no minimum stay and cancellation requires two weeks' notice.
CREDIT CARDS	MasterCard, Visa
BREAKFAST	Full breakfast is served in the dining room and includes hot coffee, juice, tea, fresh fruit from the garden, fresh strawberry waffles, and homemade granola. Lunch, dinner, and special meals are also available. The berries (marion, blue, rasp, and straw) are homegrown.
AMENITIES	Robes, hair dryers, gas-log fireplace, air conditioning in guest rooms, afternoon tea, private sunbathing veranda, award-winning rose garden, deck, gazebo, quiet tree-lined historic street, convenient parking.
RESTRICTIONS	No smoking, no pets
REVIEWED	*Fodor's, Northwest Best Places, Better Homes & Gardens*
MEMBER	Oregon Bed & Breakfast Guild
KUDOS/COMMENTS	"Beautifully furnished and a lovely garden make this B&B a feast for the eyes; breakfast is a feast as well."

HERON HAUS

2545 NW Westover Road, Portland, OR 97210   503-274-1846
Julie Keppeler, Innkeeper
WEBSITE *europa.com/~hhaus*

LOCATION	Northwest Portland.
OPEN	All year
DESCRIPTION	A large, 1904 Tudor inn located in the exclusive residential area of Northwest Hills, decorated with contemporary furnishings. Listed on the National and State Historic Registers.
NO. OF ROOMS	Six rooms with private bathrooms.
RATES	Year-round rates are $95-105 for a single and $135-350 for a double. There is no minimum stay and cancellation requires two weeks' notice.
CREDIT CARDS	MasterCard, Visa
BREAKFAST	Continental breakfast is served in the dining room and includes cut fresh fruit, pastry basket with 10 different kinds of pastry, fresh-baked breads, and three kinds of cereal.

Heron Haus, Portland

AMENITIES	Robes, fireplaces, TV, data ports, phones, pool, off-street parking, reading areas.
RESTRICTIONS	No smoking, no pets, children over 10 are welcome.
REVIEWED	Weekends for Two in the Pacific Northwest, The Best Places to Kiss in the Northwest, Recommended Country Inns, Best Places to Stay in the Pacific Northwest, Fodor's Pacific North Coast, Frommer's Seattle & Portland
MEMBER	Unique Northwest Country Inns, Independent Innkeepers Association, Portland Area Innkeepers Association

HOLLADAY HOUSE BED & BREAKFAST

1735 NE Wasco Street, Portland, OR 97232   503-282-3172
Mary Rose, Innkeeper

LOCATION	Two-and-a-half miles from downtown Portland.
OPEN	All year
DESCRIPTION	A 1922 three-story western family inn located in a quiet neighborhood near the mall, light rail, and restaurants.
NO. OF ROOMS	Two rooms with one shared bathroom. Mary recommends the room with the balcony.
RATES	Call for year-round rates.
CREDIT CARDS	MasterCard, Visa

BREAKFAST	Full breakfast is served in the dining room and includes fruit, coffee or tea, toast, homemade jam, cereal, eggs and sausage, or salmon quiche.
AMENITIES	Folk music during breakfast (if desired), piano and organ, travel advice to local scenic spots.
RESTRICTIONS	No smoking. Niki is the friendly resident dog.
REVIEWED	*Women's Travel in Your Pocket, Lesbian & Gay Pink Pages, CitySmart*
MEMBER	Portland Metro Innkeepers Association

HOSTESS HOUSE BED & BREAKFAST

5758 NE Emerson, Portland, OR 97218   503-282-7892
Milli Laughlin, Innkeeper
EMAIL hostesshouse@juno.com   WEBSITE www.bbchannel.com

LOCATION	Fifteen minutes from downtown Portland. Take 60th Street to Emerson. The B&B is the eighth house on the left side of the street.
OPEN	All year
DESCRIPTION	A 1956 two-story contemporary host home in a residential neighborhood, close to the city and the wilderness.
NO. OF ROOMS	One room with a private bathroom and two rooms share one bathroom.
RATES	March through October, rates are $60-65 for a single or double with a private bathroom and $45-55 for a single or double with a shared bathroom. November through February, rates are reduced by 10 percent. There is a two-night minimum stay from March through October. Cancellation requires 48 hours' notice.
CREDIT CARDS	No
BREAKFAST	Full breakfast is served in the dining room and includes fruit, pastry, muffins, cereals, yogurt, granola, bacon, and eggs. Guests' input is always appreciated and special menus are available by request.
AMENITIES	Flowers, air conditioning, some handicapped access.
RESTRICTIONS	No smoking, no pets. Crib available.
MEMBER	Oregon Bed & Breakfast Guild

Irvington Inn

2727 NE 21st Street, Portland, OR 97212   503-280-2299

Kennedy School

5736 NE 33rd Avenue, Portland, OR 97211   503-249-3983
WEBSITE www.mcmenamins.com

Knott Street Inn Bed & Breakfast

2331 NE Knott, Portland, OR 97212   503-249-1855
Jeanne Dreyer, Innkeeper   FAX 503-280-1812
WEBSITE www.citysearch.com/pdx/knotstreet

The Lion & Rose Victorian B&B

1810 NE 15th, Portland, OR 97212   503-287-9245
Kay Peffer, Innkeeper   800-955-1647
EMAIL lionrose@ix.netcom.com   FAX 503-287-9247
WEBSITE www.lionrose.com

LOCATION	In the historic Irvington district of Portland.
DESCRIPTION	A restored 1906 Queen Anne Victorian with period decor, listed on the National Historic Register.
NO. OF ROOMS	Five rooms with private bathrooms and one room with a shared bathroom.
RATES	Please call for current rates and cancellation information.
CREDIT CARDS	American Express, MasterCard, Visa
BREAKFAST	Full gourmet breakfast is served in the dining room.
AMENITIES	English gardens, gazebo, afternoon tea.
RESTRICTIONS	No smoking, no pets
KUDOS/COMMENTS	"Impressive, awesome, excellent food, fine innkeeper."

MACMASTER HOUSE CIRCA 1895

1041 SW Vista Avenue, Portland, OR 97205	503-223-7362
Cecilia Murphy, Innkeeper	800-774-9523
WEBSITE www.macmaster.com	

KUDOS/COMMENTS   "Great experience in historic mansion." "Friendly host. Nice neighborhood."

PITTOCK ACRES BED & BREAKFAST

103 NW Pittock Avenue, Portland, OR 97210	503-226-1163
Linda & Richard Matson, Innkeepers	800-769-9774
	FAX 503-226-6116

KUDOS/COMMENTS   "Great location five minutes from city center with great overall service."

PORTLAND GUEST HOUSE

1720 NE 15th Avenue, Portland, OR 97212	503-282-1402
Susan Gisvold, Innkeeper	
EMAIL pgh@teleport.com	
WEBSITE www.teleport.com/~pgh	

LOCATION	Ten minutes from downtown Portland.
DESCRIPTION	A restored 1890 Victorian guesthouse.
NO. OF ROOMS	Rooms with private or shared bathrooms.
RATES	Year-round rates are $75-85 for a single or double with a private bathroom, $55-65 for a single or double with a shared bathroom, and $95 for a double in a suite. Cancellation requires one week's notice.
CREDIT CARDS	American Express, MasterCard, Visa (payment with credit cards incurs a 5 percent charge)
BREAKFAST	Full breakfast is served in the dining room or in the rose garden.
AMENITIES	Bicycle storage, air conditioning, rose garden.
RESTRICTIONS	No smoking, no pets

PORTLAND'S WHITE HOUSE BED & BREAKFAST

1914 NE 22nd Avenue, Portland, OR 97212
Lanning Blanks & Steve Holden, Innkeepers
EMAIL pdxwhi@aol.com
WEBSITE www.portlandswhitehouse.com

503-287-7131
800-272-7131
FAX 503-249-1641

LOCATION	Located in the heart of historic Irvington, minutes from downtown Portland.
OPEN	All year
DESCRIPTION	A stately 1911 three-story Greek revival mansion restored to its original splendor, with circular drive and classic Greek columns, decorated with bronze and crystal chandeliers and period antiques. Listed on the National and State Historic Registers.
NO. OF ROOMS	Nine rooms with private bathrooms. Try the Chauffeur's Quarter.
RATES	Year-round rates are $98-159 for a single or double. There is no minimum stay and cancellation requires seven days' notice.
CREDIT CARDS	American Express, Discover, MasterCard, Visa
BREAKFAST	Full breakfast is served in the dining room and includes seasonal fresh fruit, lox eggs Benedict, and housemade muffins.
AMENITIES	Facilities for meetings, weddings, and retreats; guestrooms are climate controlled; fountains, courtyard gardens, a grand dining room with period furnishings; feather beds; private telephones; data ports.
RESTRICTIONS	No smoking, no pets. Kelly and Francine are the resident Scotties "that own the house."
REVIEWED	*The Best Places to Kiss in the Northwest, Best Places in Portland, Northwest Best Places*
MEMBER	Oregon Bed & Breakfast Guild, Oregon Restaurant Association, Portland Metro Innkeepers Association
KUDOS/COMMENTS	"Enchanting history and antiques in a beautiful walking neighborhood." "A touch of elegance. A beautiful wedding setting."

SAUVIE ISLAND BED & BREAKFAST

26504 NW Reeder Road, Portland, OR 97231-1424
Marie & AJ Colasurdo, Innkeepers

503-621-3216

LOCATION	Located 30 minutes from Portland's city center. From either I-405 or I-5, follow signs for US-30 West/St. Helens, which becomes NW

	St. Helens Road. Continue past the St. Johns Bridge to the Sauvie Island exit on your right. Go to Reeder Beach.
OPEN	All year
DESCRIPTION	A 1988 one-story contemporary host home situated on the Columbia River.
NO. OF ROOMS	Two rooms with private bathrooms. Marie and AJ recommend the River Room.
RATES	Year-round rates are $60-75 for a single or double. There is no minimum stay and cancellation requires 72 hours' notice.
CREDIT CARDS	No
BREAKFAST	Full breakfast is served in the dining room and includes melon and blueberries, egg soufflé, and cinnamon rolls.
AMENITIES	Piano, outdoor spa, air conditioning.
RESTRICTIONS	No smoking, no pets. Max is the resident dalmatian.
REVIEWED	*Sunset* magazine

SULLIVAN'S GULCH B&B

1744 NE Clackamas Street, Portland, OR 97232   503 331-1104
Gordon "Skip" Rognlien & Jack Robinson, Innkeepers   FAX 503 331-1575
EMAIL thegulch@teleport.com   WEBSITE www.teleport.com/~thegulch/

LOCATION	Just east of the Lloyd Center, I-5 exit 302A or I-84 exit 1.
OPEN	All year
DESCRIPTION	A 1906 two-story Portland Craftsman host home, "Frank Lloyd Wright meets Buffalo Bill," a comfortable, art-filled home. Not Laura Ashley! "We celebrate diversity."
NO. OF ROOMS	Two rooms with private bathrooms and two rooms with one shared bathroom. Try the Northwest Room.
RATES	High-season rates are $85 for a single or double with a private bathroom and $70 for a single or double with a shared bathroom. Regular rates are $75 for a single or double with a private bathroom and $60 for a single or double with a shared bathroom. There is a minimum stay during holiday weekends and cancellation requires 48 hours' notice.
CREDIT CARDS	American Express, MasterCard, Visa
BREAKFAST	Continental-plus is served in the dining room, in the garden, or on the decks in summer. Breakfast includes fresh fruit, juices, coffee or tea, croissants or English muffins, granola or cereals, steel-cut oatmeal in winter.

AMENITIES	Rooms with private baths have private phone lines; all rooms have refrigerators, cable TV, and ceiling fans.
RESTRICTIONS	No smoking, children over 10 are welcome. Well-behaved pets are welcome. Shonka is the friendly resident Lab/shepherd.
REVIEWED	*Fodor's Gay America, Fodor's Gay USA*
MEMBER	Portland Metro Innkeepers Association
KUDOS/COMMENTS	"Friendly. Close to shopping and restaurants. Nice residential area."

TERWILLIGER VISTA BED & BREAKFAST

515 SW Westwood Drive, Portland, OR 97201   503-244-0602
Dick & Jan Vatert, Innkeepers   888-244-0602
WEBSITE www.site-works.com/tvista

LOCATION	Take I-5 exit 297, and go 1.5 miles up Terwilliger Boulevard. Take a hard left onto Westwood; the B&B is the second house on the right. Park in front of the brick wall.
OPEN	All year
DESCRIPTION	A 1940 two-story colonial with traditional and art deco decor.
NO. OF ROOMS	Five rooms with private bathrooms.
RATES	Year-round rates are $80-145 for a single or double. There is no minimum stay and cancellation requires six days' notice.
CREDIT CARDS	MasterCard, Visa
BREAKFAST	Full breakfast is served in the dining room and features a healthy, low-fat menu with dishes such as asparagus soufflé and wild-rice corn fritters. Special meals are available for those with food allergies.
AMENITIES	Port and sherry in the library; guest refrigerators full of juice, soft drinks, and water; air conditioning; terraces; special soaps.
RESTRICTIONS	No smoking, no pets, children over 10 are welcome.
REVIEWED	*Bed & Breakfast Encyclopedia of America Historic Inns, Fodor's*
MEMBER	Professional Association of Innkeepers International

THREE B'S AT MARKET

1704 SE 22nd Avenue, Portland, OR 97214

KUDOS/COMMENTS   "Sweet innkeeper. Her place is clean, clean, clean." "A down-home place where hospitality shines."

TUDOR HOUSE BED & BREAKFAST

2321 NE 28th Avenue, Portland, OR 97212   503-287-9476
Milan Larsen, Innkeeper   800-786-9476
WEBSITE www.moriah.com/tudor   FAX 503-288-8363

A VILLA BED & BREAKFAST

3032 NE Rocky Butte Road, Portland, OR 97220   503-252-4492
EMAIL edbobbieritt@msn.com   FAX 503-251-9183
WEBSITE www.a-villa.com

WESTLUND'S RIVER'S EDGE BED & BREAKFAST

22502 NW Gillihan Road, Portland, OR 97231   503-621-9856
Beverley & Harold Westlund, Innkeepers   FAX 503-621-9784
EMAIL rivers-edge1@juno.com   WEBSITE www.riversedge-bb.com

KUDOS/COMMENTS   "Beautiful location on the Columbia River."

THE WOVEN GLASS INN

14645 Beef Bend Road, Tigard, OR 97224   503-590-6040
Renee & Paul Giroux, Innkeepers   800-484-2192
    FAX 503-590-6511

LOCATION   From Portland, drive south 8 miles on I-5 to Highway 99 west (Tigard exit 294). Go south on Highway 99 for 4 miles to Beef Bend Road. Turn right and drive 1.8 miles.

OPEN	All year
DESCRIPTION	A 1938 two-story rambling farmhouse decorated with fine art, tile, and wood floors, on 1.5 acres in wine country.
NO. OF ROOMS	Two rooms with private bathrooms. Try the French Room.
RATES	Year-round rates are $65-75 for a single or double. There is no minimum stay and cancellation requires seven days' notice for a full refund.
CREDIT CARDS	Visa (to hold rooms only).
BREAKFAST	Full breakfast served in the dining room includes fresh fruit, juice, crepes, coffee, and tea.
AMENITIES	Flowers in season, robes upon request, hot tub on deck, air conditioning in French Room, guest refrigerator, gourmet teas and coffee in sitting room, Steinway piano, two floor looms, stained-glass windows throughout the house.
RESTRICTIONS	No smoking. Felix is the resident tabby.
REVIEWED	*The Official Guide to American Historical Inns*
MEMBER	Portland Metro Innkeepers Association, Inns of Washington County

PRAIRIE CITY

Aptly named for the surrounding grasslands, Prairie City sprang up during the Gold Rush to house a surfeit of miners pouring in from the surrounding hills. Explore the Strawberry Mountain Wilderness and the Blue Mountains.

STRAWBERRY MOUNTAIN INN

HCR 77, Box 940, Prairie City, OR 97869
Linda & Bill Harrington, Innkeepers
EMAIL linda@eoni.com
WEBSITE www.strawberry@moriah.com

541-820-4522
800-545-6913
FAX 541-820-4622

LOCATION	A quarter mile past the Chevron station on the north side of Highway 26E in Prairie City, 13 miles east of John Day.
OPEN	All year
DESCRIPTION	A 1910 three-story late Victorian inn with dormered roof, original oval leaded-glass windows, wraparound covered front porch, with traditional Queen Anne period decor, located on 3 lovely acres.
NO. OF ROOMS	One room with private bathroom and four rooms share two bathrooms. The Harringtons recommend the Blue Room.

RATES	Year-round rates are $95 for a single or double with a private bathroom, $65-85 for a single or double with a shared bathroom, $165 for the suite, and $385 for the entire B&B. There is no minimum stay and cancellation requires 10 days' notice or the first night is charged.
CREDIT CARDS	American Express, Diners Club, Discover, MasterCard, Visa
BREAKFAST	Full gourmet breakfast is served in the dining room and includes fruit, fresh juice, coffee or tea, fresh homemade muffins or bread, an egg dish or deep-dish apple-cinnamon pancakes, and breakfast meat. Reservations for "guest chef" dinners must be made 10 days in advance.
AMENITIES	Hot tub, horse stable and pasture, terry robes in rooms, small-group meeting facilities, fax, in-room phones, champagne or sparkling cider for honeymoons and anniversaries, breakfast by candlelight with classical music, pool table, full library, game table, TV/VCR, video movie library.
RESTRICTIONS	No smoking, no pets inside the inn (separate facilities available). Deja is the poodle and Duke and Duchess are the Maine Coon cats.
REVIEWED	America's Historic Inns

PRINEVILLE

Established in 1863, Prineville is central Oregon's oldest town. Rock hounds flock to Prineville to climb the rimrocks. Ochoco Lake offers a host of year-round outdoor activities. For a romantic evening, check out the Crooked River dinner train.

THE ELLIOTT HOUSE

305 W First Street, Prineville, OR 97754   541-416-0423
Andrew & Betty Wiechert, Innkeepers
EMAIL andybet@ibm.net   WEBSITE www.empnet.com/elliotthouse/

LOCATION	From Bend, take Highway 97 north to Redmond, turn east onto Highway 126 to Prineville, and go 18 miles. The B&B is west of the Prineville courthouse off Highway 126.
OPEN	All year
DESCRIPTION	A 1908 three-story Queen Anne Victorian with a wraparound porch, Tuscan columns, bay windows, a scrolled iron gate, and decorated with antiques. Listed on the National and State Historic Registers.

The Elliott House, Prineville

NO. OF ROOMS	One room with a private bathroom and two rooms share one bathroom.
RATES	Year-round rates are $70 for a single or double with a private or shared bathroom. There is no minimum stay and cancellation requires two weeks' notice.
CREDIT CARDS	No
BREAKFAST	Full breakfast is served by candlelight in the dining room and includes fresh-ground coffee, fresh-squeezed orange juice, homemade applesauce, and fresh strawberry crepes. Special meals are accommodated.
AMENITIES	Flower gardens, complimentary golf club use, complimentary bicycle use, iced tea and cookies served on the patio in spring, hot tea or coffee and warm cookies served in the parlor in winter, 1916 Wurlitzer player piano and 1906 Edison phonograph in the parlor, TV and videos in the attic hideaway.
RESTRICTIONS	No smoking, no pets, children over 12 are welcome. Suzi and Stanley are the Siamese and Persian cats, and Mattie Lou and Winnie Pooh are the golden retriever and great Pyranees. The cats are house cats and might slip into guestrooms if the doors are not closed. The dogs do not have run of the house.
REVIEWED	*Fodor's Bed & Breakfasts and Country Inns*
KUDOS/COMMENTS	"Warm and inviting. Friendly hosts who made one feel at home."

PROSPECT

This small logging town lies along scenic Highway 62, the road to Crater Lake, at the southern edge of Umpqua National Forest. The Rogue Umpqua Divide Wilderness Area is to the north and the Sky Lake and Mountain Lakes Wilderness Areas are to the east. Lost Creek Reservoir is just to the south.

PROSPECT HISTORICAL HOTEL/MOTEL AND DINNERHOUSE

391 Mill Creek Dr, Prospect, OR 97536　　　541-560-3664
Mike & Jo Turner, Innkeepers　　　　　　　800-944-6490
Spanish spoken　　　　　　　　　　　　　　541-560-3825

LOCATION	Located on Highway 62 (Crater Lake Highway) midway between Crater Lake National Park and Medford, in the small logging town of Prospect.
OPEN	All year
DESCRIPTION	A renovated 1889 three-story stagecoach inn furnished with period antiques and situated on 5.5 semi-wooded acres.
NO. OF ROOMS	Eight rooms with private bathrooms.
RATES	May through September, rates are $60-80 for a single or double. October through April, rates are $50-70 for a single or double. There is no minimum stay and cancellation is required by 4 p.m. on the day of arrival.
CREDIT CARDS	Diners Club, Discover, MasterCard, Visa
BREAKFAST	Continental breakfast is served in the parlor and includes muffins, fruit, coffee, and tea. Dinner, group, and vegetarian meals are also available.
AMENITIES	Free parking, 5.5 semi-wooded acres with horseshoe pits, gazebo, and barbecue area. Meeting facilities and air conditioning.
RESTRICTIONS	No smoking and no pets in the hotel. Both are allowed in some of the motel units. Dewey and Teddie are the two resident dogs named after two of the famous guests of the hotel, i.e., Teddy Roosevelt. They are kept company by Tsunami, their feline counterpart.
REVIEWED	*Frommer's, Fodor's Northwest USA, Oregon Discovery Guide, Lonely Planet*

RAINIER

This historic river town's namesake mountain rises as a magnificent backdrop to the northeast. Prescott Beach is a great place to hang out and admire the Columbia River.

1888 HOUSE

713 W "B" Street, Rainier, OR 97048   503-556-1888

REDMOND

Perched on a plateau at just over 3,000 feet and surrounded by junipers, Redmond offers the best of Oregon's high desert country. The Deschutes River is a stone's throw away. Rock hounds flock to nearby Smith Rock State Park for the superb rock-climbing. The Peterson Rock Garden is worth exploring and kids certainly enjoy Operation Santa Claus, a reindeer ranch. The Deschutes County Fair gets under way at the end of July.

LLAST CAMP LLAMAS BED & BREAKFAST

4555 NW Pershall Way, Redmond, OR 97756   541-548-6828
Aileen & Buck Adams, Innkeepers

ROSEBURG

The Roseburg area now has eight wineries, all open for tours and tastings much of the year. Wildlife Safari allows you to drive through rolling country to see a quasi-natural wildlife preserve, with predators discreetly fenced from their prey, and to watch baby animals up close. The Douglas County Museum of History and Natural History imaginatively displays logging, fur-trapping, and pioneer items in one of the handsomest contemporary structures you'll find.

HOKANSON'S GUEST HOUSE

848 SE Jackson, Roseburg, OR 97470   541-672-2632
John & Victoria Hokanson, Innkeepers   FAX 541-672-5111

OPEN	All year
DESCRIPTION	An 1882 three-story Gothic revival with Victorian decor, listed on the National and State Historic Registers.
NO. OF ROOMS	Two rooms with private bathrooms. Try the Marietta Room.
RATES	June through October, rates are $75-95 for a single or double. November through May, rates are $65-85 for a single or double. There is no minimum stay and cancellation requires 72 hours' notice.
CREDIT CARDS	Discover, MasterCard, Visa
BREAKFAST	Full three-course breakfast is served in the front parlor.
AMENITIES	Central air conditioning, 1920s piano in parlor, TV, phone, clawfoot tubs with bath salts and bubble bath.
RESTRICTIONS	No smoking inside, children over 10 are welcome. Fritz is the resident bobtailed tabby.

HOUSE OF HUNTER

813 SE Kane, Roseburg, OR 97470
Walt & Jean Hunter, Innkeepers
WEBSITE www.wizzards.net/hunter

541-672-2335
800-540-7704
FAX 541-957-0998

THE UMPQUA HOUSE

840 Oak View Drive, Roseburg, OR 97470
Rhoda & Allen Mozorosky, Innkeepers

541-672-4353

SALEM

Recent remodeling and restoration have spruced up both the state capitol and the surrounding blocks, the most attractive part of town. The 1938 capitol has an art-deco-cum-grandiose-classical look and is worth a visit, especially since the fix-up from earthquake damage earlier this decade. Handsome parks flank the building, and just behind is Willamette University, the oldest university in the West. Across the road from Willamette University is Historic Mission Mill Village. The impressive 42-acre cluster of restored buildings from the 1800s includes a wool mill, a parsonage, a Presbyterian church, and several homes.

BETHEL HEIGHTS FARM BED & BREAKFAST

6055 Bethel Heights Road NW, Salem, OR 97304   503-364-7688

KUDOS/COMMENTS   "Outstanding lodging and meals."

BOOKMARK BED & BREAKFAST

975 "D" Street NE, Salem, OR 97301   503-399-2013

COTTON WOOD COTTAGE BED & BREAKFAST

960 "E" Street NE, Salem, OR 97301   503-362-3979
Bill & Donna Wickman, Innkeepers   800-349-3979
EMAIL ctnwdctg@open.org   WEBSITE www.open.org/ctnwdctg/

LOCATION   Take the Market Street exit (256) off I-5 and go 1.6 miles to Summer Street. Turn left and go 2 blocks to "E" Street. Turn left, and the B&B is on the right between Summer and Capitol.

OPEN   All year

Cottono Wood Cottage Bed & Breakfast, Salem

DESCRIPTION	A 1924 three-story English cottage with "eclectic but comfortable" decor, located near the state capitol and the heart of Oregon wine country.
NO. OF ROOMS	Two rooms share one bathroom. Try the Pansey Room.
RATES	Year-round rates are $55-60 for a single or double. There is no minimum stay and cancellation requires seven days' notice (barring certain extenuating circumstances).
CREDIT CARDS	Bank Americard, Diners Club, Discover, MasterCard, Visa
BREAKFAST	Full breakfast is served in the dining room on china with antique silver. The menu is selected the previous evening, but will include fruit, juice, hot drinks, and various entrées.
AMENITIES	Robes, bath sheets, cable TV, library, cats, English car in garage, on-street parking, but above all, hospitality.
RESTRICTIONS	Smoking outdoors on deck only, no pets, children over 12 are welcome. Merry is the resident cat, and there is reportedly another kitten on the way. "Cats must like guests to be allowed in this house," says Bill.
MEMBER	Professional Association of Innkeepers International, Marion/Lane County Bed & Breakfasts

EAGLE CREST BED & BREAKFAST

4401 Eagle Crest NW, Salem, OR 97304 503-364-3960
Greg & Sharon White, Innkeepers
EMAIL *ecrest1@juno.com*
WEBSITE *www.eaglecrest1.com*

MARQUEE HOUSE

333 Wyatt Court NE, Salem, OR 97301 503-391-0837
Rickie Hart, Innkeeper 800-949-0837
EMAIL *rickiemh@open.org* FAX 503-391-1713
WEBSITE *www.oregonlink.com/marquee/*

LOCATION	One and a half miles from I-5 using the Market Street exit (256). Travel west on Market to 17th and turn left (south). Pass through two major intersections and turn right on Center. Wyatt Court is five houses past the Battery Exchange, on the right.
OPEN	All year

Marquee House, Salem

DESCRIPTION	A 1938 two-story Mount Vernon colonial inn with movie-themed rooms furnished with antiques.
NO. OF ROOMS	Three rooms with private bathrooms and two rooms share one bathroom. Rickie recommends the Auntie Mame.
RATES	Year-round rates are $75-90 for a single or double with a private bathroom and $55-60 for a single or double with a shared bathroom. The entire B&B rents for $405. There is a minimum stay during holidays and Willamette University events and cancellation requires 48 hours' notice (14 days during holidays and university events).
CREDIT CARDS	Discover, MasterCard, Visa
BREAKFAST	Full breakfast is served in the dining room or on the veranda during summer. Breakfast features seasonal ingredients comprising a variety of menus, with special attention to presentation. Courses include juice, fruit, oatmeal custard, a savory dish, meat, and pastry. Dietary needs are accommodated.
AMENITIES	Evening movie showing with popcorn, candy, and beverages; his and her hammock swing chairs overlooking the creek; data ports and desks for business travelers; butler's basket with free travel amenities; room for small meetings and intimate celebrations; murder mystery weekends; air conditioners in rooms; and ceiling fans.
RESTRICTIONS	No smoking, no pets, children over 14 are welcome.
REVIEWED	*Northwest Best Places, Fodor's, Frommer's, Oregon: Off the Beaten Path, The Official Guide to American Historic Inns*
MEMBER	Oregon Bed & Breakfast Guild, Professional Association of Innkeepers International

RATED	AAA 2 Diamonds
KUDOS/COMMENTS	"Interesting, quiet, accommodating hostess, comfortable with attractive decor." "Interesting historic house with old-time movie theme." "An absolutely delightful B&B with a warm, friendly, helpful innkeeper. Located in a spectacular creekside setting."

MEADOW VIEW INN BED & BREAKFAST

11221 Steinkamp Road SE, Aumsville, OR 97325　　503-749-1344
Ernie & Jona Ingram, Innkeepers
WEBSITE *www.wvi.com/~dhull/meadowview*

LOCATION	Just east of Salem.
DESCRIPTION	An octagon-shaped home with 16-foot cedar ceilings, wainscoting, and traditional decor.
NO. OF ROOMS	Two rooms with private bathrooms.
RATES	Year-round rates are $45-55 for a single or double.
CREDIT CARDS	No
RESTRICTIONS	No smoking, no pets

STATE HOUSE BED & BREAKFAST

2146 State Street, Salem, OR 97301　　503-588-1340
Mike & Judy Winsett, Innkeepers　　800-800-6712
WEBSITE *www.teleport.com/~mikwin*

STONE LION INN

4692 Lancaster Drive NE, Salem, OR 97305　　503-463-6374

VISTA PARK BED & BREAKFAST

480 Vista Avenue SE, Salem, OR 97302
Janet, John, & Joi Whitney, Innkeepers
EMAIL welcome@vistapark.com
WEBSITE www.vistapark.com

503-588-0698
888-588-0699
FAX 503-588-0698

LOCATION	From the center of town at State and Commercial, head south on Commercial for 2.5 miles and turn left onto Vista. Go to the fourth driveway on the right.
OPEN	All year
DESCRIPTION	A 1933 2½-story Normandy Tudor host home decorated with simple elegance and surrounded by beautiful gardens.
NO. OF ROOMS	Two rooms with private bathrooms. Try the Garden Room.
RATES	Year-round rates are $60-90 for a single or double. There is a two-night minimum stay during community events and holidays, and cancellation requires 48 hours' notice with a 10 percent charge.
CREDIT CARDS	Discover, MasterCard, Visa
BREAKFAST	Full breakfast is served in the dining room and includes juice; coffee, tea, or hazelnut praline hot chocolate; fresh fruit; waffles; Dutch babies; quiche; frittatas; Octoberfest sausage; homemade turkey sausage; and fresh breads.
AMENITIES	Fresh flowers, feather mattress toppers, the Garden Room features a romantic fireplace filled with candles, homemade cookies, swimming pool in summer, gardens, croquet, a well-stocked reading room, plenty of off-street parking, picnic area, ceiling fans in rooms, living room and dining room suitable for small meetings and events.
RESTRICTIONS	No smoking, no pets. Salem is the resident Scottish fold cat.
MEMBER	Mid-Willamette Valley Bed & Breakfast Association, Salem Convention and Visitors Association

SANDY

Highway 26 divides into one-way avenues through the town of Sandy on the way to Mount Hood. Named for the nearby river, Sandy offers a white-steepled church, antique shops, a weekend country market, ski rentals, and big fruit stands that purvey the local fruits, vegetables, wines, juices, and filberts. The Oregon Candy Farm, 5.5 miles east of Sandy on Highway 26, features Bavarian truffles along with hand-dipped chocolates and caramels.

BROOKSIDE BED & BREAKFAST

45232 SE Paha Loop, Sandy, OR 97055   503-668-4766
WEBSITE *www.ideal-web.com/brookside*

LOCATION	On the Mount Hood Loop.
DESCRIPTION	A 1948 host home with views of Mount Hood.
NO. OF ROOMS	One room with a private bathroom and four rooms share bathrooms.
RATES	Year-round rates are $35-65 for a single or double.
BREAKFAST	Full breakfast is served.
RESTRICTIONS	No smoking

FERNWOOD AT ALDER CREEK

54850 E Highway 26, Sandy, OR   503-622-3570

SCAPPOOSE

Scappoose ("gravelly plain") is about 40 minutes northwest of Portland on Highway 30. J. J Coons Marine Park, a wildlife preserve on Coon Island, can only be reached by boat. It's a fun place for a picnic.

BARNSTORMER BED & BREAKFAST

53758 W Lane Road, Scappoose, OR 97056   503-543-2740
EMAIL *barnstormer@columbia-center.org*   FAX 503-543-4704
WEBSITE *www.moriah.com/barnstormer*

DESCRIPTION	A restored farmhouse, built in the early 1900s, decorated with antiques, and situated on 4 acres
NO. OF ROOMS	Five rooms with private bathrooms.
RATES	Year-round rates are $55-95 for a double. Romance packages and discounts for multinight stays are available. Cancellation requires 72 hours' notice for a refund of deposit.
CREDIT CARDS	MasterCard, Visa
BREAKFAST	Full country breakfast is served. There is a full-service restaurant on-site.
AMENITIES	Player piano; TV/VCR; microwave; snacks; room with sitting area, feather bed, and Jacuzzi; biplane rides.
RESTRICTIONS	No smoking. Please ask about children and pets.

MALARKEY RANCH INN B&B

55948 Columbia River Highway, Scappoose, OR 97056   503-543-5244

SEASIDE

One hundred years ago, affluent Portland beachgoers rode Columbia River steamers to Astoria and then hopped a stagecoach to Seaside, the Oregon Coast's first resort town. The place has become more crowded ever since. The hordes mill along Broadway, eyeing the entertainment parlors, taffy concessions, and bumper cars, and then emerge at the Prom, the 2-mile-long cement "boardwalk" that's ideal for strolling. Lately, they also head for the newly constructed outlet mall along Highway 101 on the town's north end. Surf fishing is popular, particularly at the south end of town in the cove area. Steelhead and salmon can be taken (in season) from the Necanicum River, which flows through town. Occasional minus tides provide good razor clamming along the wide, flat beach.

10TH AVENUE INN

125 10th Avenue, Seaside, OR 97138   503-738-0643
Francie & Vern Starkey, Innkeepers   800-569-1114
EMAIL 10aveinn@seasurf.net   FAX 503-717-1688
WEBSITE www.obbg.org (look under Coast, then Seaside)
OPEN   All year

DESCRIPTION	A 1908 three-story host home and cottage decorated with some antiques.
NO. OF ROOMS	Four rooms with private bathrooms.
RATES	Year-round rates are $55-75. Please call for cancellation information.
CREDIT CARDS	American Express, Discover, MasterCard, Visa
BREAKFAST	Full breakfast is served.
AMENITIES	Very close to the beach.
RESTRICTIONS	No smoking, no pets
MEMBER	Oregon Bed & Breakfast Guild
KUDOS/COMMENTS	"Friendly couple, easy to talk with. Good breakfast. Great location."

ANDERSON'S BOARDING HOUSE BED & BREAKFAST

208 N Holladay Drive, Seaside, OR 97138   503-738-9055
Barbara Harlan Edwards, Innkeeper   800-995-4013
EMAIL bedwards@transport.com

LOCATION	Take Highway 101 into Seaside. When coming from the north, turn right onto Third Avenue and go to the dead end at Holladay Drive. Coming from the south, turn left onto Second Avenue and go to the dead end at Holladay Drive. Located two blocks north of town.
OPEN	All year
DESCRIPTION	An 1898 two-story transitional Victorian host home with a white picket fence and spacious porch, decorated with antiques and overlooking the Necanicum River.
NO. OF ROOMS	Five rooms with private bathrooms. Barbara recommends room 5.
RATES	Year-round rates are $75-85 for a single or double. There is a minimum stay during high season and cancellation requires five days' notice.
CREDIT CARDS	MasterCard, Visa
BREAKFAST	Full breakfast is served in the dining room and includes coffee and tea, juice, fruit, an entrée such as gourmet pancakes, French toast, an egg dish, and baked goods.
AMENITIES	Fresh flowers, several rooms with clawfoot tubs, wheelchair ramp, information regarding sights and activities.

RESTRICTIONS	No smoking, no pets, children over 3 are welcome. Beatie is the resident cat.
REVIEWED	*Northwest Best Places, Recommended Country Inns, Fodor's, Driving the Pacific Coast*
MEMBER	Oregon Bed & Breakfast Guild
KUDOS/COMMENTS	"Very well furnished, excellent breakfast, warm and inviting, very hospitable."

COUNTRY RIVER INN

1020 N Holladay Drive, Seaside, OR 97138   503-738-8049
Steve & Janet Mathews, Innkeepers   800-605-3337
EMAIL *crinn@clatsop.com*   FAX 503-738-6208
WEBSITE *www.clatsop.com*

LOCATION	From Highway 101 in Seaside, take N 21st Avenue west for two blocks to N Holladay and go south one block.
OPEN	All year
DESCRIPTION	A 1989 two-story contemporary inn with country decor.
NO. OF ROOMS	Sixteen rooms with private bathrooms.
RATES	May through September, rates are $55-84 for a single. October through April, rates are $45-75 for a single. There is a minimum stay and cancellation requires 48 hours' notice.

Country River Inn, Seaside

CREDIT CARDS	Discover, MasterCard, Visa
BREAKFAST	Full breakfast is served in the dining room and includes freshly ground Starbucks coffee, tea, orange juice, an entrée (usually French toast, some sort of pancake, or an egg dish). Special meals are available for groups.
AMENITIES	One room is handicapped accessible, meeting room available with the rental of five or more rooms, six rooms with river views.
RESTRICTIONS	No smoking, no pets. Otto and Bandit are the resident dogs. They are not permitted in the guests' quarters.
MEMBER	Oregon Lodging Association
RATED	AAA 1 Star

CUSTER HOUSE BED & BREAKFAST

811 First Avenue, Seaside, OR 97138   503-738-7825
Helen & George A. Custer, Innkeepers   800-738-7852
Fluent German spoken   FAX 503-738-4324
EMAIL custerbb@seasurf.com   WEBSITE www.clatsop.com/custer

LOCATION	Sixth house west of Highway 101 on First Avenue in Seaside.
OPEN	All year
DESCRIPTION	A 1900 two-story Queen Anne inn listed on the Seaside Historic Inventory.
NO. OF ROOMS	Three rooms with private bathrooms. The Custers recommend room 1.
RATES	May 15 through October 15, rates are $75 for a single or double. October 15 through May 15, rates are $65 for a single or double. There is a two-night minimum stay and cancellation requires 72 hours' notice.
CREDIT CARDS	American Express, Diners Club, Discover, MasterCard, Visa
BREAKFAST	Full breakfast is served.
RESTRICTIONS	No smoking, no pets
MEMBER	Oregon Bed & Breakfast Guild

GILBERT INN BED & BREAKFAST

341 Beach Drive, Seaside, OR 97138
Carole & Dick Rees, Innkeepers
EMAIL gilbert@west-connect.com
WEBSITE www.clatsop.com/gilbertinn

503 738-9770
800-410-9770
FAX 503-717-1070

LOCATION	Eighty miles northwest of Portland. Take Highway 26, turn left at the City Center exit, and left again at Avenue A. Head west to the beach.
OPEN	February through December
DESCRIPTION	An 1892 three-story Queen Anne Victorian inn—a classic Victorian beach house with 10-foot ceilings, original fir walls and ceilings, and French country decor. Listed on the Oregon Historic Register.
NO. OF ROOMS	Ten rooms with private bathrooms. Try the Turret Room.
RATES	Year-round rates are $89-105 for a single or double and $105 for the suite. There is a two-night minimum stay on weekends, three nights during some summer holidays. Cancellation requires five days' notice.
CREDIT CARDS	American Express, Discover, MasterCard, Visa
BREAKFAST	Full breakfast is served in the breakfast room and might include stuffed French toast with apricot sauce, fresh fruit, juice, coffee, tea, hot chocolate, and cider.
AMENITIES	Bath items provided; coffee room; sherry; fresh fruit; magazines; cards and games; garden; facilities for weddings, retreats, and receptions; close to town and the beach.
RESTRICTIONS	No smoking, no pets. Gilbert the Great, the resident Siamese cat, is gorgeous and knows it. He is king of the parlor.
REVIEWED	*Northwest Best Places, The Best Places to Kiss in the Northwest, Fodor's Travel Guide—West Coast, Recommended Country Inns, Wake Up and Smell the Coffee*
MEMBER	American Bed & Breakfast Association, Professional Association of Innkeepers International, Oregon Lodging Association
RATED	AAA 3 Diamonds, ABBA 3 Crowns, Mobil 3 Stars, *Best Places to Kiss* 3 Lips
KUDOS/COMMENTS	"Very well appointed, classic styling, good food and atmosphere."

THE GUEST HOUSE BED & BREAKFAST

486 Necanicum Drive, Seaside, OR 97138 800-340-8150
WEBSITE *www.moriah.com/inns*

RIVERSIDE INN B&B

430 S Holladay Drive, Seaside, OR 97138 503-738-8254
Judy & Larry Heth, Innkeepers 800-826-6151
EMAIL *riverside@riversideinn.com* FAX 503-738-7375
WEBSITE *www.riversideinn.com*

LOCATION	Along the Necanicum River
DESCRIPTION	A refurbished 1907 inn with antiques and country decor.
NO. OF ROOMS	Eleven rooms with private bathrooms.
RATES	Year-round rates are $55-99 for a double. Ask about off-season discounts. There is no minimum stay and cancellation requires notice.
CREDIT CARDS	American Express, Discover, MasterCard, Visa
BREAKFAST	Full breakfast is served in the dining room or library.
AMENITIES	Gardens, barbecues.
RESTRICTIONS	No smoking inside, no pets, well-behaved children are welcome.
REVIEWED	*Northwest Best Places*, *The Best Places to Kiss in the Northwest*, *America's Wonderful Little Hotels & Inns*

SAND DOLLAR B&B

606 N Holladay Drive, Seaside, OR 97138 800-738-3491
Bob & Nita Hempfling, Innkeepers
WEBSITE *www.ohwy.com*

Sea Side Inn, Seaside

SEA SIDE INN

581 S Promenade, Seaside, OR 97138　　　　503-738-6403
Susan Peters, Innkeeper　　　　　　　　　　800-772-7766
WEBSITE *www.seasideinnbandb.com*　　　FAX 503-738-6634

LOCATION	Take Highway 101 north into Seaside, turn left (toward the ocean) onto Avenue "G", drive six blocks to Beach Drive, and turn left.
OPEN	All year
DESCRIPTION	A seaside, 1994 four-story contemporary inn with eclectic decor and theme rooms.

NO. OF ROOMS	Fourteen rooms with private bathrooms. Susan recommends the Northwest Timber Room.
RATES	May through September, rates are $105-159 for a single or double and $225 for a suite. October through April, rates are $99-149 for a single or double and $199-225 for a suite. There is no minimum stay and cancellation requires five days' notice.
CREDIT CARDS	Discover, MasterCard, Visa
BREAKFAST	Full breakfast is served in the dining room and includes fresh fruit, juice, pastry, coffee, tea, and a choice of omelets or eggs, French toast or pancakes, hashbrowns, and ham, bacon, or link sausage. Dinner is served Saturday nights. For large groups, all meals are available with advance notice.
AMENITIES	Rooms with one- and two-person jetted tubs; many rooms with gas fireplaces; robes, TV/VCR, telephone, heat pumps, and air conditioners in rooms; an oceanfront room with handicapped access; complete bar; licensed massage therapist; cozy library; conference room that seats up to 20.
RESTRICTIONS	No smoking. Rosie is the resident Maltese and Teddy is the Maltese/terrier mix.
REVIEWED	The Best Places to Kiss in the Northwest, Frommer's

SUMMER HOUSE BED & BREAKFAST

1221 N Franklin, Seaside, OR 97138　　　　　503-738-5740
Jack & Lesle Palmeri, Innkeepers　　　　　　800-745-2378
EMAIL summerhs@seasurf.com
WEBSITE www.ohwy.com/or/s/summerbb.htm

SHERIDAN

Sheridan sits snug between Portland and Oregon's central coast off Highway 18 in the very heart of Oregon's celebrated wine country.

BRIGHTRIDGE FARM BED & BREAKFAST

18575 SW Brightridge Road, Sheridan, OR 97378　　　503-843-5230
Bettyanne & Dick Shoaff, Innkeepers
EMAIL brightridge@macnet.com

Brightridge Farm Bed & Breakfast, Sheridan

LOCATION	Take Highway 18 west from McMinnville 9 miles to Bellevue. Turn right at Lawrence Gallery onto Muddy Valley Road. Turn left onto Latham Road and go 2 miles to Brightridge Road. Turn right. The B&B is the second driveway on the right.
OPEN	All year
DESCRIPTION	A 1978 two-story farmhouse on a 10-acre hillside, decorated with contemporary country furnishings, and situated in the heart of wine country.
NO. OF ROOMS	Two rooms with private bathrooms.
RATES	Year-round rates are $90 for the entire B&B. There is a two-day minimum stay during holiday weekends and cancellation requires seven days' notice.
CREDIT CARDS	No
BREAKFAST	Full breakfast includes juice, fresh fruit scones/muffins, sausage (turkey and chicken only), and a main dish. Everything is homemade using organic ingredients whenever possible.
AMENITIES	Flowers, robes, flexible breakfast time, turndown service; homemade cookies, tea/coffee any time; maps to area wineries; front porch with rocking chairs.
RESTRICTIONS	No smoking, no pets, no children. Tootsiebell is the resident barn cat, and there are small-breed Shetland sheep grazing the land. They are raised for their wool, are of a variety of colors, and are friendly.

MEMBER	Yamhill County Bed & Breakfast Association, Mid-Willamette Valley Bed & Breakfast Association
KUDOS/COMMENTS	"Well-kept contemporary country home with breathtaking views, comfortable rooms, and above-average breakfasts."

MIDDLE CREEK RUN BED & BREAKFAST

25400 Harmony Road, Sheridan, OR 97378   503-843-7606
John Tallerino & Marc Randall, Innkeepers

LOCATION	Eighteen miles west of McMinnville, 30 miles from the Oregon Coast off Highway 18.
OPEN	All year
DESCRIPTION	A 1901 two-story rural Queen Anne Victorian on 23 landscaped acres, with high-country Victorian decor, a floor-to-ceiling stained-glass window in the formal dining room, wraparound porches, and an upstairs veranda.
NO. OF ROOMS	Three rooms with private bathrooms and two rooms share one bathroom. Try the Oak Room.
RATES	Year-round rates are $95-125 for a single or double with a private bathroom, $80 for a single or double with a shared bathroom, and $125 for a suite. There is no minimum stay and cancellation requires two weeks' notice for a full refund.
CREDIT CARDS	No
BREAKFAST	Full three-course breakfast is served in the dining room. The menu may include a first course of fresh mango/banana or orange/ginger muffins; a second course of herbed egg crepe stuffed with wild mushrooms and green tomatoes with herbed goat cheese or spicy smoked sausage and spinach over sweet potato polenta nests with herbed goat cheese and toasted pine nuts; and a third course of seasonal fruit clafouti with marscapone cheese or fresh peach coffeecake soaked in rum and topped with fresh berries and a blueberry glaze. All items are made from scratch and feature local or homegrown produce.
AMENITIES	Fresh flowers in rooms, truffles on pillows, turndown service, robes, hot tub, refreshments during the stay, meeting facilities, weddings, receptions, retreats, nature walks in woods.
RESTRICTIONS	Smoking on porches only, children over 15 are welcome. Kona is the resident Lab and Mouse is the cat. They are also the tour guides through the woods.
REVIEWED	America's Favorite Inns, B&Bs, & Small Hotels; The Best Places to Kiss in the Northwest

Middle Creek Run Bed & Breakfast, Sheridan

MEMBER   Mid-Willamette Bed & Breakfast Association

KUDOS/COMMENTS   "Beautiful restoration of Victorian. Great food and service. Attention to detail."

SHERIDAN COUNTRY INN

1330 W Main Street, Sheridan, OR 97378   503-843-3226

SILVERTON

At the junction of Highways 213 and 214, Silverton is about a half hour outside of Salem and an hour south of Portland. A short drive down Highway 214 takes you to Silver Falls State Park. In September, nearby Mount Angel celebrates Oktoberfest, and there are tulip and iris festivals in season.

ABIQUA CREEK FARMS BED & BREAKFAST

11672 Nusom Road, Silverton, OR 97381   503-873-6878
Chris & Betty Roemer, Innkeepers   FAX 503-873-6878
EMAIL abqacrkbb@aol.com

LOCATION	Two miles south of Mount Angel, 2.5 miles north of Silverton, and 15 miles east of Salem and I-5.
OPEN	All year
DESCRIPTION	A 1962 two-story Cape Cod country inn with country decor on Abiqua Creek.
NO. OF ROOMS	Two rooms share one bathroom.
RATES	Year-round rates are $50 for a single or double. There is no minimum stay and cancellation requires seven days' notice.
CREDIT CARDS	No
BREAKFAST	Full breakfast is served in the kitchen and usually consists of fruit, juice, a variety of egg dishes (such as frittata or cheese omelet), Belgian waffles with strawberries, or French toast.
AMENITIES	Air conditioning, handicapped access, flowers, candy, wine, a pond with goldfish and koi. Close to covered bridges, wineries, and antique shopping.
RESTRICTIONS	No smoking, no pets. There are two well-mannered, gentle German shepherds in residence.
REVIEWED	*Oregon Wine* magazine
MEMBER	Marion-Polk Bed & Breakfast Society, Oregon Lodging Association

THE EGG CUP INN BED & BREAKFAST

11920 Sioux Street, Silverton, OR 97381 503-873-5497
Lolita & Elmer Valkenaar, Innkeepers

MARVIN GARDENS GUEST HOUSE

511 S Water Street, Silverton, OR 97381 503-873-2683
Valeria & Ron Stanley, Innkeepers
EMAIL *Broccoli@cyberis.net*
WEBSITE *www.silvertonor.com*

LOCATION	Traveling south on I-5, exit at Woodburn/Mount Angel. Travel 11 miles to downtown historic Silverton. Traveling north on I-5, exit at Silverton and follow signs 15 miles to downtown historic Silverton.
OPEN	All year
DESCRIPTION	A 19th-century two-story Victorian farmhouse.

NO. OF ROOMS	Two rooms with one shared bathroom. Valeria and Ron recommend the Blue Room.
RATES	Year-round rates are $75 for a single or double. The Suite is $120. Call about the minimum-stay policy April through November, and cancellation requires 36 hours' notice.
CREDIT CARDS	Discover
BREAKFAST	Continental-plus is served in the dining room or breakfast nook and includes heart-healthy foods. Special meals are available upon request.
AMENITIES	Computers, laundry, patio in luscious surroundings.
RESTRICTIONS	No smoking, children over 8 are welcome.

SISTERS

Named after the three mountain peaks that dominate the horizon (Faith, Hope, and Charity), this little community is becoming a bit of a mecca for tired urban types looking for a taste of cowboy escapism. On a clear day (and there are about 250 of them a year here), Sisters is exquisitely beautiful. Surrounded by mountains, trout streams, and pine and cedar forests, this little town capitalizes on the influx of winter skiers and summer camping and fishing enthusiasts. Sisters hosts 56,000 visitors for each of four shows during its annual June rodeo. It also has the world's largest outdoor quilt show each July, with 800 quilts hanging from balconies and storefronts.

CONKLIN'S GUEST HOUSE, A BED & BREAKFAST

69013 Camp Polk Road, Sisters, OR 97759	541-549-0123
Frank & Marie Conklin, Innkeepers	800-549-4262
WEBSITE *www.informat.com/bz/conklins*	541-549-4481

LOCATION	A quarter mile north of Sisters on Camp Polk Road. Across the road from Sisters Eagle Airport.
OPEN	All year
DESCRIPTION	Sprawling white farmhouse with wraparound porch, nestled among stately pines.
NO. OF ROOMS	Five rooms with private bathrooms
RATES	June through December, rates are $90-140 for a single or double and $140 for a suite. January through May rates are $70-120 for a single or double and $120 for a suite. There is no minimum stay and a 24-hour cancellation policy.

Conklin's Guest House, A Bed & Breakfast, Sisters

CREDIT CARDS	No
BREAKFAST	Full breakfast is served in the dining room.
AMENITIES	Pool, two ponds with catch-and-release fishing, piped music in room, flowers, robes, air-conditioning, handicapped access.
RESTRICTIONS	No smoking, pets on leash outside, children over 12 are welcome. Ducks and chickens are resident critters.
REVIEWED	*Northwest Best Places, Best Places to Stay in the Pacific Northwest, The Best Places to Kiss in the Northwest, American Historic Inns, Northwest Discoveries, Quick Escapes in the Pacific Northwest, Frommer's Washington & Oregon, Fodor's Pacific Northwest*
MEMBER	Oregon Bed & Breakfast Guild, Oregon Lodging Association
RATED	AAA 3 Diamonds, ABBA 3 Crowns
KUDOS/COMMENTS	"A beautiful place. Great view, nicely decorated. Wonderful owners."

HOSPITALITY HOUSE

PO Box 1971, Sisters, OR 97759　　　　　　　　　　　　541-549-4909

RAGS TO WALKERS GUEST RANCH

17045 Farthing Lane, Sisters, OR 97759
Bonnie & Neal Halous
EMAIL rags@bendnet.com
WEBSITE www.bendnet.com/rags

541-548-7000
800-422-5622
FAX 541-923-5107

LOCATION	Take Highway 126 from Sisters 5 miles to Redmond; turn right on Cloverdale Road. Go 2 miles, turn left on Farthing Lane, and take a right at the first driveway.
OPEN	All year
DESCRIPTION	A 1990 two-story B&B with wraparound porch and views of the Cascade Mountains.
NO. OF ROOMS	Five rooms with private bathrooms and two rooms with one shared bathroom.
RATES	Year-round rates are $95-150 for a suite. There is no minimum stay and cancellation requires 30 days' notice.
CREDIT CARDS	MasterCard, Visa
BREAKFAST	Full breakfast is served in the dining room and includes fresh fruit, fresh-squeezed orange juice, entreé, and fresh-baked bread.
AMENITIES	Horse ranch, trout-stocked ponds, bikes, pool tables, fresh cookies.
RESTRICTIONS	No smoking
KUDOS/COMMENTS	"Great for country and animal lovers—horses, space, views, near a charming town."

Rags to Walkers Guest Ranch, Sisters

SQUAW CREEK

68733 Junipine Lane, Sisters, OR 97759
Susie & Keith Johnson, Innkeepers
EMAIL squawcreek@moriah.com
WEBSITE www.moriah.com

541-549-4312
800-930-0055
FAX 541-549-4312

LOCATION	One and a half miles northeast of Sisters, just off Highway 126 on Junipine Lane.
OPEN	All year
DESCRIPTION	A 1970 two-story country inn with high vaulted ceilings, natural woods, and a wraparound deck, situated on 8.5 acres of aspen groves and ponderosa pines with a creek meandering through the property.
NO. OF ROOMS	Four rooms with private bathrooms.
RATES	Year-round rates are $85 for a single or double. There is no minimum stay and cancellation requires 72 hours' notice.
CREDIT CARDS	MasterCard, Visa
BREAKFAST	Big country breakfast is served.
AMENITIES	Jacuzzi on deck, TV/VCR, movies, coffee, goodies, robes, private entrances.
RESTRICTIONS	No smoking. April is the resident black Lab.
REVIEWED	Hot Showers, Soft Beds & Dayhikes in the Central Cascades; Oregon's Sisters Country
MEMBER	Oregon Lodging Association
KUDOS/COMMENTS	"Nice country setting and very nice innkeepers."

SIXES

On Scenic Highway 101, Sixes is just east of Cape Blanco State Park. Check out the historic Cape Blanco lighthouse, and in spring and fall, be vigilant for whales moving stealthily along the coast. The Elk and Sixes Rivers boast fine salmon and steelhead fishing.

SIXES RIVER HOTEL

93316 Sixes River Road, Sixes, OR 97476
Bert & Elizabeth Teitzel, Innkeepers
EMAIL innkeeper@sixeshotel.com
WEBSITE www.sixeshotel.com

541-332-3900
800-828-5161
FAX 541-332-9063

LOCATION	Twenty-two miles south of Bandon and 5 miles north of Port Orford on Highway 101. About halfway between mileposts 295 and 296, turn east onto Sixes River Road. The hotel driveway is the first driveway on the right (0.25 mile from Highway 101).
OPEN	All year
DESCRIPTION	A meticulously restored 1895 two-story Victorian hotel decorated with antiques, collectibles and original period art, and situated on 8 acres along the Sixes River close to the ocean. Listed on the National Historic Register.
NO. OF ROOMS	Four rooms with private bathrooms.
RATES	June through September, rates are $85-95 for a single or double and $340 for the entire inn. October through May, rates are $60-70 for a single or double and $250 for the entire inn. There is no minimum stay and cancellation requires 24 hours' notice.
CREDIT CARDS	American Express, MasterCard, Visa
BREAKFAST	Full breakfast is served in the dining room and includes juice, fruit bowl or plate, homemade muffins, biscuits and/or bread, a meat/egg entrée, and a bottomless cup of coffee or tea. A limited menu is offered as a convenience to guests if needed.
AMENITIES	Afternoon refreshments including coffee, tea, soft drinks, beer, wine, and pastry; air conditioning; fresh flowers in rooms; early morning coffee; movies in rooms; horseshoes; croquet; bicycles; recreation room with pool table.
RESTRICTIONS	No smoking, no pets. Ashley is the resident dachshund.
MEMBER	Oregon Bed & Breakfast Guild

STAYTON

About 30 minutes southeast of Salem, Stayton was named to honor the man who erected a sawmill there in 1866, around which the town soon grew. Sublimity is close by and connected by a bike path.

BIRD & HAT INN—B&B

717 N Third Avenue, Stayton, OR 97383   503-769-7817

Our Place in the Country Bed & Breakfast

9297 Boedigheimer Road, Stayton, OR 97385
Dave & Lynn Sweetland, Innkeepers
WEBSITE www.wvi.com/~ourplace

503-769-4555
FAX 503-769-4556

Sublimity

A nice (sublime even) little community about 20 minutes southeast of Salem, Sublimity is connected by a lovely bike bath with its neighbor city Stayton.

Silver Mountain Bed & Breakfast

4672 Drift Creek Road SE, Sublimity, OR 97385
Jim & Shirley Heater, Innkeepers
WEBSITE www.angelfire.com/or/VPNCTA

503-769-7127
800-952-3905

Summer Lake

Take Highway 31 just a few miles south of La Pine and head east to the high desert and Summer Lake. You'll pass Fort Rock, where Klamath Indians found refuge when Mount Mazama exploded 6,800 years ago. Woven sandals found in one of Fort Rock's caves carbon-dated to 9,000 years ago, and archaeological studies have found Klamath-style artifacts that date back 13,000 years in the old lake bed.

Summer Lake Inn

31501 Highway 31, Summer Lake, OR 97640
Darrell Seven & Jean Sage, Innkeepers
WEBSITE www.summerlakeinn.com

541-943-3983
800-261-2778
FAX 541-943-3352

SUMPTER

The town's name was intended to be a tribute to Fort Sumter (of Civil War fame) but it suffered from a misspelling that rendered it Sumpter. Established in the 1860s, it is an old gold-mining town.

SUMPTER BED & BREAKFAST

PO Box 40, Sumpter, OR 97877　　　　　　　　　　　800-640-3184
WEBSITE www.moriah.com/inns

THE DALLES

The Dalles is the historical stop along this stretch, especially now that the long-awaited $21.6-million Columbia Gorge Discovery Center has opened at Crate's Point. For centuries, this area was the meeting place for Native Americans. In the early 1800s, Hudson's Bay trappers (Edward Crate was one of them) lived here. In the 1840s, it was the official end of the Oregon Trail. Gold miners loaded up at The Dalles. Thomas Condon, Oregon's father of geology, got his start here amid local basalts. At the Columbia Gorge Discovery Center, learn about 40 million years of geology and natural history and the last 10,000 years of human occupation of the Columbia Gorge.

BOARDING HOUSE

207 W Fourth Street, The Dalles, OR 97058　　　　　541-296-5299

CAPTAIN GRAY'S GUEST HOUSE

210 W Fourth Street, The Dalles, OR 97058　　　　　541-298-8222
　　　　　　　　　　　　　　　　　　　　　　　　　800-448-4729

THE COLUMBIA HOUSE

525 E Seventh Street, The Dalles, OR 97058　　　　　541-298-4686
　　　　　　　　　　　　　　　　　　　　　　　　　800-807-2668

WINDRIDER INN

200 W Fourth Street, The Dalles, OR 97058   541-296-2607

TILLAMOOK

A broad, flat expanse of bottomland created by the confluence of three rivers (Tillamook, Trask, and Wilson), Tillamook is best known as dairy country. On the north end of town along Highway 101 sits the home of Tillamook cheese, the Tillamook County Creamery Association plant and visitors center. The tour is self-guided, but interesting. Afterward, nibble the free cheese samples, buy a scoop of Tillamook ice cream, or visit the restaurant and gift shop. Be prepared for hordes of tourists year-round. Bear Creek Artichokes (in Hemlock, 11.5 miles south of Tillamook, and closed in winter) features a first-class selection of fruits, veggies, and herbs.

BLUE HAVEN INN

3025 Gienger Road, Tillamook, OR 97141   503-842-2265
Joy & Ray Still, Innkeepers
EMAIL JaR@oregoncoast.com

LOCATION	Two miles south of Tillamook at the blinking yellow caution light. Turn off Highway 101 onto Gienger Road and go west 0.75 mile.
OPEN	All year
DESCRIPTION	A 1916 three-story Craftsman host home with French silk wallcoverings, furnished with antiques and collectibles, and situated on 2 acres. Listed on the State Historic Register.
NO. OF ROOMS	One room with a private bathroom and two rooms with one shared bathroom.
RATES	Year-round rates are $85 for a single or double with a private bathroom, $70 for a single or double with a shared bathroom, and $225 for the entire B&B. Cancellation requires 48 hours' notice.
CREDIT CARDS	American Express, MasterCard, Visa
BREAKFAST	Full breakfast is served in the formal dining room on fine bone china with gold flatware and crystal. Breakfast includes buttermilk biscuits, eggs, meat, waffles, stuffed French toast, gourmet pancakes, coffeecake, Dutch babies, eggs Benedict, or breakfast strata.
AMENITIES	Robes in shared bathrooms; library of videos, books, games; TV and music; fresh flowers in season; beverage service.

RESTRICTIONS	No smoking, no pets, children over 5 are welcome.
REVIEWED	The Official Guide to American Historic Bed & Breakfasts, Great Affordable Bed & Breakfast Getaways, The Complete Guide to American Bed & Breakfasts, Bed & Breakfast Homes: Best of the West Coast

WHISKEY CREEK BED & BREAKFAST

7500 Whiskey Creek Road, Tillamook, OR 97141   503-842-2408
Allison Asbjornsen & Forrest Dickerson, Innkeepers

LOCATION	West of Tillamook, follow the signs to Cape Lookout State Park and you will see the B&B.
OPEN	All year
DESCRIPTION	A 1900 two-story country inn with rough-cut wood interior, built by a Danish sawmill owner using spruce cut and milled at the site.
NO. OF ROOMS	One room with a private bathroom and two rooms with one shared bathroom.
RATES	Year-round rates are $95 for a single or double with a private bathroom, $75 for a single or double with a shared bathroom, and $120 for a suite. There is no minimum stay and cancellation requires 24 hours' notice.
CREDIT CARDS	MasterCard, Visa
BREAKFAST	Full breakfast is served in the dining room and includes coffee, tea, muffins, juice, Swedish pancakes, fruit, and oysters (hangtown fry). Dinner is available by arrangement.
AMENITIES	Massage, small gallery on-site (owner/operator is an artist).
RESTRICTIONS	No smoking. Children are welcome.
REVIEWED	*Fodor's, Where to Find the Oregon in Oregon*

VALE

The Oregon Trail passed by here. Check out the wagon ruts still visible at Keeney Pass and the murals of pioneers that are painted on walls around town. For outdoor activities, head south to Owyhee River and Reservoir or west to Bully Creek Reservoir.

1911 SEARS & ROEBUCK HOME

484 N 10th Street, Vale, OR 97918   541-473-9636
Judith A. Gallant, Innkeeper
EMAIL wobarj@micron.net

LOCATION	From I-84, take the Ontario exit and follow Highway 20/26 for 14 miles to Vale. Enter Vale, turn right onto 10th Street (at Logans Foodtown), and go one block.
OPEN	All year
DESCRIPTION	A two-story Victorian inn ordered from the Sears-Roebuck Catalog in 1911, with comfortable, period decor.
NO. OF ROOMS	Six rooms share four bathrooms. Try Lisa's room.
RATES	Year-round rates are $45-85 for a single or double, $350 for the guesthouse, and $250 for the entire inn. There is no minimum stay and cancellation requires 48 hours' notice.
CREDIT CARDS	No
BREAKFAST	Continental-plus is served in the dining room and includes local home-baked pastries, bagels, croissants, granolas, an array of fruit, milk, tea, coffee, cocoa, and juice. Egg and croissant breakfast sandwiches are also available. Full country breakfasts are available for special occasions.
AMENITIES	Full kitchen and barbecue available for guests' use; privacy and full use of the home (hostess does not live in the home); horse stabling and dog kennels on premises; heated game-cleaning room for hunters; laundry facilities; air conditioning in each room; big-screen cable TV; horse-drawn carriage rides, includes narrated tour of Vale's magnificent murals depicting the Oregon Trail.
RESTRICTIONS	Smoking outdoors only. Montgomery is the miniature mule.
MEMBER	Oregon Lodging Association

VERNONIA

Vernonia is an old logging town on the Nehalem River. Today the old mill pond is called Lake Vernonia and is stocked with a variety of fish.

VERNONIA INN

900 Madison Avenue, Vernonia, OR 97064　　　　　　503-429-4006

VIDA

MCKENZIE RIVER INN

49164 McKenzie Highway, Vida, OR 97488　　　　　　541-822-6260

WALDPORT

Waldport is a town in coastal limbo, overshadowed by its larger, better-known neighbors—Newport to the north and Yachats to the south. Not to worry; Waldport has much to recommend it, including the lovely Alsea River estuary, untrampled beaches at either end of town, and a city center unspoiled by tourism. At the south end of the Alsea Bay Bridge (beautifully rebuilt in 1991) is an interpretive center with historic transportation displays. There's good clamming and crabbing in the bay. The remote, pocket-size Drift Creek Wilderness is tucked into the Coast Range halfway between Seal Rock and Waldport.

CLIFF HOUSE—YAQUINA JOHN POINT

1450 SW Adahi Avenue, Waldport, OR 97394　　　　541-563-2506
Gabrielle, Innkeeper　　　　　　　　　　　　　FAX 541-563-4393
EMAIL clifhos@pioneer.net　　　　　　　WEBSITE www.virtualcities.com

WELCHES

Welches sits at the western entrance to Mount Hood National Forest on Highway 26. Check out Multnomah Falls and the Columbia River Gorge Loop.

DOUBLEGATE INN B&B

26711 E Welches Road, Welches, OR 97067 503-622-4859
Gary & Charlene Poton, Innkeepers FAX 503-622-4859
EMAIL dgatebnb@teleport.com WEBSITE www.mthoodlodging.com

LOCATION	From Portland, take Burnside Road to Highway 26 east and head toward Mount Hood. After going through Sandy, continue for 18 miles to the next signal and turn right onto Welches Road and go 1 mile. The inn is on the right. Coming west around Mount Hood from Hood River, take Highway 35 to Highway 26 and go west. Turn left onto Welches Road when you come to the first signal at the bottom of the mountain.
OPEN	All year
DESCRIPTION	A 1920s-era two-story shingled "storybook" cottage in a wonderful mountain setting with English countryside decor.
NO. OF ROOMS	Three rooms with private bathrooms. The owners' favorite is the English Country Suite.
RATES	Year-round rates are $95-120 for a single or double. There is a two-night minimum stay on weekends or an additional $30 for one night. Cancellation requires seven days' notice with a $10 charge.
CREDIT CARDS	American Express, Discover, MasterCard, Visa
BREAKFAST	Full three-course breakfast is served in the dining room or on the upper deck or lower patio. Honeymooners are always offered breakfast en suite, others by request. Breakfast includes a fruit dish, baked items, fresh-ground coffee, teas, and an entrée such as vegetarian quiche, lumberjack hash, stuffed French toast with shoulder bacon, and good-morning parfaits.
AMENITIES	Chocolate chip cookies; robes; snacks such as mozzarella cheese sticks with jalapeno-pepper jelly dip; guest refrigerator stocked with sodas and a microwave with popcorn; extensive video library; coffee, hot chocolate, and teas always available; hot cider in the cooler months; guestrooms have cassette player and selection of romantic tapes; guest lounge with TV/VCR and a library; pond with waterfall; herbal courtyard filled with delightful fragrances; upper deck surrounded by tall cedars with the sounds of the Salmon River rushing by; private baths with spas or soaking tubs; complimentary sparkling cider or champagne for birthdays, anniversaries, and honeymoons.

RESTRICTIONS	No smoking inside, no pets, children over 14 are welcome.
REVIEWED	Fodor's, Oregon: Off the Beaten Path, Recommended Bed & Breakfasts: Pacific Northwest, The Romantic Pacific Northwest
MEMBER	Associated Bed & Breakfasts of Mount Hood and Northern Willamette Valley, Professional Association of Innkeepers International, Oregon Lodging Association

OLD WELCHES INN BED & BREAKFAST

26401 E Welches Road, Welches, OR 97067 503-622-3754
Judith & Ted Monoun, Innkeepers 503-622-5370
EMAIL oldwelchesinn@bbdirectory.com
WEBSITE www.bbdirectory.com/inn/oldwelchesinn

LOCATION	Just east of Portland on Highway 26. The inn is 1 mile south of Highway 26 on Welches Road, across from the golf meadows in Welches Valley.
OPEN	All year
DESCRIPTION	A three-story 1890 colonial inn with a mix of antiques and contemporary furniture.
NO. OF ROOMS	Three rooms with private bathrooms.

Old Welches Inn Bed & Breakfast, Welches

RATES	Year-round rates are $95-145 for a single or double and $130-180 for a private guesthouse. There is a minimum stay from January 15 through May 15 and cancellation requires seven days' notice (holidays: 20 days' notice).
CREDIT CARDS	American Express, Discover, MasterCard, Visa
BREAKFAST	Full breakfast is served in the dining room and includes sausage cakes, herbed potatoes, omelets, biscuits, applecake, fruit plate, coffee, and juice.
AMENITIES	Homemade goodies and beverages at all times, wine in the afternoon, custom robes, fresh flowers, champagne for special occasions, chocolates on pillows.
RESTRICTIONS	No smoking, no pets, children over 12 are welcome. Sadie is the resident doggie.
REVIEWED	*Northwest Best Places; Complete Guide to B&Bs, Inns, & Guesthouses; National Trust Guide to Historic B&B's, Inns and Small Hotels; Annual Directory of American and Canadian B&Bs; Oregon: Off the Beaten Path; Hot Showers, Soft Beds, and Dayhikes in the Central Cascades*
MEMBER	Professional Association of Innkeepers International, Association of Bed & Breakfasts of Mount Hood and Northern Willamette Valley

SUITE RIVER BED & BREAKFAST

PO Box 530, Welches, OR 97067
EMAIL *patsteve@mornet.com*

503-622-3547
888-886-6820

WEST LINN

On the banks of the Willamette River, West Linn features a system of locks originally constructed in the 1870s. There's a nice waterfront park with a footbridge over to Cedar Oak Island.

RIVERBEND HOUSE

949 Willamette Falls Drive, West Linn, OR 97068   503-557-1662

Swift Shore Chalet Bed & Breakfast

1190 Swift Shore Circle, West Linn, OR 97068 503-650-3853
Nancy & Horace Duke, Innkeepers

Westfir

This former logging town flanks the North Fork of the Middle Fork of the Willamette River, excellent for fishing for rainbow trout. The Aufderheide National Scenic Byway winds east out of Westfir into the heart of the Cascades, meandering along the river, and is popular with bicyclists, although heavy snowfall closes the route from November until early April.

Westfir Lodge, a Bed & Breakfast Inn

47365 1st Street, Westfir, OR 97492 541-782-3103
Gerry Chamberlain & Ken Symons, Innkeepers FAX 541-782-3103

LOCATION   Travel 35 miles east of Eugene on Highway 58 to the Westfir exit and go 3 miles. The inn is across from the long, red, covered bridge.

OPEN   All year

Westfir Lodge, a Bed & Breakfast Inn, Westfir

DESCRIPTION	Two-story lodge that was the original offices for the Westfir lumber companies, renovated and furnished with antiques.
RATES	Year-round rates are $40-60 for a single or double. Ask about a reservation/cancellation policy.
CREDIT CARDS	No
BREAKFAST	Full English breakfast is served in the dining room and includes coffee, tea, fresh fruit cup, eggs, broiled tomato, banger sausages, crepes or pancakes, scones, and muffins.
AMENITIES	Evening dessert, fresh flowers in rooms, robes, air conditioning, handicapped accessible.
RESTRICTIONS	No smoking, no pets, children are welcome.
REVIEWED	*Northwest Best Places, Lonely Planet, Fodor's Northwest, America's Best B&Bs*
MEMBER	Bed & Breakfast Association of Oregon, Oregon Lodging Association

WESTON

TAMARACK INN BED & BREAKFAST

62388 Highway 204, Weston, OR 97886　　　541-566-9348
Tom & Eileen Moon, Innkeepers　　　　　　800-662-9348

YACHATS

Yachats (pronounced "ya-hots") means "at the foot of the mountain." Tide pools teeming with marine life dot the rocky shoreline; above loom spectacular headlands affording excellent ocean and whale-watching vistas. The Yachats River intersects downtown and empties into the Pacific, providing a playground for seabirds, seals, and sea lions. Between April and October, sea-run smelt (sardinelike fish) are harvested in the coast's sandy coves (visit Smelt Sands State Park, on the town's north end, for a look). The town has a hip, arts-community flavor, with an interesting mix of aging counterculturalists, yuppies, and tourists. Yachats is situated at the threshold of the spectacular 2,700-acre Cape Perpetua Scenic Area. Hiking trails lead to isolated coves and rocky ledges constantly bombarded by ocean waves. Other paths head deep into bona fide rain forest. Driving along Highway 101 provides an exhilarating journey, packed with panoramas of rugged cliffs abutting the ever-changing Pacific.

BURD'S NEST INN B&B

664 Yachats River Road, Yachats, OR 97498   541-547-3683
Joni & Big Burd Bicksler, Innkeepers
WEBSITE www.moriah.com/inns

KITTIWAKE BED & BREAKFAST

95368 Highway 101 S, Yachats, OR 97498   541-547-4470
Brigitte & Joseph Szewc, Innkeepers   FAX 541-547-4415
EMAIL jszewc@orednet.org   WEBSITE www.ohwy.com/or/k/kittiwbb.htm

LOCATION	At mile marker 171.2 on Highway 101. Approximately 7 miles south of Yachats and 17 miles north of Florence.
OPEN	All year
DESCRIPTION	A 1990s two-story contemporary host home.
NO. OF ROOMS	Two rooms with private bathrooms. Joseph and Brigitte recommend room 2.
RATES	Year-round rates are $125-140. There is a two-night minimum stay on weekends and cancellation requires two weeks' notice.
CREDIT CARDS	American Express, Discover, MasterCard, Visa
BREAKFAST	Full breakfast is served in guestrooms on weekdays. On weekends breakfast is available at the $140 room rate.
AMENITIES	Afghans, magazines, coffee bar, guest refrigerator, down duvets, glycerine soap.
RESTRICTIONS	No smoking, no pets, no children. No candles or incense, and no

Kittiwake Bed & Breakfast, Yachats

hiking boots in the house.

KUDOS/COMMENTS "Beautiful location on an ocean bluff. Very attractive and comfortable."

MORNING STAR

95668 Highway 101, Yachats, OR 97498 541-547-4412
Susan Hanson, Innkeeper FAX 541-547-4621
EMAIL artgal@teleport.com WEBSITE *www.teleport.com/~artgal*

OPEN	All year
DESCRIPTION	A 1995 traditional inn with antiques and eclectic decor, overlooking a spectacular oceanfront bluff.
NO. OF ROOMS	Three rooms with private bathrooms.
RATES	Year-round rates are $85-150 for a single or double. There is a minimum stay during long weekends and cancellation requires seven days' notice.
CREDIT CARDS	American Express, MasterCard, Visa
BREAKFAST	Full breakfast is served in the dining room and includes fresh-baked scones, baked eggs, coconut pancakes, coffee, and juice.
AMENITIES	Robes in rooms, outdoor hot tub, flowers.
RESTRICTIONS	No smoking, no pets, children over 14 are welcome. Ozzie and Emmy are the resident tabbies and Baby is the Yorkie.
REVIEWED	*The Best Places to Kiss in the Northwest*

Morning Star, Yachats

NEW ENGLAND HOUSE BED & BREAKFAST

227 Shell Street, Yachats, OR 97498 541-547-4799
EMAIL nehouse@pioneer.net 800-508-6455

THE OREGON HOUSE

94288 Highway 101, Yachats, OR 97498 541-547-3329
WEBSITE www.oregonhouse.com

THE SANDERLING BED & BREAKFAST

7304 SW Pacific Coast Highway, Yachats, OR 97498 541-563-4752
Pat & Ernie, Resident Innkeepers

SEA QUEST BED & BREAKFAST

95354 Highway 101, Yachats, OR 97498 541-547-3782
Elaine & George, Innkeepers 800-341-4878
EMAIL seaquest@newportnet.com 541-547-3719
WEBSITE www.seaq.com

LOCATION	Mile marker 171–172, 19 miles north of Florence, 6 miles south of Yachats.
OPEN	All year
DESCRIPTION	A 1900 two-story remodeled inn, made of cedar and glass and located 100 feet from the ocean. The inn has wraparound decks and is situated on 2.5 acres.
NO. OF ROOMS	Five rooms with private bathrooms.
RATES	Call for year-round rates. There is a minimum stay on holidays and weekends and cancellation requires seven days' notice.
CREDIT CARDS	Discover, MasterCard, Visa
BREAKFAST	Full breakfast is served in the Great Room and features a breakfast bar with homemade granola, fresh fruit, stuffed croissants, crepes,

AMENITIES	Chilean puffs, and fresh-baked bundt cakes. Sitting areas; overstuffed chairs; floor-to-ceiling used-brick fireplaces; coffee, tea, cocoa, cookies, and pastries all day; private Jacuzzi tubs; private entryways to beach.
RESTRICTIONS	Children over 14 are welcome. Resident pets are a schnauzer named Sebastian, a yorkipoo named Murphy, and a cat named Clouseau.
REVIEWED	*The Best Places to Kiss in the Northwest; Weekends for Two; Northwest Best Places; America's Favorite Inns, B&Bs, & Small Hotels; Recommended Country Inns; Oregon Discovery Guide; Fodor's—The Best B&B's; Fodor's Pacific Northwest*
MEMBER	Eugene Area Bed & Breakfast Association
KUDOS/COMMENTS	"Fantastic. A world away from everyday." "Wonderfully warm innkeepers, fabulous views of the ocean. Very, very relaxing, romantic getaway."

SERENITY BED & BREAKFAST

5985 Yachats River Road, Yachats, OR 97498   541-547-3813
WEBSITE *www.ohwy.com/or/s/serenibb.htm*

ZIGGURAT BED & BREAKFAST

95330 Highway 101, Yachats, OR 97498   541-547-3925
Mary Lou Cavendish, Innkeeper
WEBSITE *www.newportnet.com/ziggurat*

YONCALLA

This is prime covered-bridge territory, just east of I-5, midway between Eugene and Roseberg, in lovely western Oregon hill country. Check out historic Homestead Park or sample the local wines.

Tuckaway Farm Inn, Yoncalla

TUCKAWAY FARM INN

7179 Scotts Valley Road, Yoncalla, OR 97499   541-849-3144
Steve & Rosalind Dix, Innkeepers
WEBSITE *www.moriah.com/tuckaway*

LOCATION	Seven miles east of Highway 15, about halfway between Roseburg and Eugene and 11 miles from the small town of Yoncalla.
OPEN	All year
DESCRIPTION	A 1920s-era two-story Craftsman farmhouse decorated with American and family heirloom antiques, overlooking a valley amid 34 acres of forests and pastures.
NO. OF ROOMS	Three rooms with private bathrooms. Try the Bradford Room.
RATES	Year-round rates are $75-85 for a single or double. There is no minimum stay.
CREDIT CARDS	MasterCard, Visa
BREAKFAST	Full breakfast is served in the dining room and includes fresh-squeezed orange juice, Full City coffee, seasonal fruit, egg dishes, pancakes, waffles, and/or home-baked scones and muffins.
AMENITIES	Intimate guest sitting room with fireplace, books, games, video library, classic farmhouse front porch overlooking valley, open-air spa, peace and quiet, no freeway noise, sirens, or "urban buzz."
RESTRICTIONS	Smoking limited to certain areas, children over 12 are welcome, younger children will be considered by special arrangement. Two dogs, seven cats, and 20 Romney sheep roam the farm.
MEMBER	Eugene Area Bed & Breakfast Association

INDEX

10th Avenue Inn 185
1888 House 177
1911 Sears & Roebuck Home 206
2310 Lombard Bed & Breakfast 151
A Demain "Until Tomorrow"
   Bed & Breakfast 38
A-1 Krumdieck Kottage 77
A-Dome Studio Bed & Breakfast 2
Abernathy's Bed & Breakfast 161
Abiqua Creek Farms Bed & Breakfast .. 195
Adams Cottage Bed & Breakfast 3
Ainsworth House Bed & Breakfast ... 153
Albion Inn 3
Aloha Junction Inn & Gardens
   Bed & Breakfast 43
Anderson's Boarding House
   Bed & Breakfast 186
Anne Hathaway's Cottage 3
Antique Rose Inn 4
Apple Inn Bed & Breakfast 69
Applegate River Lodge 1
Arbors Bed & Breakfast, The 128
Arden Forest Inn 5
Ashberry Inn 5
Ashland Patterson House 5
Ashland's English Country Cottage .. 6
Ashland's Main Street Inn 7
Ashwood, The 65
Astoria Inn Bed & Breakfast 31
Atavista Farm Bed & Breakfast 57
Atherton Place 77
Avalon Bed and Breakfast 105
Baer House B&B 39
Bailey's Cedar House
   Bed & Breakfast 41
Baker Street Bed & Breakfast 129
Balch Hotel 73
Bandon Beach House 41
Bar M Dude Ranch 1
Barnstormer Bed & Breakfast 184
Bayberry Inn 7
Beach Street Bed & Breakfast 41
Beckley House Bed & Breakfast ... 152
Bed & Breakfast on the Green, A ... 66
Benjamin Young Inn 32
Beryl House Bed & Breakfast 106
Bethel Heights Farm
   Bed & Breakfast 179
Bird & Hat Inn—B&B 201
Black Bart Bed & Breakfast 118

Blackberry Inn Bed & Breakfast 63
Blue Bucket Inn at 3E Ranch
   Bed & Breakfast 58
Blue Haven Inn 204
Blue Heron Inn 85
Boarding House 203
Boarding House Inn 119
Bookmark Bed & Breakfast 179
Brautigam House at Kensington
   Park, The 44
Brey House "Ocean View"
   Bed & Breakfast Inn 125
Bridal Veil Lodge Bed & Breakfast .. 51
Bridge Creek Flora Bed & Breakfast
   Inn 91
Brier Rose Inn Bed & Breakfast 1
Brightridge Farm Bed & Breakfast .. 192
Brightwood Guesthouse
   Bed & Breakfast 51
Brookings South Coast Inn 53
Brookside Bed & Breakfast 184
Brown's Bed & Breakfast 106
Bruno Ranch Bed & Breakfast 51
Burd's Nest Inn B&B 213
C&J Lodge Bed & Breakfast 129
Cadbury Cottage 7
Camille's Bed & Breakfast 77
Campbell House, a City Inn 77
Cannon Beach Hotel 60
Captain Gray's Guest House 203
Carousel House Bed & Breakfast ... 69
Carpenter Hill Inn 135
Century Garden Bed & Breakfast .. 161
Chamberlain House Bed & Breakfast .. 65
Chandlers' Bed, Bread & Trail Inn .. 117
Channel House Bed & Breakfast 72
Chanticleer Inn 8
Chapman House Bed & Breakfast 67
Chart House Lodge, Outfitter
   and Bed & Breakfast 54
Cherry Hill Farm 139
Chetco River Inn 54
Clarity Cottage and Suite 8
Clear Creek Bed & Breakfast 105
Clementine's Bed & Breakfast 33
Cliff House—Yaquina John Point .. 207
Clinkerbrick House 162
Colonel Silsby's Bed & Breakfast Inn .. 8
Columbia House, The 203
Columbia River Inn B&B 33

Conklin's Guest House,
    A Bed & Breakfast 197
Coolidge House Bed & Breakfast 9
Coos Bay Manor Bed & Breakfast 63
Cotton Wood Cottage
    Bed & Breakfast 179
Cottonwood Bed & Breakfast 107
Country Inn The City 45
Country River Inn 187
Country Willows B&B Inn 10
Countryside Inn Bed & Breakfast 121
Courtyard Inn 67
Cowslip's Belle Bed & Breakfast 11
Cricketwood Country B&B 45
Custer House Bed & Breakfast 188
Daniel's Roost Bed & Breakfast 12
Diamond Stone Guest
    Lodge & Gallery 122
Dorie's Inn 157
Doublegate Inn B&B 208
Drift Inn Bed & Breakfast 49
Eagle Crest Bed & Breakfast 180
Eagle's View Bed & Breakfast 155
Edwin K Bed & Breakfast 86
Egg Cup Inn Bed & Breakfast, The 196
Elkqua Lodge 74
Elliott House, The 174
Enchanted Cottage 126
Endicott Gardens Bed & Breakfast 94
Entheos Estate 142
Erin Lodge 62
Excelsior Inn 78
Fadden's Inn 12
Falcon's Crest Inn 97
Fernwood at Alder Creek 184
Fish House Inn 71
Flery Manor 99
Floras Lake House by the Sea 123
Fort Smith Bed & Breakfast 78
Franklin Street Station
    Bed & Breakfast 33
Frenchglen Hotel 92
Gahr Farm B&B Cottage 130
Gardiner Guest House 93
Gaslight Inn, The 88
Gazebo 46
Gedney Gardens 162
General Hooker's Bed & Breakfast 162
George Hyatt House Bed & Breakfast
    Inn, The 76
Georgian House Bed & Breakfast 163
Getty's Emerald Garden
    Bed & Breakfast 79

Gilbert Inn Bed & Breakfast 189
Gorge View Bed & Breakfast 107
Gracie's Landing Bed & Breakfast 72
Grandview Bed & Breakfast 34
Granny Franny's Farm 98
Grant House 39
Grapevine Inn 13
Green Gables Bed & Breakfast 145
Green Springs Inn 13
Guest House Bed & Breakfast, The 190
Hackett House 108
Hanson Country Inn, The 67
Harrison House Bed and Breakfast 67
Havenshire Bed & Breakfast 37
Hell's Canyon Bed & Breakfast 155
Heron Haus 164
Hersey House and Bungalow 14
Heryford House Bed & Breakfast 123
Historic Broetje House 136
Historic Henkle House
    Bed & Breakfast 70
Historic Oregon Hotel
    Bed & Breakfast 137
Historic Orth House B&B
    "The Teddy Bear Inn" 112
Historic River House, The 42
Hokanson's Guest House 177
Holladay House Bed & Breakfast 165
Holmes Sea Cove Bed & Breakfast 55
Home by the Sea Bed & Breakfast 160
Home Farm 101
Honker Inn Bed & Breakfast 142
Hood River Hotel and Pasquale's
    Ristorante 108
Horseshoe Ranch 90
Hospitality House 198
Hostess House Bed & Breakfast 166
House of Hunter 178
Howell's Bed & Breakfast 138
Hudson House Bed & Breakfast 62
Inn at Aurora 36
Inn at Nesika Beach 94
Inn at the Gorge—Bed & Breakfast 110
Iris Inn, The 15
Iron Gate Estate Bed & Breakfast 119
Irvington Inn 167
Itty Bitty Inn Motel Bed & Breakfast ...151
Ivy Creek Bed & Breakfast 136
Ivy House, The 101
Jacksonville Inn 114
Jessell House 16
Johnson House Bed & Breakfast 87
Juniper Acres Bed & Breakfast 46

220

Kelty Estate Bed & Breakfast 123
Kennedy School 167
Kerbyville Inn 118
Kittiwake Bed & Breakfast 213
Kjaer's House in the Woods 79
Knott Street Inn Bed & Breakfast 167
Lake House Bed & Breakfast, The 154
Lakecliff Estate Bed & Breakfast 110
Land's Inn Bed & Breakfast 119
Lara House Bed & Breakfast 47
Laurel Street Inn 16
Lawnridge House 102
Lighthouse Bed & Breakfast 42
Lily of the Field Bed & Breakfast 69
Lion & Rose Victorian B&B, The 167
Lithia Rose Bed & Breakfast 16
Lithia Springs Inn 17
Llast Camp Llamas Bed & Breakfast . . .177
Lowden's Beachfront B&B 55
Lozier's Country Loft Bed & Breakfast . .76
Macmaster House Circa 1895 168
MacPherson Inn Bed & Breakfast 69
Main Street Bed & Breakfast 89
Malarkey Ranch Inn B&B 185
Maple River 53
Marjon Bed & Breakfast Inn 124
Marquee House 180
Marvin Gardens Guest House 196
Maryellen's Guest House
 Bed & Breakfast 80
Mattey House Bed & Breakfast 131
McCall House Bed & Breakfast 17
McCully House Inn, The 115
McGarry House Bed & Breakfast 80
McGillivray's Log Home
 Bed & Breakfast 75
McKenzie River Inn 207
McKenzie View, a Riverside
 Bed & Breakfast 80
Meadow View Inn Bed & Breakfast 182
Middle Creek Run Bed & Breakfast . . .194
Mill Inn Bed & Breakfast 48
Moloney's Inn Bed & Breakfast 81
Morical House Garden Inn 18
Morning Star 214
Morrison Cottage 136
Mosier House Bed & Breakfast, The . . .139
Mount Ashland Inn 18
Mount Hood Bed & Breakfast 140
Mount Hood Hamlet 141
Mount Hood Manor 98
Mount Reuben Inn 93
Mousetrap Inn 18

Nehalem River Inn 142
Neil Creek House Bed & Breakfast 20
New England House Bed & Breakfast . .215
Newport Belle Bed & Breakfast 146
Nightin' Gail's Inn 20
O'Brien House 91
Oak Hill Country Bed & Breakfast 21
Oak Street Cottages 21
Oak Street Station Bed & Breakfast 21
Oak Street Victorian B&B 87
Oar House Bed & Breakfast 146
Ocean House 147
Ocean Memories—A Touch of Elegance
 on the Oregon Coast 126
Officers Inn Bed & Breakfast 105
Old Parkdale Inn Bed & Breakfast, The 141
Old Tower House B&B, The 64
Old Welches Inn Bed & Breakfast 209
Orchard View Inn Bed & Breakfast 131
Oregon House, The 215
Osprey Inn 50
Our Place in the Country
 Bed & Breakfast 202
Oval Door Bed & Breakfast Inn, The 81
Pacific House 42
Pacific Rest Bed & Breakfast 127
Pacific View Bed & Breakfast 55
Panorama Lodge B&B 111
Parker House Bed & Breakfast, The . . .157
Parkside Cottage 21
Partridge Farm 143
Pedigrift House Bed & Breakfast 21
Peerless Hotel 23
Pine Meadow Inn Bed & Breakfast 102
Pinehurst Inn at Jenny Creek 23
Pinewood 74
Pittock Acres Bed & Breakfast 168
Place Apart Bed & Breakfast Inn, A 158
Pookie's Bed 'n Breakfast on
 College Hill 82
Portland Guest House 168
Portland's White House
 Bed & Breakfast 169
Powder River Bed & Breakfast 40
Prospect Historical Hotel/Motel
 and Dinnerhouse 176
Queen Anne Bed & Breakfast 24
Rags to Walkers Guest Ranch 199
Redwing Bed & Breakfast, The 24
Redwood Inn 142
Repose & Repast 72
River's Edge Inn 50
Riverbend House 210

221

Riverside Inn B&B 190
Rock Garden Inn 25
Rogue River Guest House 96
Romeo Inn 25
Rosebriar Hotel 35
Royal Carter House Bed & Breakfast 26
Sage Country Inn Bed & Breakfast 59
Salmon River Bed & Breakfast 155
Sand Dollar B&B 190
Sanderling Bed & Breakfast, The 215
Sandlake Country Inn 63
Sather House Bed & Breakfast, The 49
Sauvie Island Bed & Breakfast 169
Sea Cliff Bed & Breakfast 148
Sea Dreamer Inn 56
Sea Quest Bed & Breakfast 215
Sea Rose Bed & Breakfast 152
Sea Side Inn 191
Secret Garden 84
Serenity Bed & Breakfast 216
Sheridan Country Inn 195
Shrew's House 26
Silver Mountain Bed & Breakfast 202
Sixes River Hotel 200
Smith House Bed & Breakfast 143
Solace by the Sea Bed & Breakfast 148
Sonshine B&B 116
Springbrook Hazelnut Farm
    Bed & Breakfast 144
Spyglass Inn 125
Squaw Creek 200
Stang Manor Inn 121
St. Bernards, a Bed & Breakfast 61
State House Bed & Breakfast 182
State Street Inn 111
Steelblue Chameleon Lodge 160
Steelhead Run B&B/Fine Art Gallery ...93
Steiger Haus Bed and Breakfast 132
Stephanie Inn 62
Stone Lion Inn 182
Strawberry Mountain Inn 173
Suite River Bed & Breakfast 210
Sullivan's Gulch B&B 170
Summer House Bed & Breakfast 192
Summer Lake Inn 202
Summer Place Inn 26
Sumpter Bed & Breakfast 203
Sun Pass Ranch 90
Swallow Ridge 49
Swift Shore Chalet Bed & Breakfast ...211
Sylvia Beach Hotel 149
Tamarack Inn Bed & Breakfast 212
Tamarack Pines Inn 118
Terwilliger Vista Bed & Breakfast 171

The Barton House 65
This Olde House 64
Thompsons' Bed & Breakfast 120
Three B's at Market 172
Tickled Trout 76
Tolemac Inn 73
Tolle House 153
Touvelle House, The 115
Tu Tu Tun Lodge 95
Tuckaway Farm Inn 217
Tudor House Bed & Breakfast 172
Tuscany Inn 84
Tyee Lodge Oceanfront
    Bed & Breakfast 150
Umpqua House, The 178
Under the Greenwood Tree
    Bed & Breakfast 135
Vernonia Inn 207
Villa Bed & Breakfast, A 172
Villa Genovese 49
Vista Park Bed & Breakfast 183
Waterside Inn 27
Weasku Inn 104
Weisinger's Vineyard Cottage 27
Wells Ranch House Bed & Breakfast,
    The 115
Westfir Lodge, a Bed & Breakfast
    Inn 211
Westlund's River's Edge
    Bed & Breakfast 172
Whiskey Creek Bed & Breakfast 205
Whispering Pines 135
Wild River Ranch Bed & Breakfast 91
Williams House Bed & Breakfast 133
Willowbrook Inn 96
Wimer Street Inn 28
Winchester Country Inn 28
Windrider Inn 204
Wine Country Farm 70
Wolfe Manor Inn 28
Woodridge Haven Bed & Breakfast 70
Woods House Bed & Breakfast
    Inn, The 29
Woolery House Bed & Breakfast 112
Woven Glass Inn, The 172
Yankee Tinker Bed & Breakfast, The 44
Young's B&B—Tastes of Yesterday 127
Youngberg Hill Vineyard & Inn 133
Ziggurat Bed & Breakfast 216